SHATTER-STAR

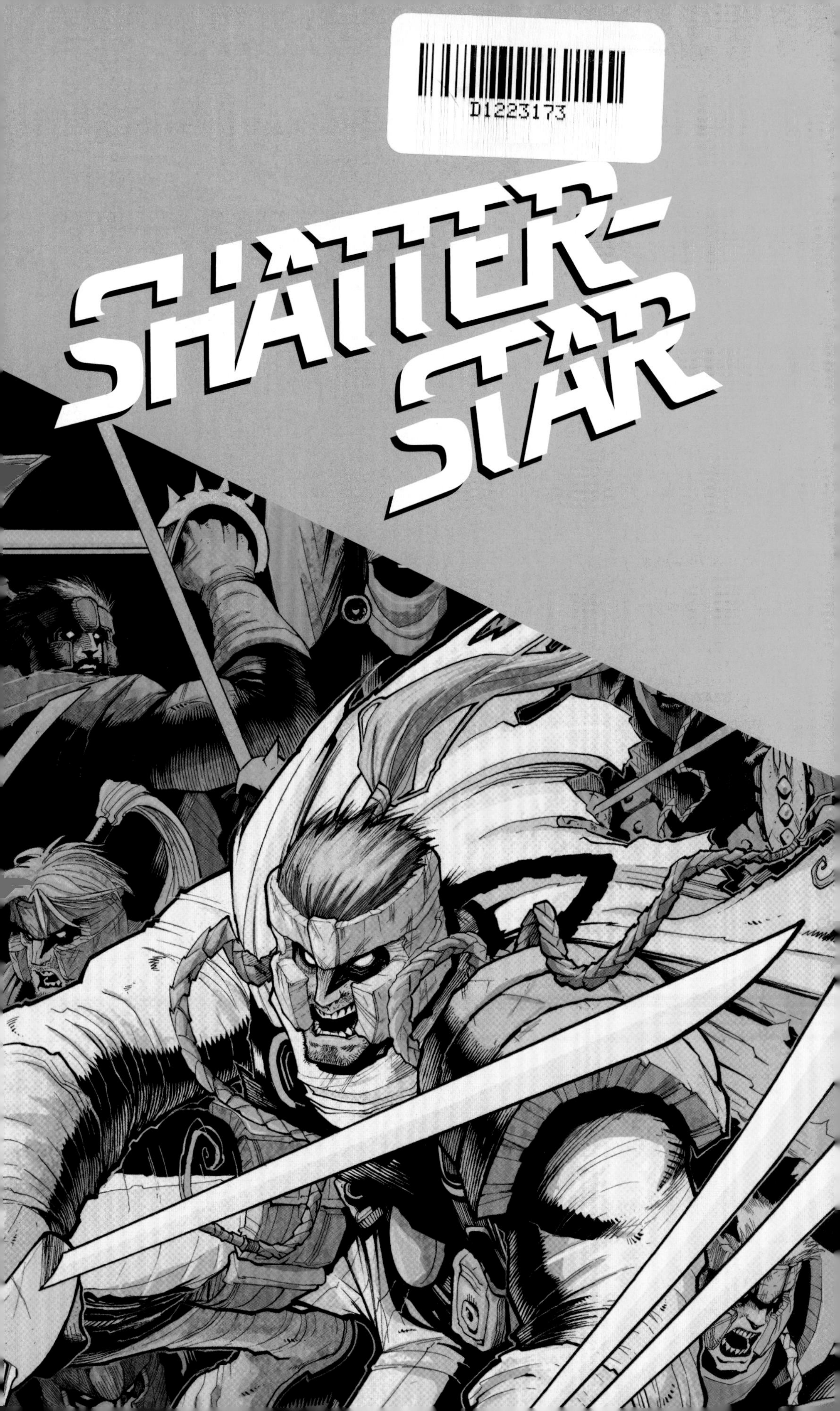

COLLECTION EDITOR
JENNIFER GRÜNWALD

ASSISTANT EDITOR
CAITLIN O'CONNELL

ASSOCIATE MANAGING EDITOR
KATERI WOODY

EDITOR, SPECIAL PROJECTS
MARK D. BEAZLEY

VP PRODUCTION & SPECIAL PROJECTS
JEFF YOUNGQUIST

SVP PRINT, SALES & MARKETING
DAVID GABRIEL

BOOK DESIGNER
JEFF POWELL

EDITOR IN CHIEF
C.B. CEBULSKI

CHIEF CREATIVE OFFICER
JOE QUESADA

PRESIDENT
DAN BUCKLEY

EXECUTIVE PRODUCER
ALAN FINE

SHATTERSTAR: REALITY STAR. Contains material originally published in magazine form as SHATTERSTAR #1-5. First printing 2019. ISBN 978-1-302-91522-3. Published by MARVEL WORLDWIDE, INC., a subsidiary of MARVEL ENTERTAINMENT, LLC. OFFICE OF PUBLICATION: 135 West 50th Street, New York, NY 10020. © 2019 MARVEL No similarity between any of the names, characters, persons, and/or institutions in this magazine with those of any living or dead person or institution is intended, and any such similarity which may exist is purely coincidental. **Printed in Canada.** DAN BUCKLEY, President, Marvel Entertainment; JOHN NEE, Publisher; JOE QUESADA, Chief Creative Officer; TOM BREVOORT, SVP of Publishing; DAVID BOGART, Associate Publisher & SVP of Talent Affairs; DAVID GABRIEL, SVP of Sales & Marketing, Publishing; JEFF YOUNGQUIST, VP of Production & Special Projects; DAN CARR, Executive Director of Publishing Technology; ALEX MORALES, Director of Publishing Operations; DAN EDINGTON, Managing Editor; SUSAN CRESPI, Production Manager; STAN LEE, Chairman Emeritus. For information regarding advertising in Marvel Comics or on Marvel.com, please contact Vit DeBellis, Custom Solutions & Integrated Advertising Manager, at vdebellis@marvel. com. For Marvel subscription inquiries, please call 888-511-5480. **Manufactured between 2/22/2019 and 3/26/2019 by SOLISCO PRINTERS, SCOTT, QC, CANADA.**

10 9 8 7 6 5 4 3 2 1

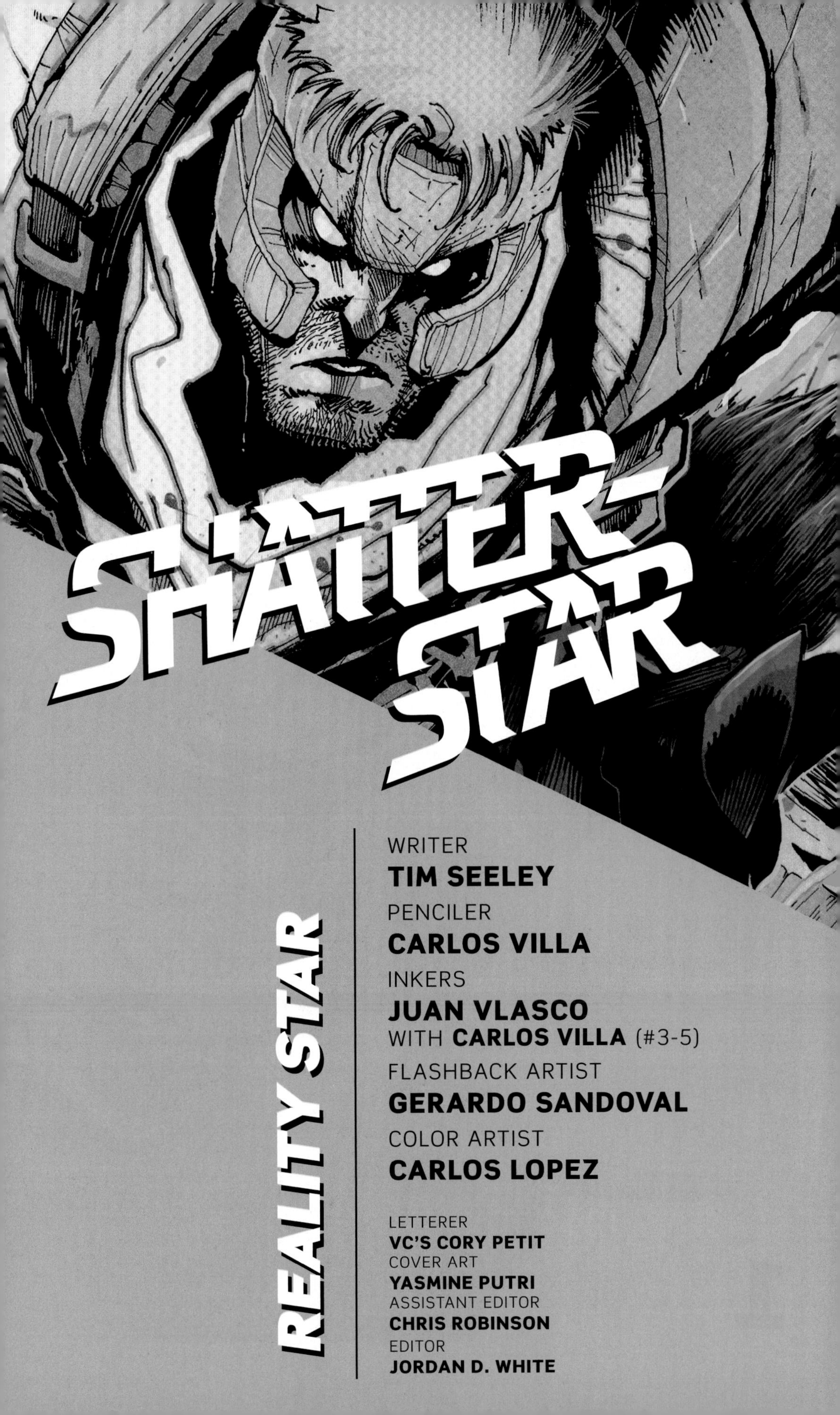

SHATTERSTAR

REALITY STAR

WRITER
TIM SEELEY

PENCILER
CARLOS VILLA

INKERS
JUAN VLASCO
WITH **CARLOS VILLA** (#3-5)

FLASHBACK ARTIST
GERARDO SANDOVAL

COLOR ARTIST
CARLOS LOPEZ

LETTERER
VC'S CORY PETIT

COVER ART
YASMINE PUTRI

ASSISTANT EDITOR
CHRIS ROBINSON

EDITOR
JORDAN D. WHITE

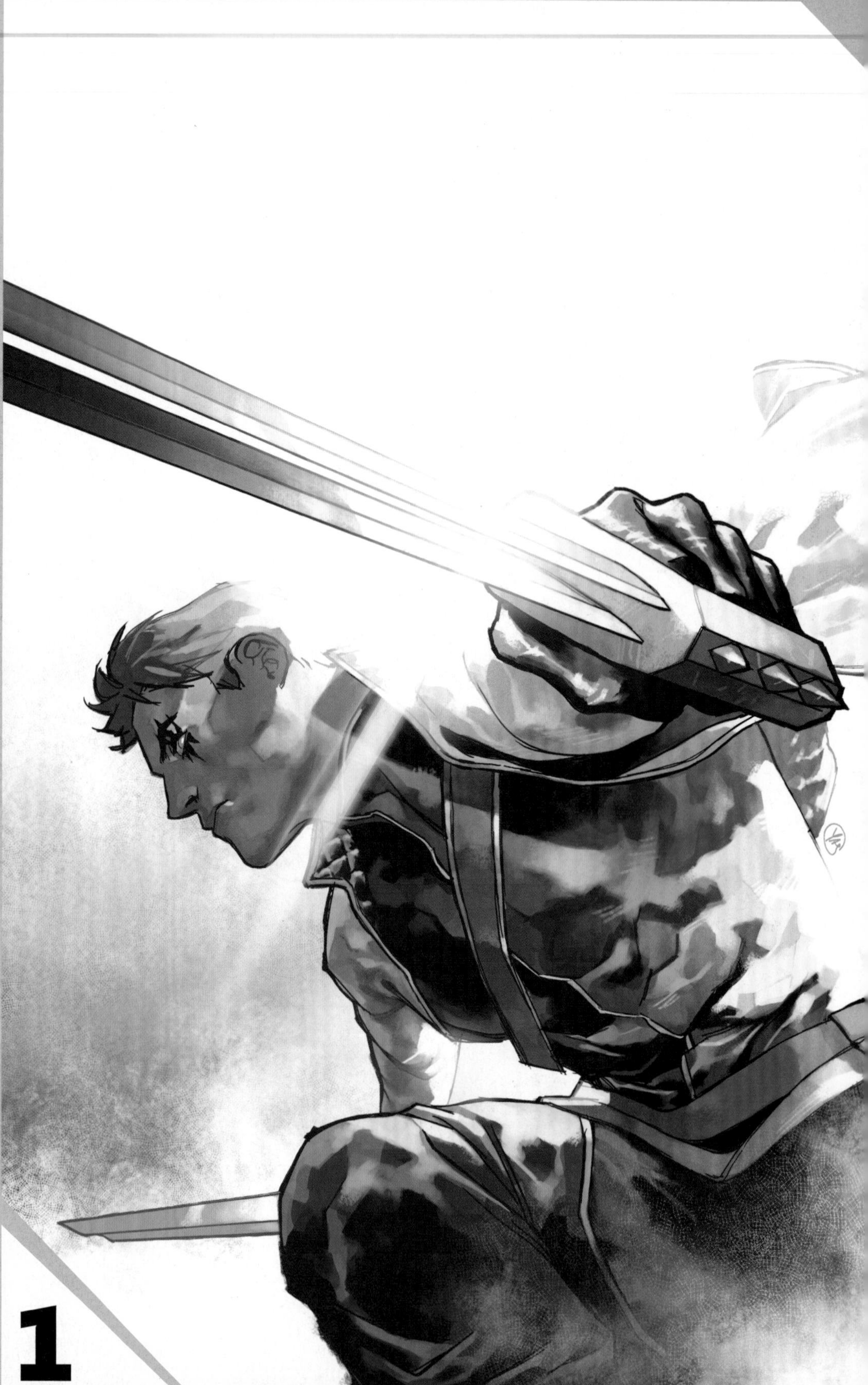
1

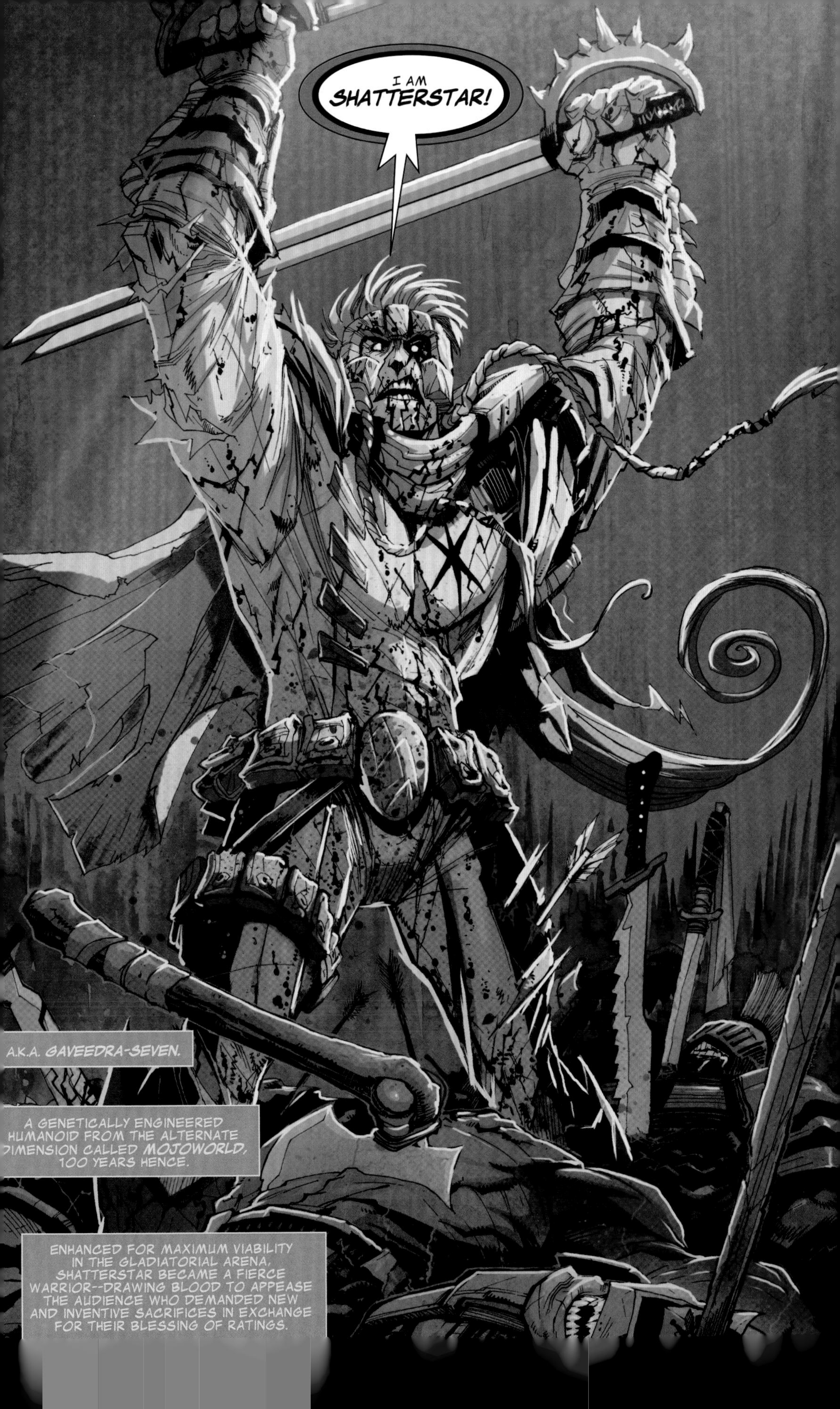
I AM SHATTERSTAR!
A.K.A. GAVEEDRA-SEVEN.
A GENETICALLY ENGINEERED HUMANOID FROM THE ALTERNATE DIMENSION CALLED MOJOWORLD, 100 YEARS HENCE.
ENHANCED FOR MAXIMUM VIABILITY IN THE GLADIATORIAL ARENA, SHATTERSTAR BECAME A FIERCE WARRIOR--DRAWING BLOOD TO APPEASE THE AUDIENCE WHO DEMANDED NEW AND INVENTIVE SACRIFICES IN EXCHANGE FOR THEIR BLESSING OF RATINGS.

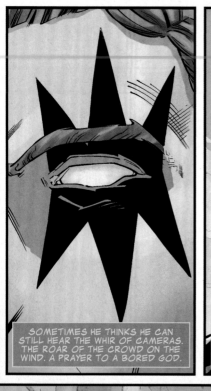

SOMETIMES HE THINKS HE CAN STILL HEAR THE WHIR OF CAMERAS. THE ROAR OF THE CROWD ON THE WIND. A PRAYER TO A BORED GOD.

BUT HE KNOWS THOSE ARE JUST ECHOES OF ANOTHER ERA...THE FADED SOUNDTRACK TO A CHARACTER HE PLAYED BEFORE HE JOINED THE REBELLIOUS CADRE ALLIANCE.

BEFORE HE TRAVELED BACK IN TIME AND THROUGH SPACE TO THE PLANET EARTH TO SEEK THE ASSISTANCE OF THE X-ME IN OVERTHROWING MOJO'S DESPOTIC RULE.

BEFORE THE CIVIL W ENDED AND HE WA LEFT A REFUGEE

BEFORE HE PUT DOWN THE SWORDS AND BECAME BEN GAVEEDRA.

NOW.

LANDLORD.

SCRRP

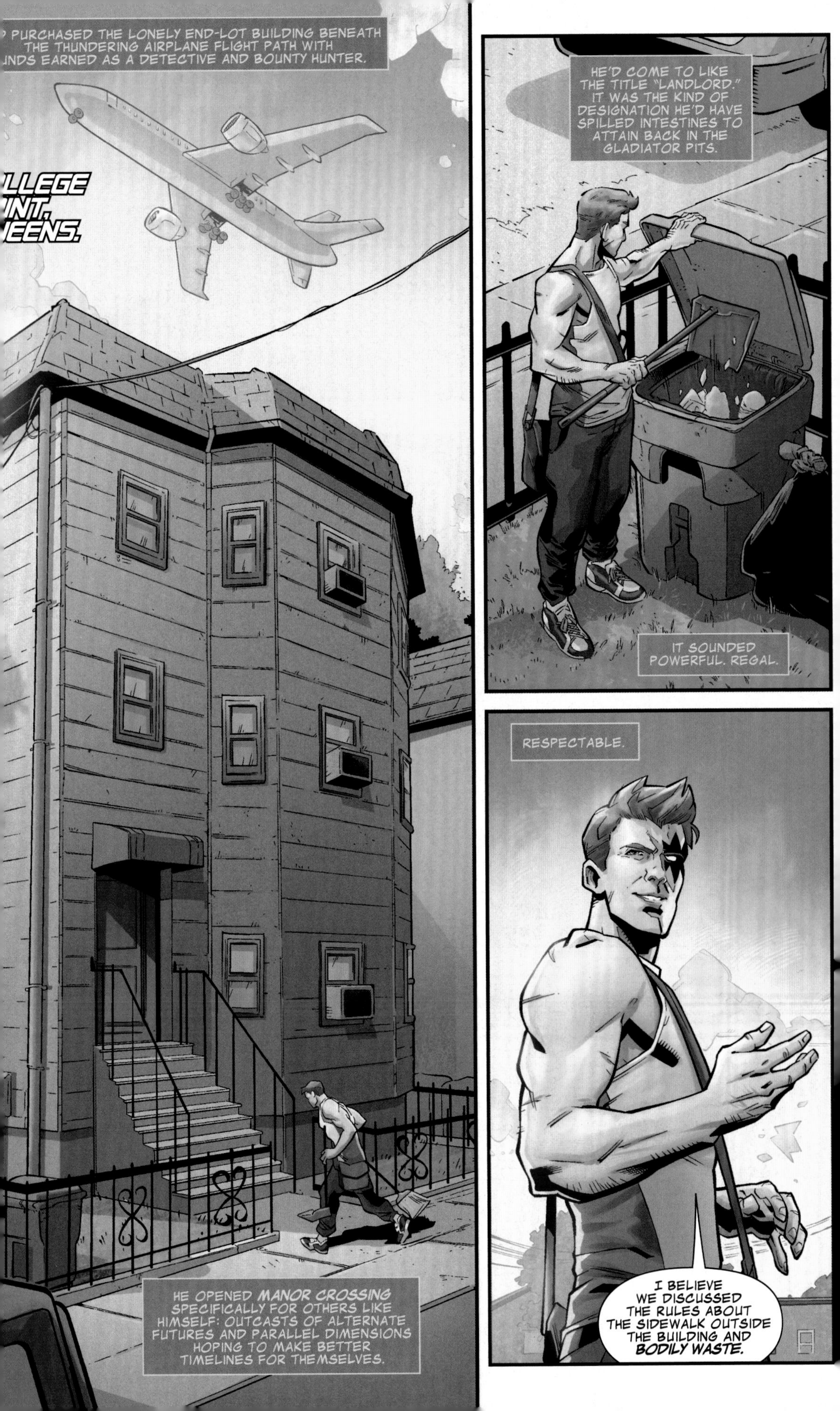
...D PURCHASED THE LONELY END-LOT BUILDING BENEATH THE THUNDERING AIRPLANE FLIGHT PATH WITH ...UNDS EARNED AS A DETECTIVE AND BOUNTY HUNTER.
...LLEGE ...INT, ...EENS.
HE OPENED MANOR CROSSING SPECIFICALLY FOR OTHERS LIKE HIMSELF: OUTCASTS OF ALTERNATE FUTURES AND PARALLEL DIMENSIONS HOPING TO MAKE BETTER TIMELINES FOR THEMSELVES.
HE'D COME TO LIKE THE TITLE "LANDLORD." IT WAS THE KIND OF DESIGNATION HE'D HAVE SPILLED INTESTINES TO ATTAIN BACK IN THE GLADIATOR PITS.
IT SOUNDED POWERFUL. REGAL.
RESPECTABLE.
I BELIEVE WE DISCUSSED THE RULES ABOUT THE SIDEWALK OUTSIDE THE BUILDING AND BODILY WASTE.

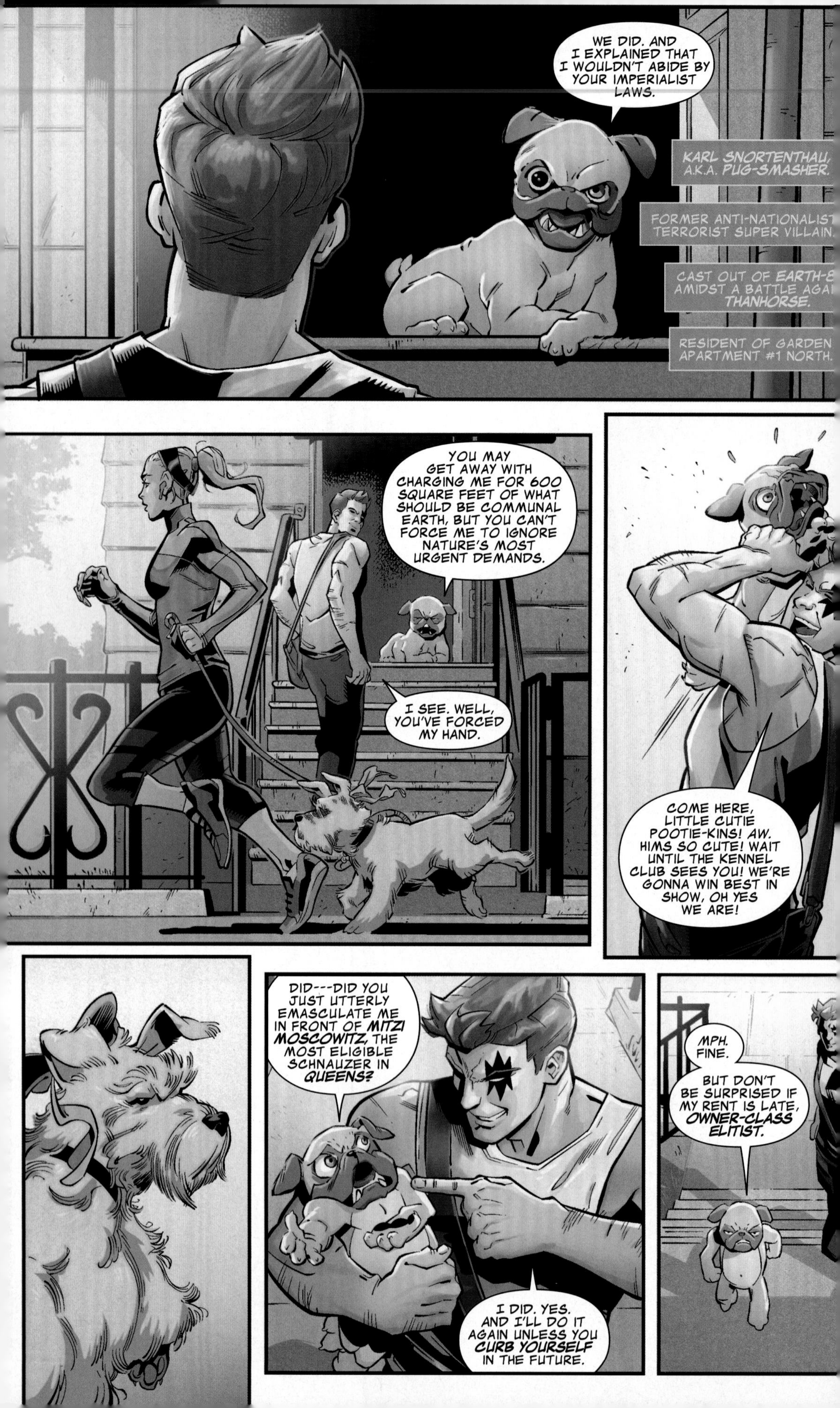

WE DID. AND I EXPLAINED THAT I WOULDN'T ABIDE BY YOUR IMPERIALIST LAWS.
KARL SNORTENTHAU, A.K.A. PUG-SMASHER.
FORMER ANTI-NATIONALIST TERRORIST SUPER VILLAIN.
CAST OUT OF EARTH-8 AMIDST A BATTLE AGAI THANHORSE.
RESIDENT OF GARDEN APARTMENT #1 NORTH.
YOU MAY GET AWAY WITH CHARGING ME FOR 600 SQUARE FEET OF WHAT SHOULD BE COMMUNAL EARTH, BUT YOU CAN'T FORCE ME TO IGNORE NATURE'S MOST URGENT DEMANDS.
I SEE. WELL, YOU'VE FORCED MY HAND.
COME HERE, LITTLE CUTIE POOTIE-KINS! AW. HIMS SO CUTE! WAIT UNTIL THE KENNEL CLUB SEES YOU! WE'RE GONNA WIN BEST IN SHOW, OH YES WE ARE!
DID---DID YOU JUST UTTERLY EMASCULATE ME IN FRONT OF MITZI MOSCOWITZ, THE MOST ELIGIBLE SCHNAUZER IN QUEENS?
I DID. YES. AND I'LL DO IT AGAIN UNLESS YOU CURB YOURSELF IN THE FUTURE.
MPH. FINE.
BUT DON'T BE SURPRISED IF MY RENT IS LATE, OWNER-CLASS ELITIST.

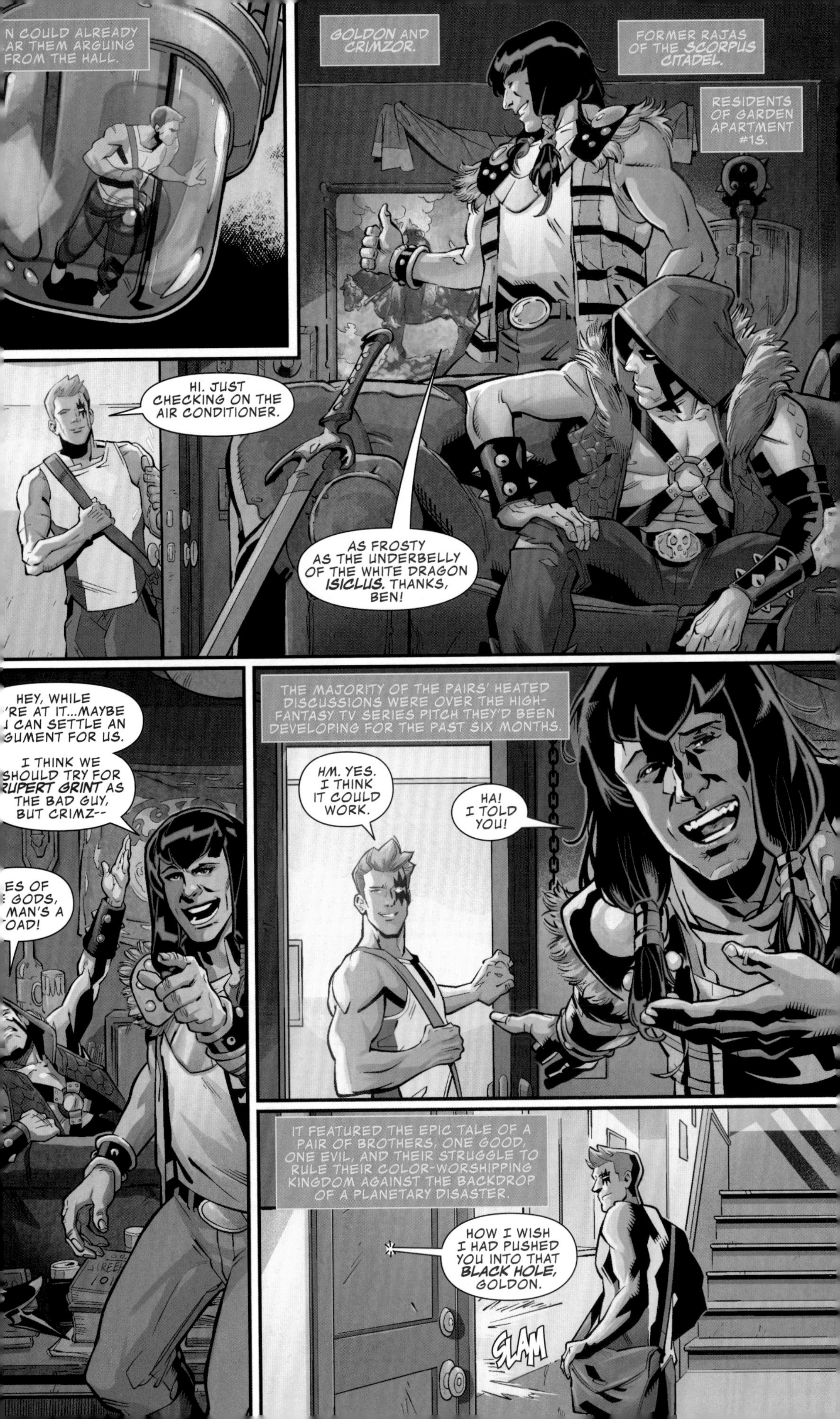

N COULD ALREADY
AR THEM ARGUING
FROM THE HALL.
GOLDON AND CRIMZOR.
FORMER RAJAS OF THE SCORPUS CITADEL.
RESIDENTS OF GARDEN APARTMENT #1S.
HI. JUST CHECKING ON THE AIR CONDITIONER.
AS FROSTY AS THE UNDERBELLY OF THE WHITE DRAGON ISICLUS. THANKS, BEN!
HEY, WHILE 'RE AT IT...MAYBE I CAN SETTLE AN GUMENT FOR US.
I THINK WE SHOULD TRY FOR RUPERT GRINT AS THE BAD GUY, BUT CRIMZ--
ES OF GODS, MAN'S A TOAD!
THE MAJORITY OF THE PAIRS' HEATED DISCUSSIONS WERE OVER THE HIGH-FANTASY TV SERIES PITCH THEY'D BEEN DEVELOPING FOR THE PAST SIX MONTHS.
HM. YES. I THINK IT COULD WORK.
HA! I TOLD YOU!
IT FEATURED THE EPIC TALE OF A PAIR OF BROTHERS, ONE GOOD, ONE EVIL, AND THEIR STRUGGLE TO RULE THEIR COLOR-WORSHIPPING KINGDOM AGAINST THE BACKDROP OF A PLANETARY DISASTER.
HOW I WISH I HAD PUSHED YOU INTO THAT BLACK HOLE, GOLDON.
SLAM

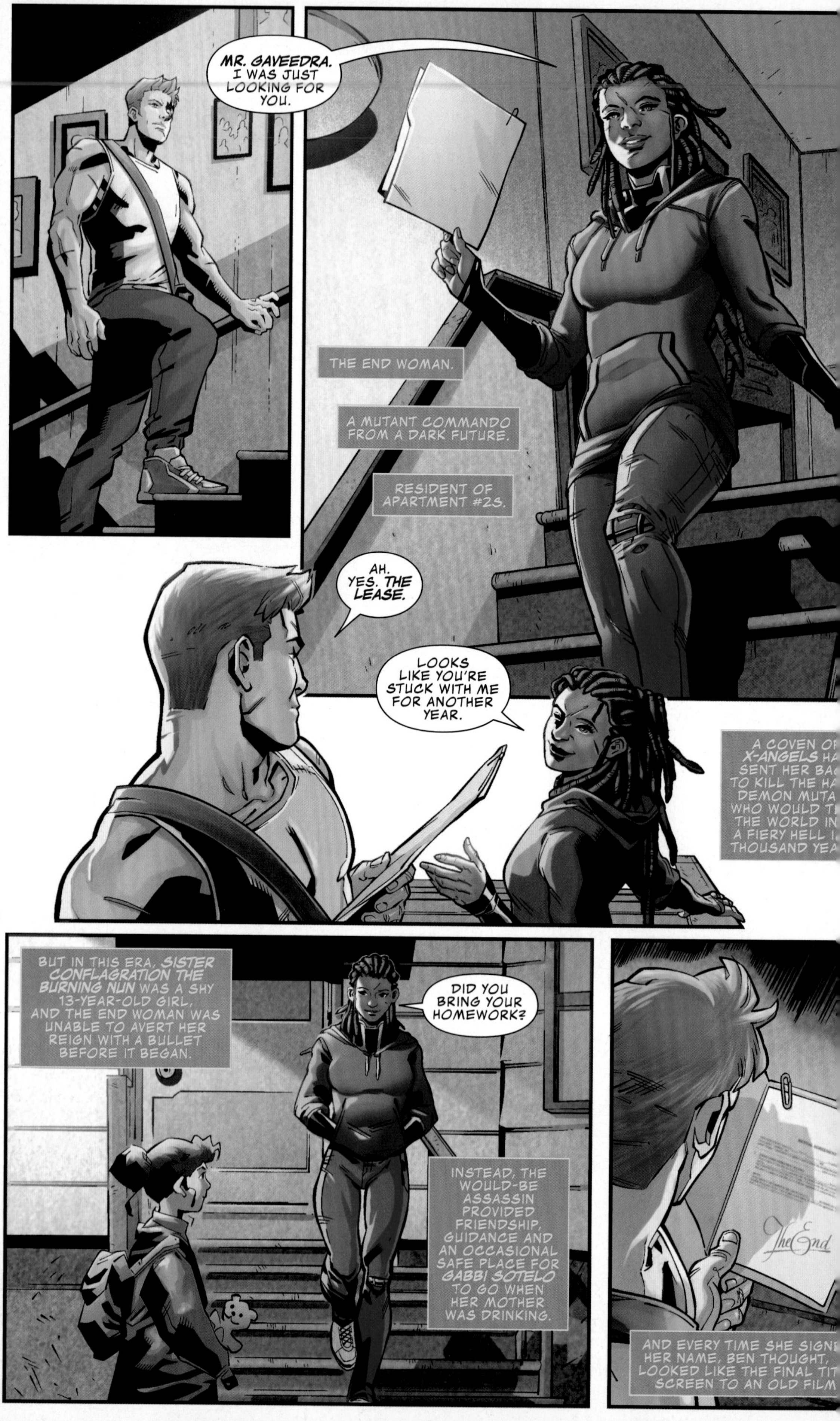
MR. GAVEEDRA. I WAS JUST LOOKING FOR YOU.
THE END WOMAN.
A MUTANT COMMANDO FROM A DARK FUTURE.
RESIDENT OF APARTMENT #2S.
AH. YES. THE LEASE.
LOOKS LIKE YOU'RE STUCK WITH ME FOR ANOTHER YEAR.
A COVEN OF X-ANGELS HA SENT HER BA TO KILL THE HA DEMON MUTA WHO WOULD T THE WORLD IN A FIERY HELL I THOUSAND YEA
BUT IN THIS ERA, SISTER CONFLAGRATION THE BURNING NUN WAS A SHY 13-YEAR-OLD GIRL, AND THE END WOMAN WAS UNABLE TO AVERT HER REIGN WITH A BULLET BEFORE IT BEGAN.
DID YOU BRING YOUR HOMEWORK?
INSTEAD, THE WOULD-BE ASSASSIN PROVIDED FRIENDSHIP, GUIDANCE AND AN OCCASIONAL SAFE PLACE FOR GABBI SOTELO TO GO WHEN HER MOTHER WAS DRINKING.
The End
AND EVERY TIME SHE SIGN HER NAME, BEN THOUGHT, LOOKED LIKE THE FINAL TIT SCREEN TO AN OLD FILM

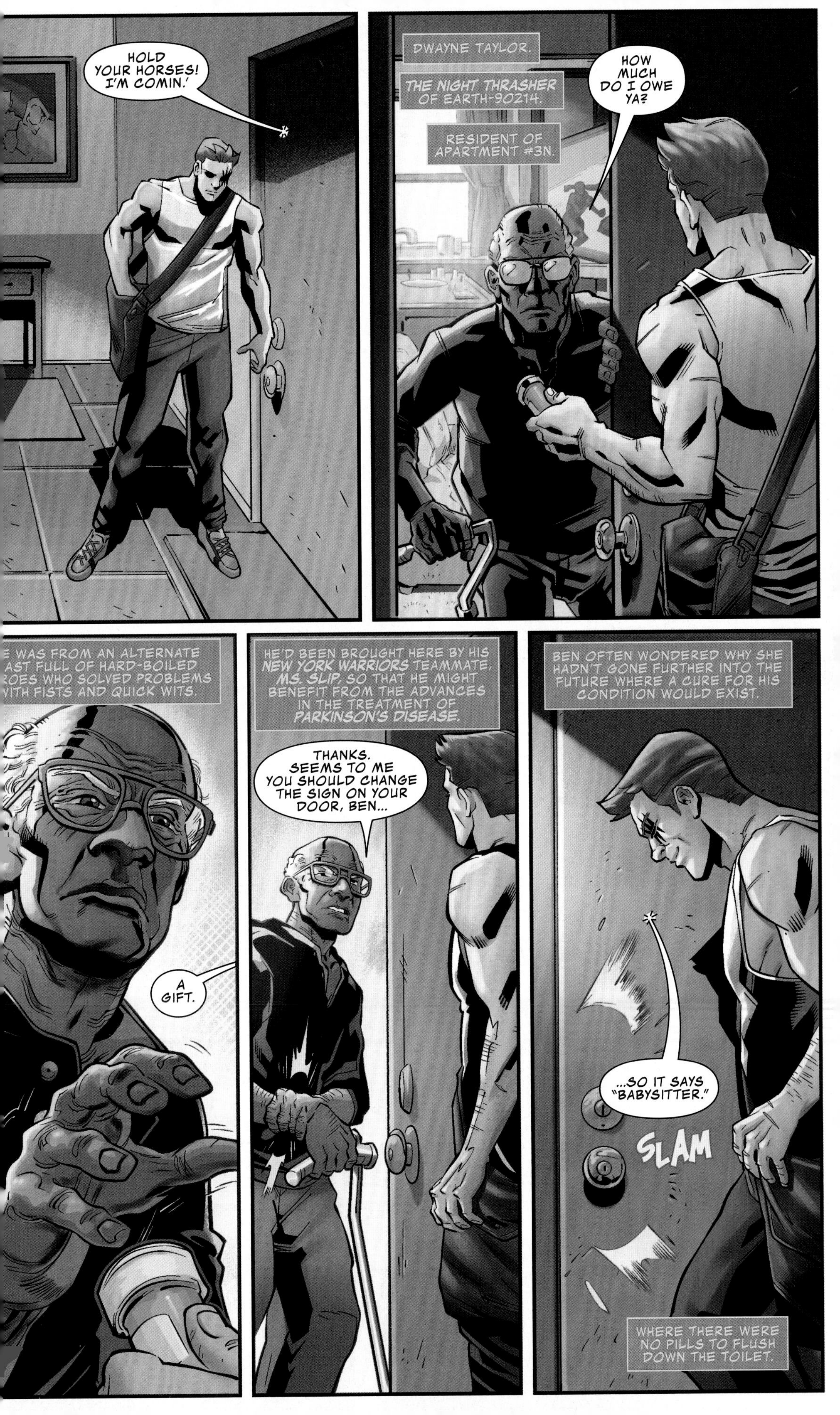
HOLD YOUR HORSES! I'M COMIN.'
DWAYNE TAYLOR.
THE NIGHT THRASHER OF EARTH-90214.
RESIDENT OF APARTMENT #3N.
HOW MUCH DO I OWE YA?
E WAS FROM AN ALTERNATE AST FULL OF HARD-BOILED ROES WHO SOLVED PROBLEMS WITH FISTS AND QUICK WITS.
A GIFT.
HE'D BEEN BROUGHT HERE BY HIS NEW YORK WARRIORS TEAMMATE, MS. SLIP, SO THAT HE MIGHT BENEFIT FROM THE ADVANCES IN THE TREATMENT OF PARKINSON'S DISEASE.
THANKS. SEEMS TO ME YOU SHOULD CHANGE THE SIGN ON YOUR DOOR, BEN...
BEN OFTEN WONDERED WHY SHE HADN'T GONE FURTHER INTO THE FUTURE WHERE A CURE FOR HIS CONDITION WOULD EXIST.
...SO IT SAYS "BABYSITTER."
SLAM
WHERE THERE WERE NO PILLS TO FLUSH DOWN THE TOILET.

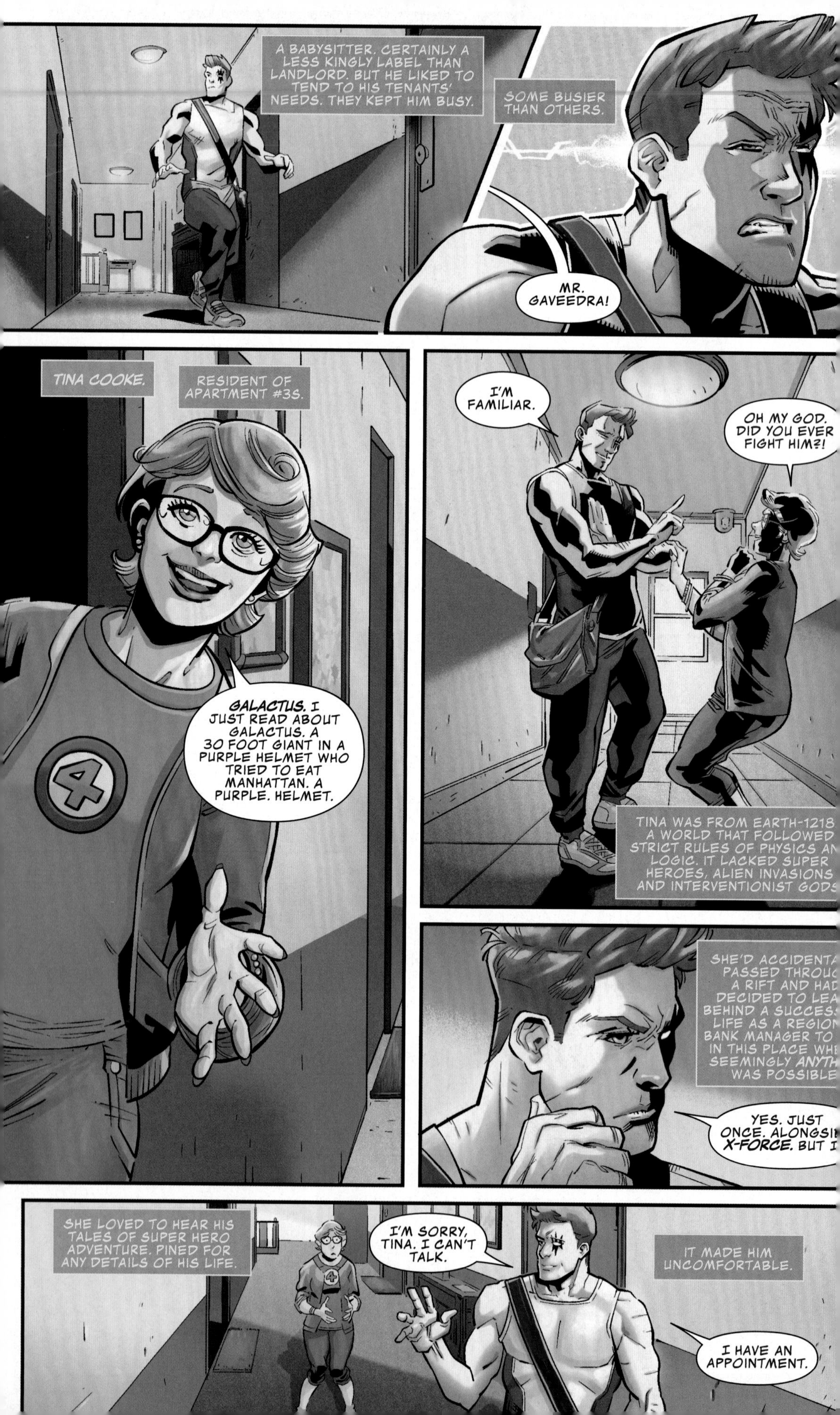
A BABYSITTER. CERTAINLY A LESS KINGLY LABEL THAN LANDLORD. BUT HE LIKED TO TEND TO HIS TENANTS' NEEDS. THEY KEPT HIM BUSY.
SOME BUSIER THAN OTHERS.
MR. GAVEEDRA!
TINA COOKE.
RESIDENT OF APARTMENT #3S.
GALACTUS. I JUST READ ABOUT GALACTUS. A 30 FOOT GIANT IN A PURPLE HELMET WHO TRIED TO EAT MANHATTAN. A PURPLE. HELMET.
I'M FAMILIAR.
OH MY GOD. DID YOU EVER FIGHT HIM?!
TINA WAS FROM EARTH-1218 A WORLD THAT FOLLOWED STRICT RULES OF PHYSICS AN LOGIC. IT LACKED SUPER HEROES, ALIEN INVASIONS AND INTERVENTIONIST GODS
SHE'D ACCIDENTA PASSED THROUG A RIFT AND HAD DECIDED TO LEA BEHIND A SUCCESS LIFE AS A REGION BANK MANAGER TO IN THIS PLACE WHE SEEMINGLY ANYTH WAS POSSIBLE
YES. JUST ONCE. ALONGSI X-FORCE. BUT I
SHE LOVED TO HEAR HIS TALES OF SUPER HERO ADVENTURE. PINED FOR ANY DETAILS OF HIS LIFE.
I'M SORRY, TINA. I CAN'T TALK.
IT MADE HIM UNCOMFORTABLE.
I HAVE AN APPOINTMENT.

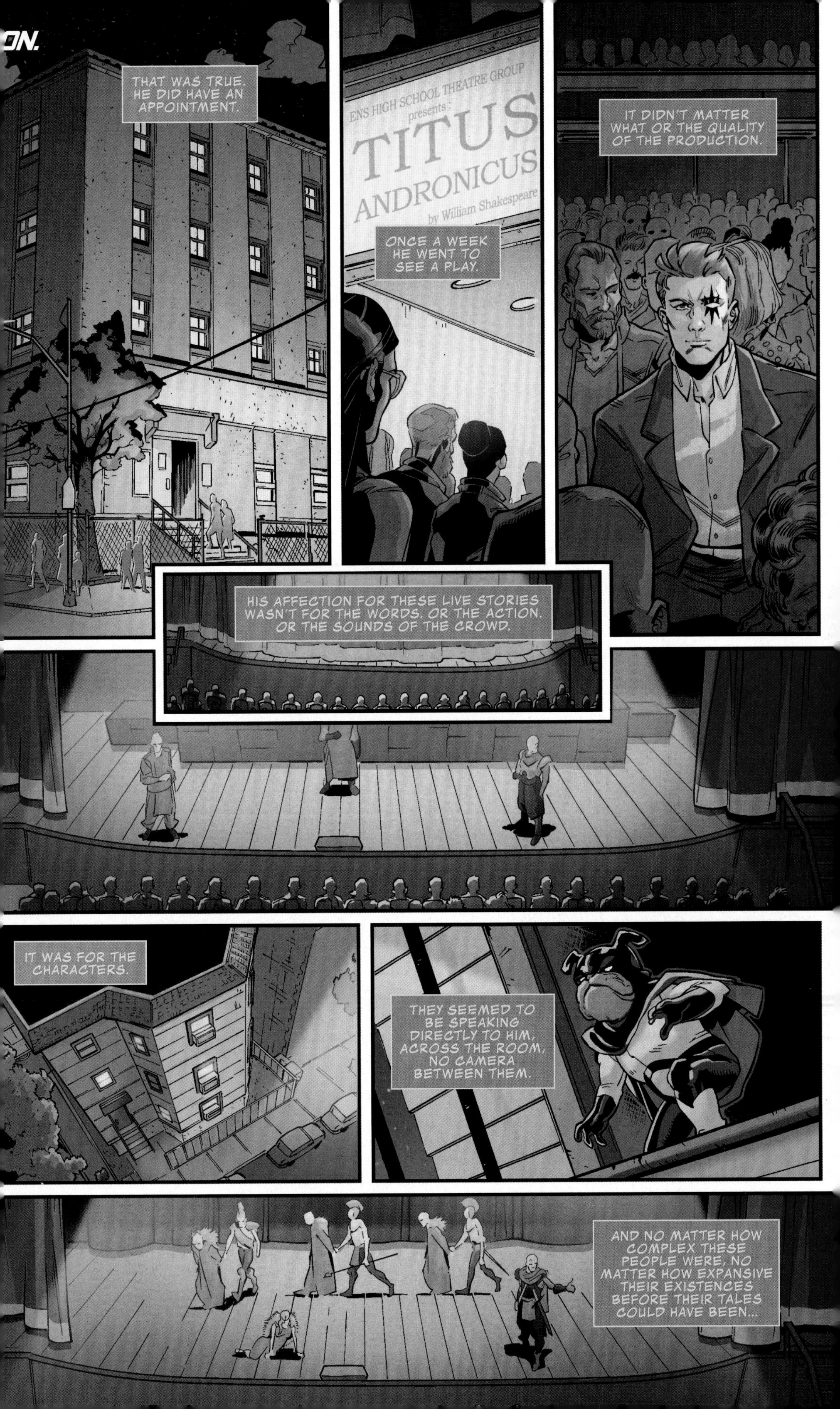
ON.
THAT WAS TRUE. HE DID HAVE AN APPOINTMENT.
ENS HIGH SCHOOL THEATRE GROUP presents : TITUS ANDRONICUS by William Shakespeare
ONCE A WEEK HE WENT TO SEE A PLAY.
IT DIDN'T MATTER WHAT OR THE QUALITY OF THE PRODUCTION.
HIS AFFECTION FOR THESE LIVE STORIES WASN'T FOR THE WORDS. OR THE ACTION. OR THE SOUNDS OF THE CROWD.
IT WAS FOR THE CHARACTERS.
THEY SEEMED TO BE SPEAKING DIRECTLY TO HIM, ACROSS THE ROOM, NO CAMERA BETWEEN THEM.
AND NO MATTER HOW COMPLEX THESE PEOPLE WERE, NO MATTER HOW EXPANSIVE THEIR EXISTENCES BEFORE THEIR TALES COULD HAVE BEEN...

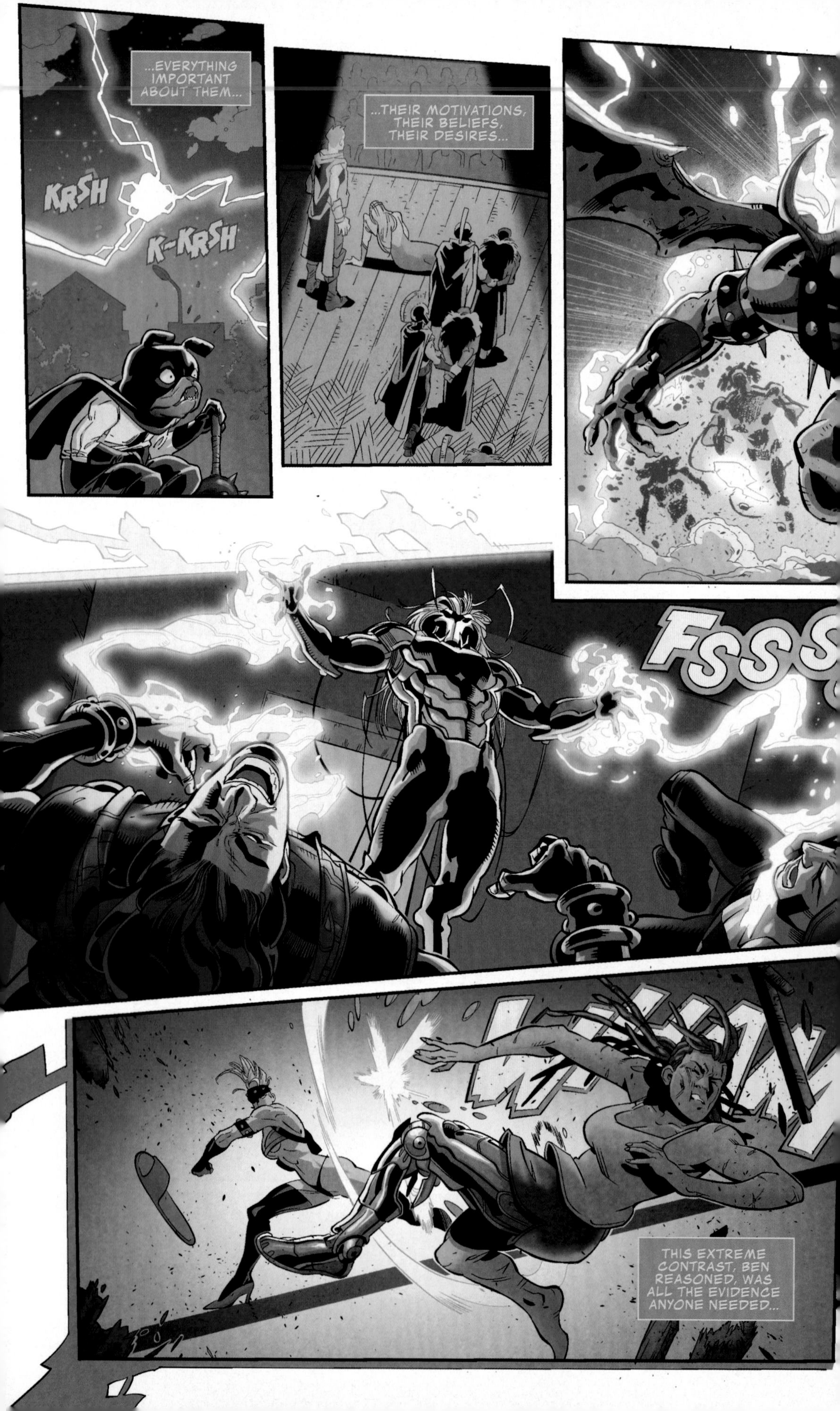
...EVERYTHING IMPORTANT ABOUT THEM...
KRSH
K-KRSH
...THEIR MOTIVATIONS, THEIR BELIEFS, THEIR DESIRES...
THIS EXTREME CONTRAST, BEN REASONED, WAS ALL THE EVIDENCE ANYONE NEEDED...

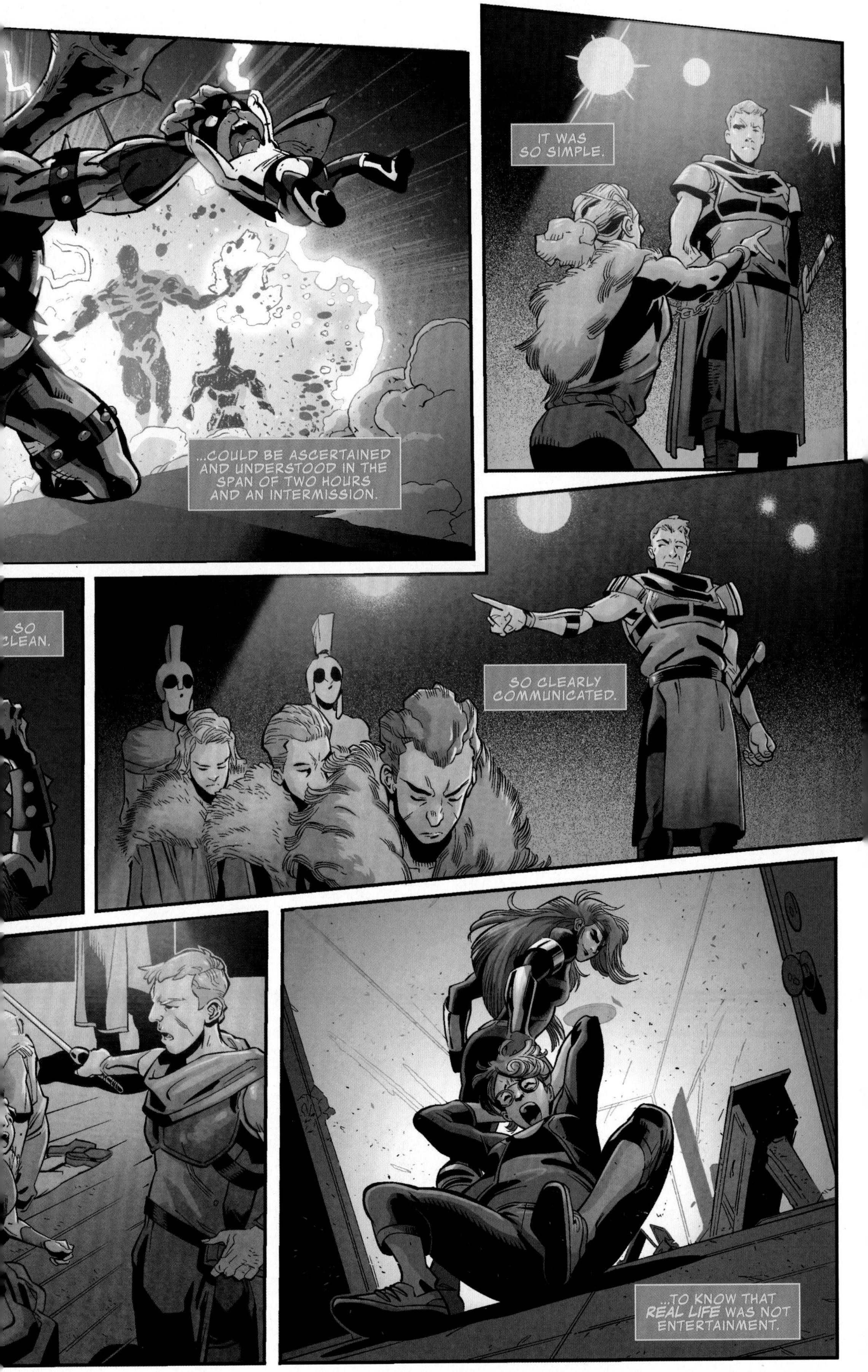
...COULD BE ASCERTAINED AND UNDERSTOOD IN THE SPAN OF TWO HOURS AND AN INTERMISSION.
IT WAS SO SIMPLE.
SO CLEAN.
SO CLEARLY COMMUNICATED.
...TO KNOW THAT REAL LIFE WAS NOT ENTERTAINMENT.

MOTIVATIONS. BELIEFS. DESIRES. IN REAL LIFE IT COULD TAKE YEARS TO ASCERTAIN THESE IN ANOTHER PERSON.

AND EVEN THEN, IT COULD BE COMPLETELY AND HOPELESSLY MISUNDERSTOOD.

BEN HAD HAD TEAMMATES. ASSOCIATES. FRIENDS, EVEN. BUT HE HAD STRUGGLED TO MAINTAIN DEEPER RELATIONSHIPS.

JULIO "RICTOR" RICHTER.

FORMER MUTANT SUPER HERO. CURRENT CLUB OWNER.

FORMER RESIDENT OF MANOR CROSSING.

BEN REMEMBERS THEIR LAST CONVERSATION. THROUGH TEARS, JULIO HAD ASKED WHY BEN'S ATTENTIONS HAD WANED, WHY HIS AFFECTIONS WERE SPURNED.

"DON'T I INTEREST YOU ANYMORE?" HE'D SAID THROUGH TEARS.

"THE WORST PART IS, I KNOW YOUR PROBLEM WITH US," HE'D SAID, GOING OUT THE DOOR.

"WE DON'T FIGHT ENOUGH."

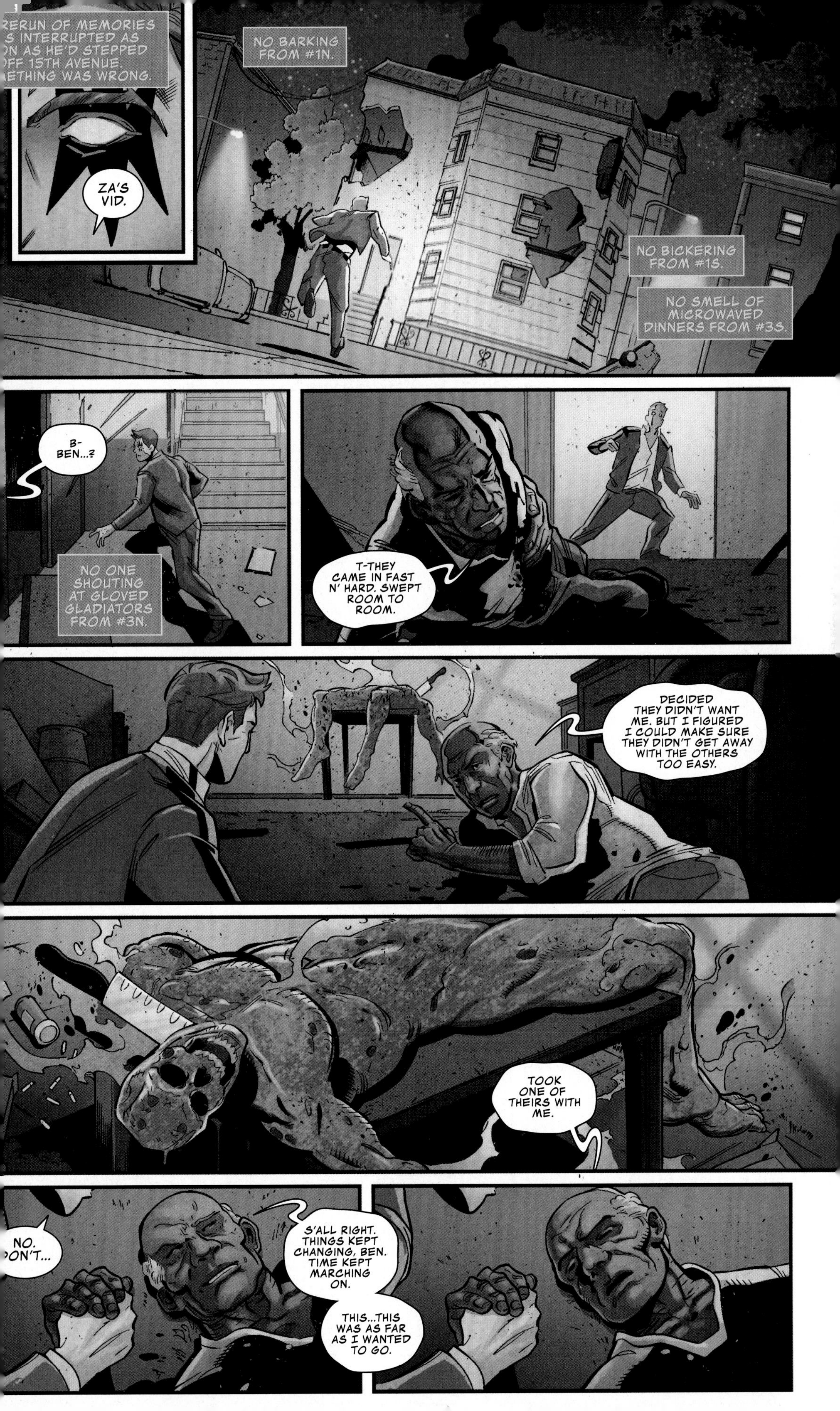

RERUN OF MEMORIES
S INTERRUPTED AS
ON AS HE'D STEPPED
OFF 15TH AVENUE.
ETHING WAS WRONG.
ZA'S VID.
NO BARKING FROM #1N.
NO BICKERING FROM #1S.
NO SMELL OF MICROWAVED DINNERS FROM #3S.
B-BEN...?
NO ONE SHOUTING AT GLOVED GLADIATORS FROM #3N.
T-THEY CAME IN FAST N' HARD. SWEPT ROOM TO ROOM.
DECIDED THEY DIDN'T WANT ME. BUT I FIGURED I COULD MAKE SURE THEY DIDN'T GET AWAY WITH THE OTHERS TOO EASY.
TOOK ONE OF THEIRS WITH ME.
NO. DON'T...
S'ALL RIGHT. THINGS KEPT CHANGING, BEN. TIME KEPT MARCHING ON.
THIS...THIS WAS AS FAR AS I WANTED TO GO.

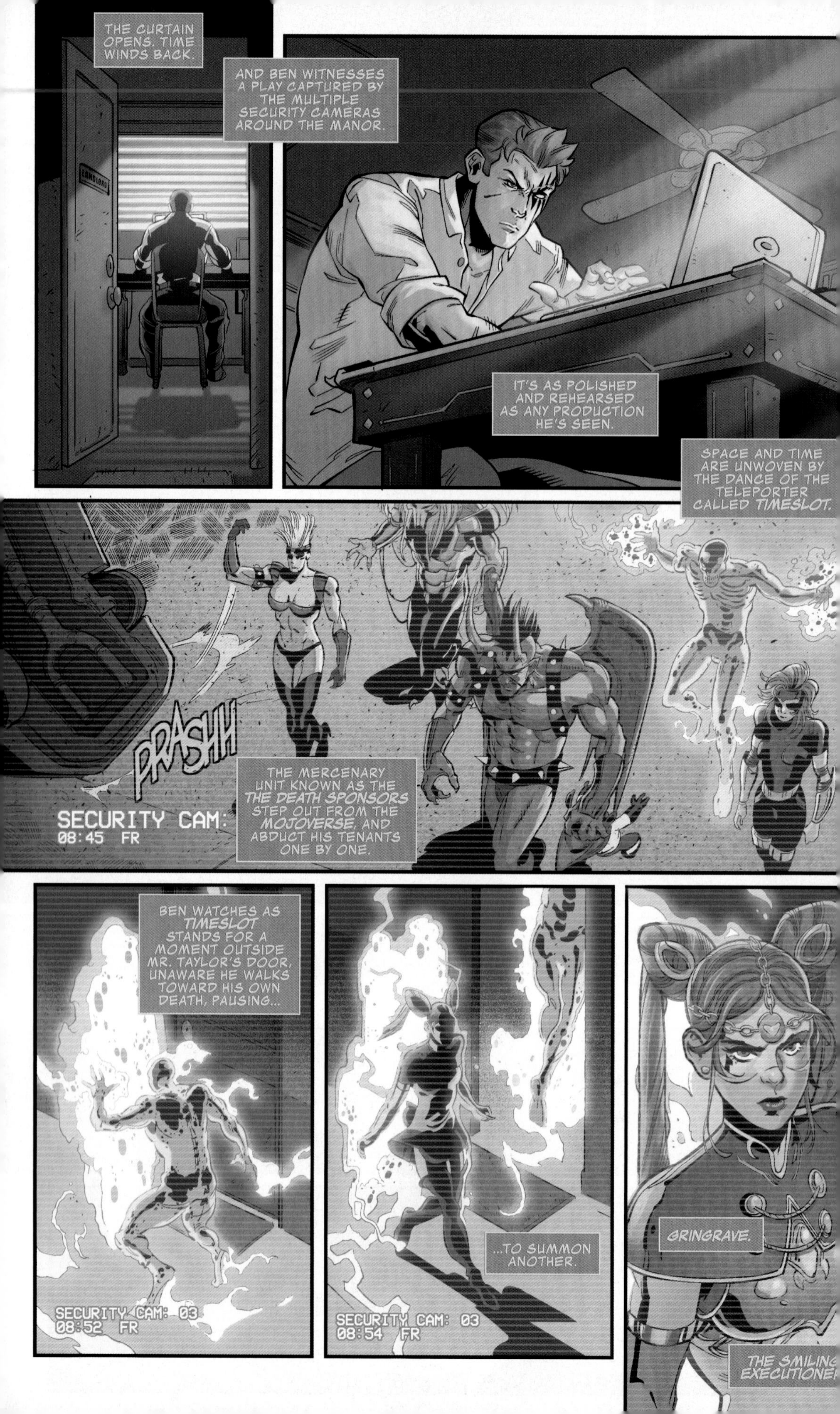
THE CURTAIN OPENS. TIME WINDS BACK.
LANDLORD
AND BEN WITNESSES A PLAY CAPTURED BY THE MULTIPLE SECURITY CAMERAS AROUND THE MANOR.
IT'S AS POLISHED AND REHEARSED AS ANY PRODUCTION HE'S SEEN.
SPACE AND TIME ARE UNWOVEN BY THE DANCE OF THE TELEPORTER CALLED *TIMESLOT.*
PRASHH
THE MERCENARY UNIT KNOWN AS THE *THE DEATH SPONSORS* STEP OUT FROM THE *MOJOVERSE,* AND ABDUCT HIS TENANTS ONE BY ONE.
SECURITY CAM:
08:45 FR
BEN WATCHES AS *TIMESLOT* STANDS FOR A MOMENT OUTSIDE MR. TAYLOR'S DOOR, UNAWARE HE WALKS TOWARD HIS OWN DEATH, PAUSING...
SECURITY CAM: 03
08:52 FR
...TO SUMMON ANOTHER.
SECURITY CAM: 03
08:54 FR
GRINGRAVE.
THE SMILING EXECUTIONE

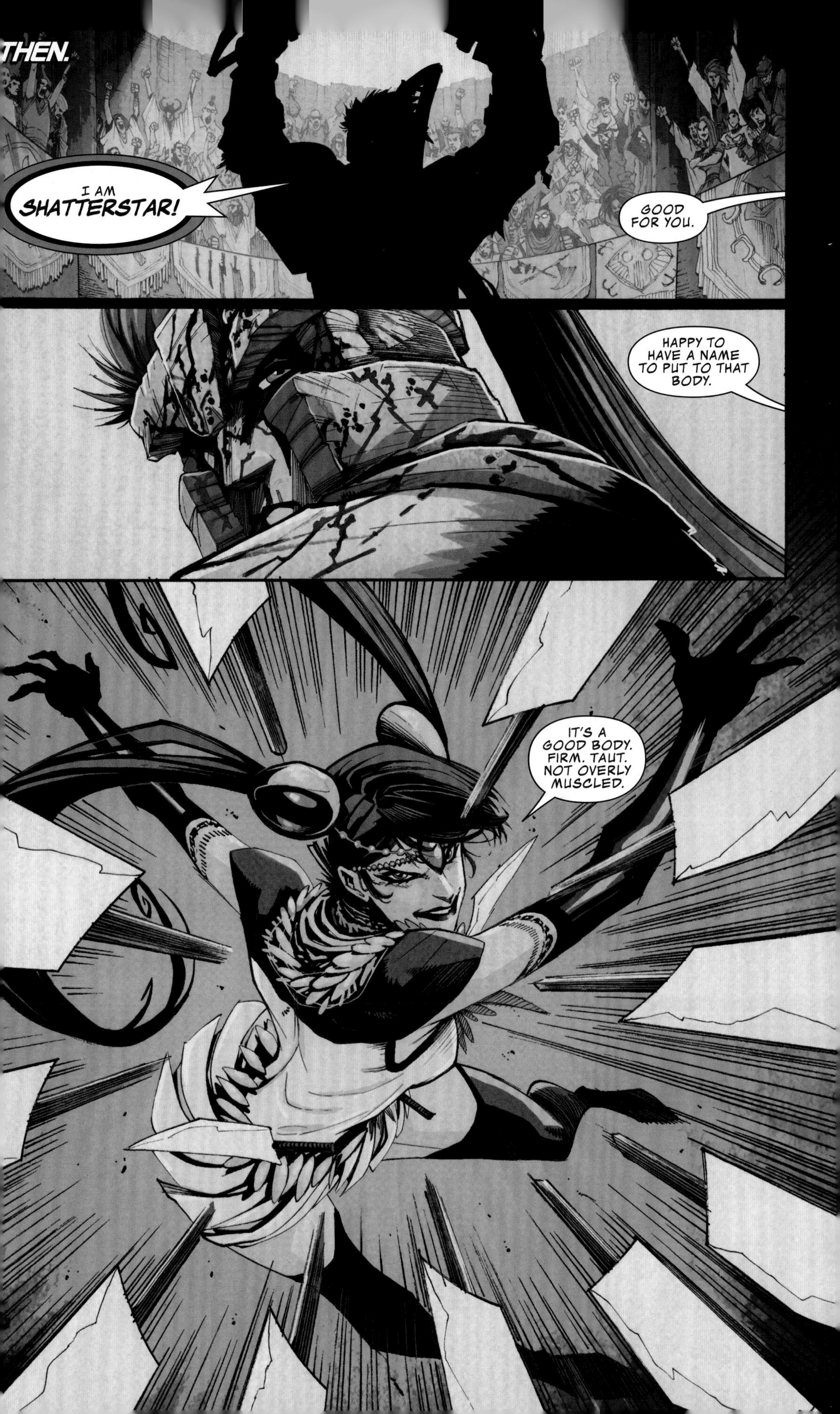
THEN.
I AM SHATTERSTAR!
GOOD FOR YOU.
HAPPY TO HAVE A NAME TO PUT TO THAT BODY.
IT'S A GOOD BODY. FIRM. TAUT. NOT OVERLY MUSCLED.

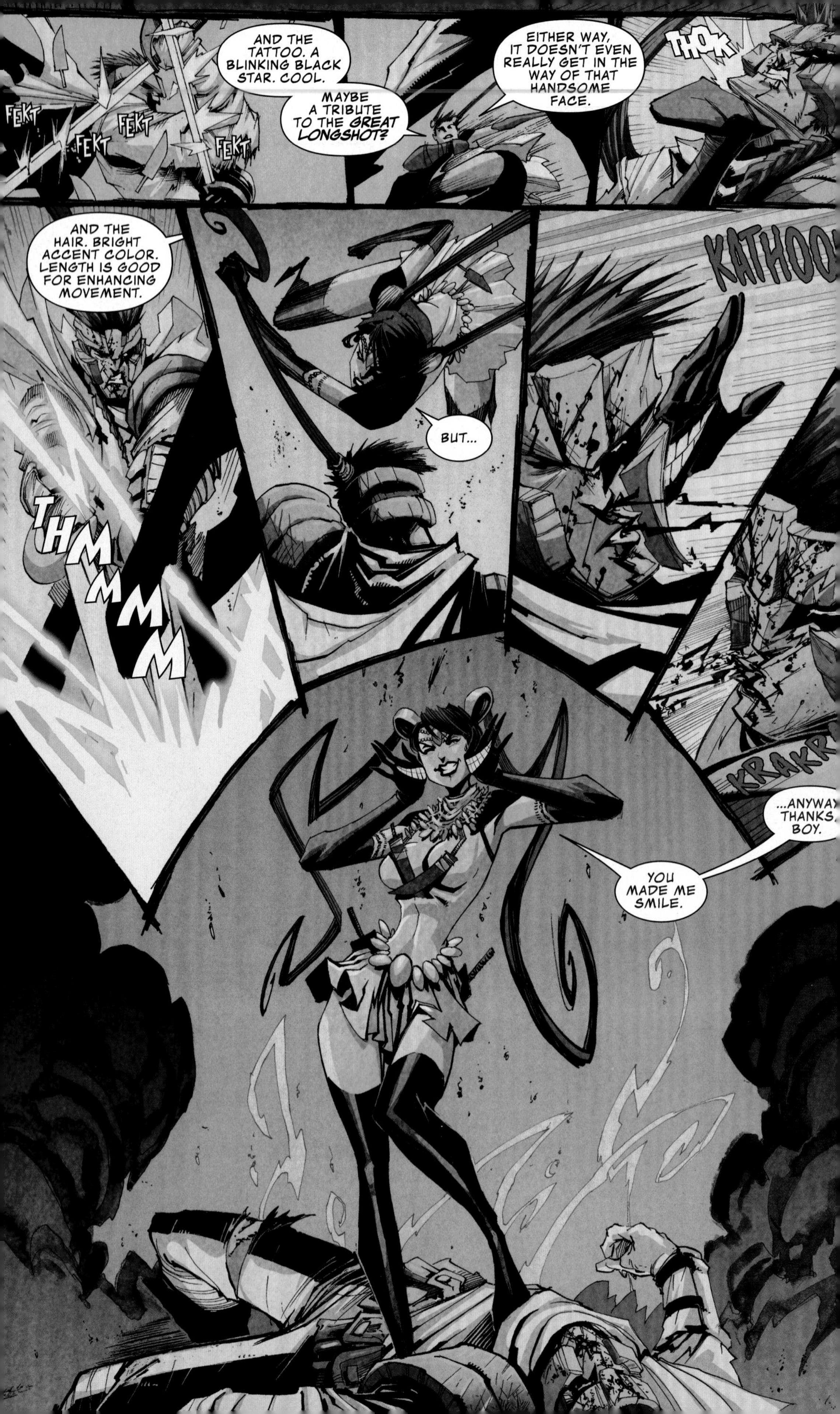
FEKT
FEKT
FEKT
FEKT
AND THE TATTOO. A BLINKING BLACK STAR. COOL.
MAYBE A TRIBUTE TO THE *GREAT LONGSHOT?*
EITHER WAY, IT DOESN'T EVEN REALLY GET IN THE WAY OF THAT HANDSOME FACE.
THOK
AND THE HAIR. BRIGHT ACCENT COLOR. LENGTH IS GOOD FOR ENHANCING MOVEMENT.
THMMMMM
BUT...
KATHOO
KRAKR
...ANYWAY THANKS, BOY.
YOU MADE ME SMILE.

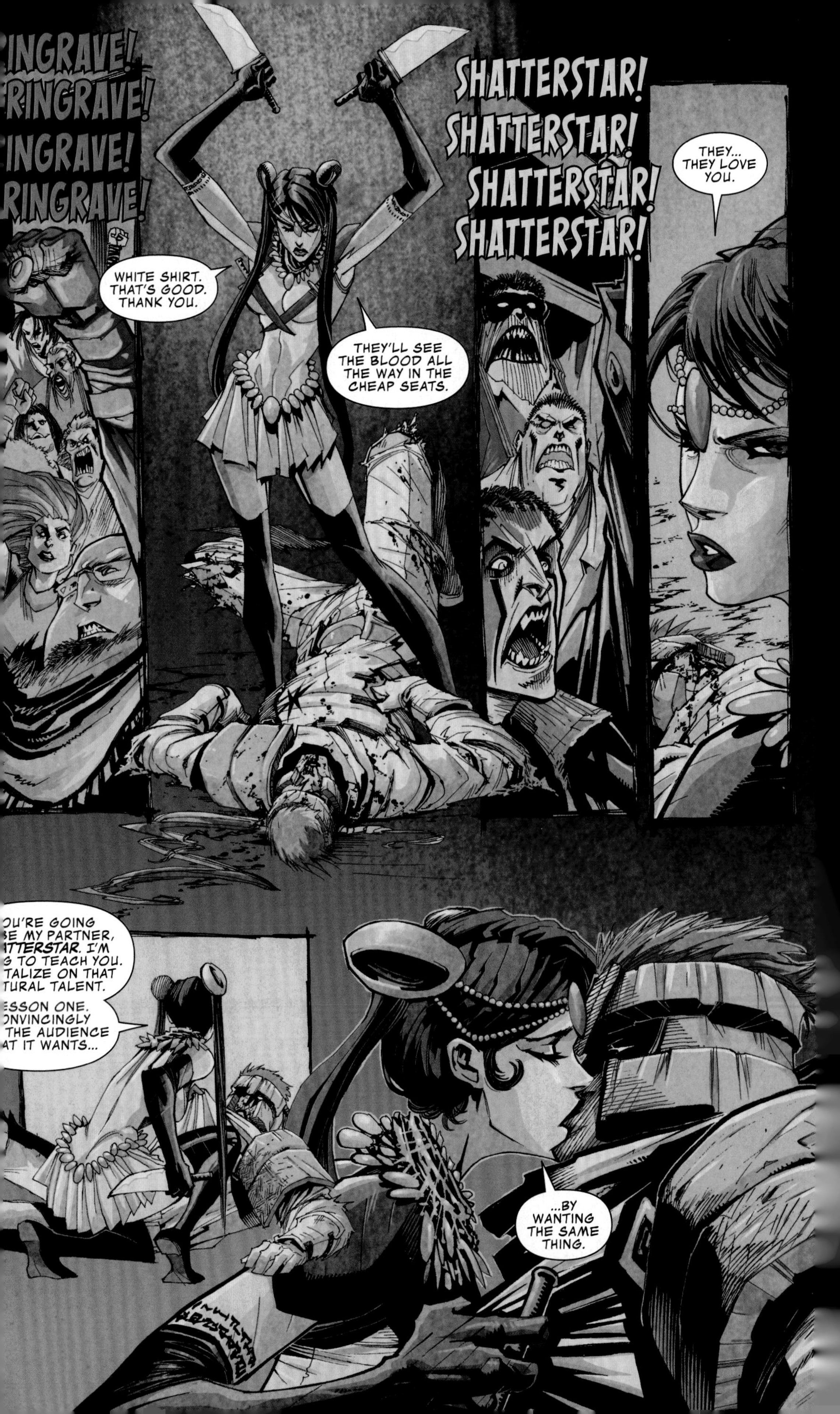

RINGRAVE!
RINGRAVE!
RINGRAVE!
RINGRAVE!
WHITE SHIRT. THAT'S GOOD. THANK YOU.
THEY'LL SEE THE BLOOD ALL THE WAY IN THE CHEAP SEATS.
SHATTERSTAR!
SHATTERSTAR!
SHATTERSTAR!
SHATTERSTAR!
THEY... THEY LOVE YOU.
OU'RE GOING BE MY PARTNER, ATTERSTAR. I'M G TO TEACH YOU. TALIZE ON THAT TURAL TALENT.
ESSON ONE. ONVINCINGLY THE AUDIENCE AT IT WANTS...
...BY WANTING THE SAME THING.

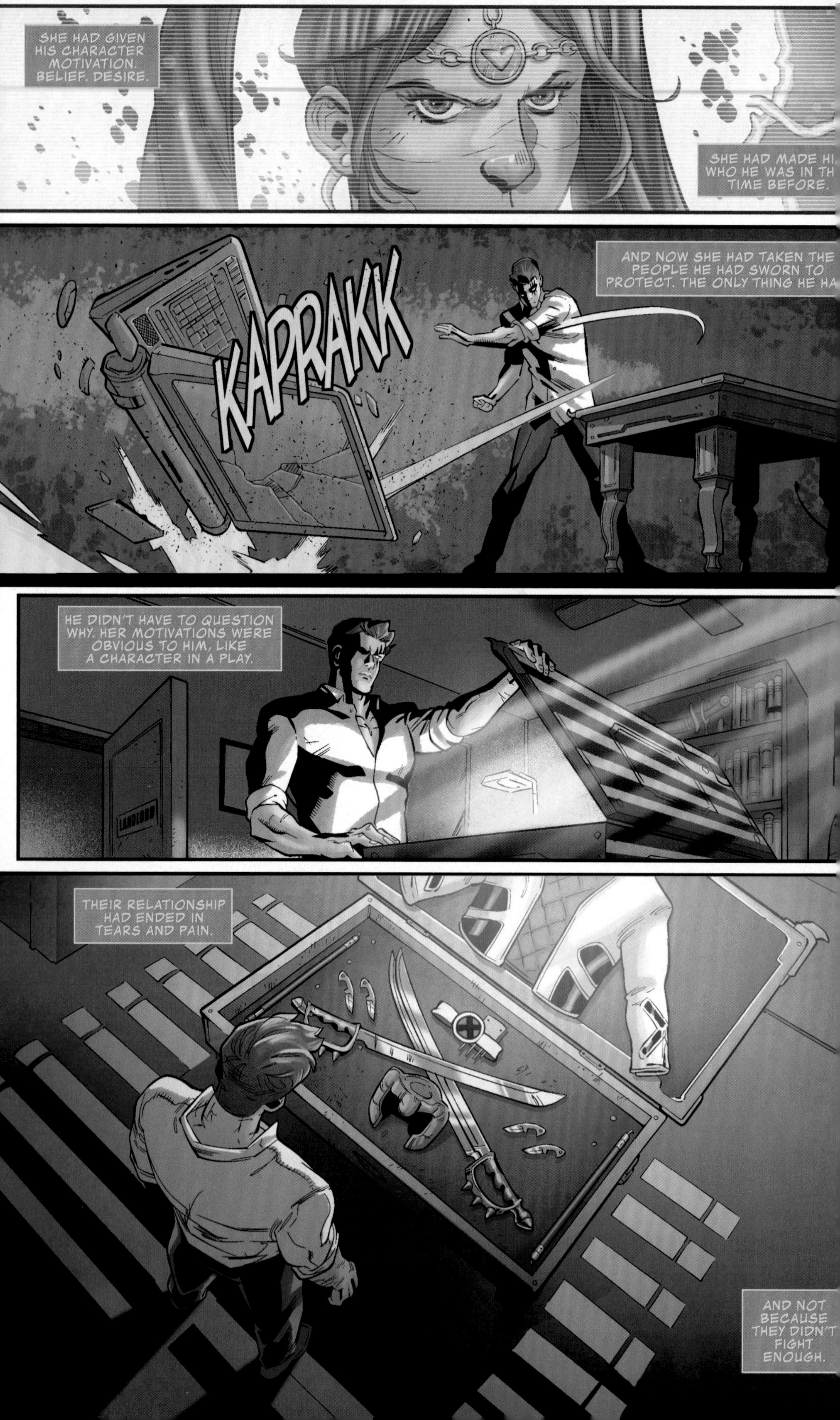
SHE HAD GIVEN HIS CHARACTER MOTIVATION. BELIEF. DESIRE.
SHE HAD MADE HI WHO HE WAS IN TH TIME BEFORE.
AND NOW SHE HAD TAKEN THE PEOPLE HE HAD SWORN TO PROTECT. THE ONLY THING HE HA
KAPRAKK
HE DIDN'T HAVE TO QUESTION WHY. HER MOTIVATIONS WERE OBVIOUS TO HIM, LIKE A CHARACTER IN A PLAY.
LANDLORD
THEIR RELATIONSHIP HAD ENDED IN TEARS AND PAIN.
AND NOT BECAUSE THEY DIDN'T FIGHT ENOUGH.

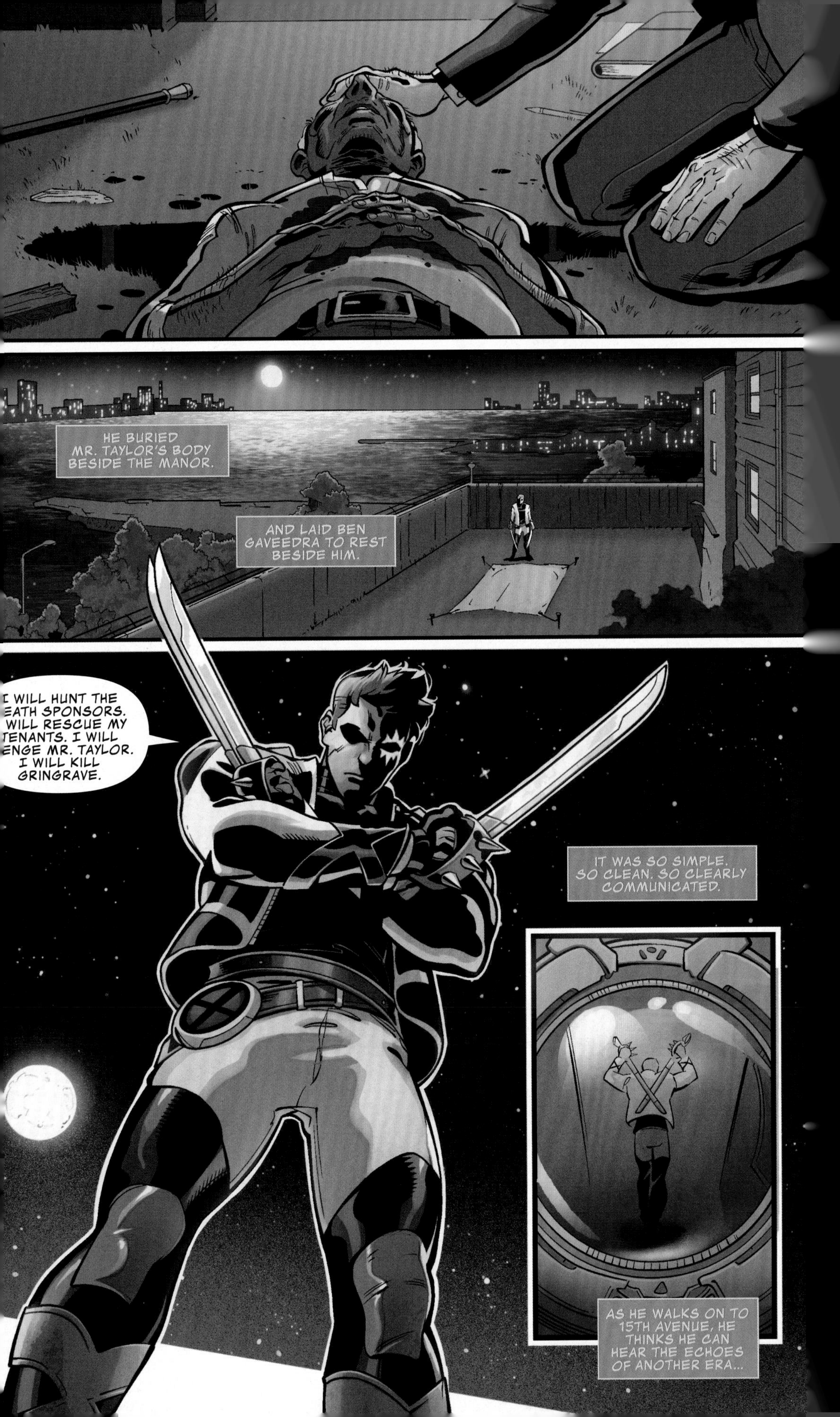
HE BURIED MR. TAYLOR'S BODY BESIDE THE MANOR.
AND LAID BEN GAVEEDRA TO REST BESIDE HIM.
I WILL HUNT THE EATH SPONSORS. WILL RESCUE MY TENANTS. I WILL ENGE MR. TAYLOR. I WILL KILL GRINGRAVE.
IT WAS SO SIMPLE. SO CLEAN. SO CLEARLY COMMUNICATED.
AS HE WALKS ON TO 15TH AVENUE, HE THINKS HE CAN HEAR THE ECHOES OF ANOTHER ERA...

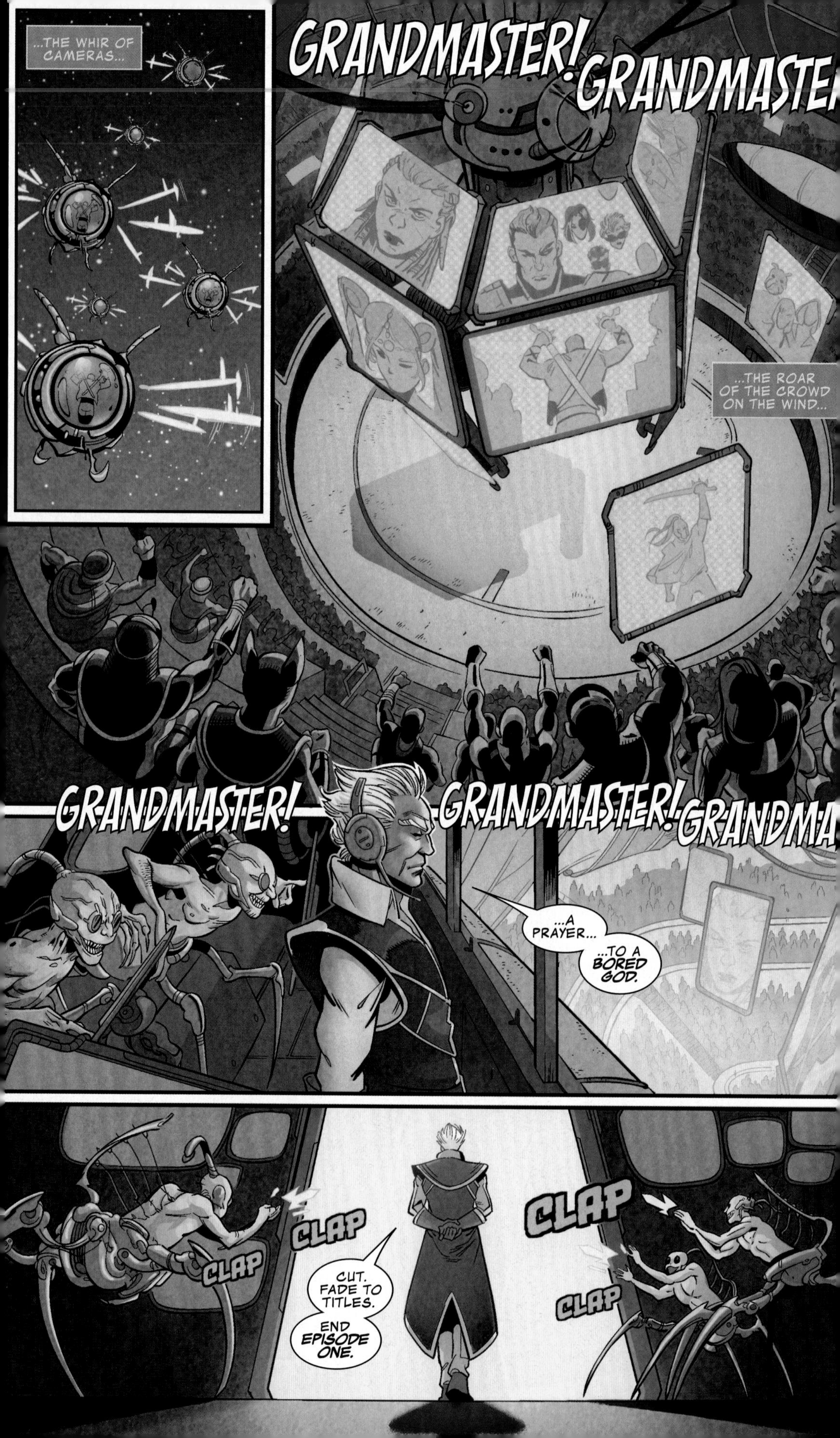
...THE WHIR OF CAMERAS...
GRANDMASTER! GRANDMASTE
...THE ROAR OF THE CROWD ON THE WIND...
GRANDMASTER! GRANDMASTER! GRANDMA
...A PRAYER...
...TO A BORED GOD.
CLAP
CLAP
CLAP
CLAP
CUT. FADE TO TITLES.
END EPISODE ONE.

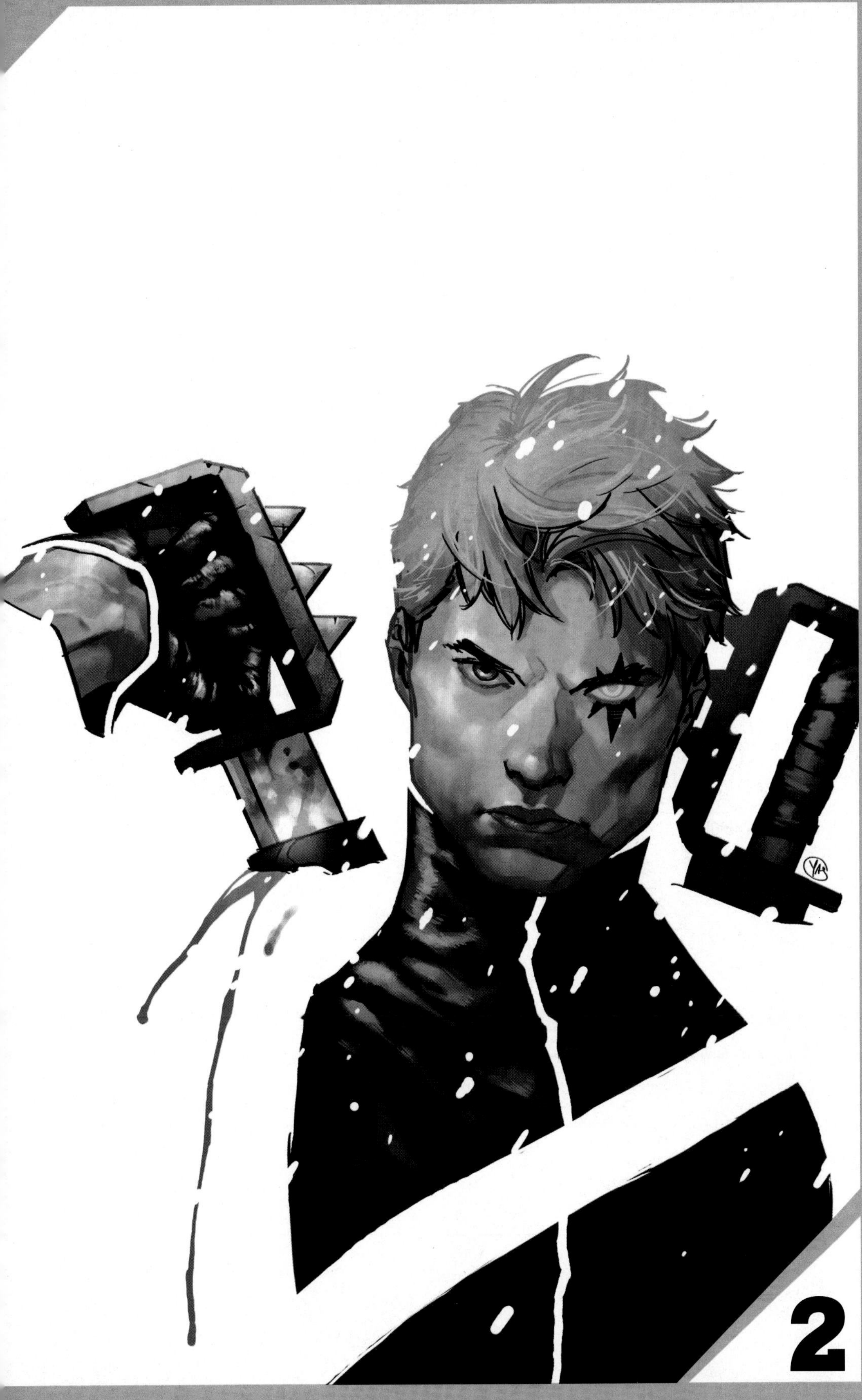
2

THE WORLD IS CALLED *HORUS IV.*

ONCE, ITS PEOPLE TRAVELED IN SILVER VESSELS ON FINGERS OF FLAME TO OTHER WORLDS, DISGUISING THEMSELVES AS GODS TO BRING AWE TO EAGER NATIVES.

CONFLICTS BETWEEN HORUSIAN NATIONS WERE SOLVED BY COMBAT AMONG THESE *MESSIANIC CHAMPIONS* WHO USED THEIR ENGINEERED STRENGTHS TO DECIDE WHO HAD THE RIGHT TO RULE.

RECENT PLANETWIDE ECONOMIC AND ENVIRONMENTAL COLLAPSE HAD ELIMINATED EMPIRES AND FRIVOLOUS INTERSTELLAR TRAVEL.

BUT THE HORUSIANS STILL DESIRE *WORSHIP.*

WATHROM

THEY STILL DESIRE *CONFLICT.*

UNFORTUNATELY, THE OLD SLAM-BANG MASH-UPS JUST AREN'T DOING IT ANYMORE.

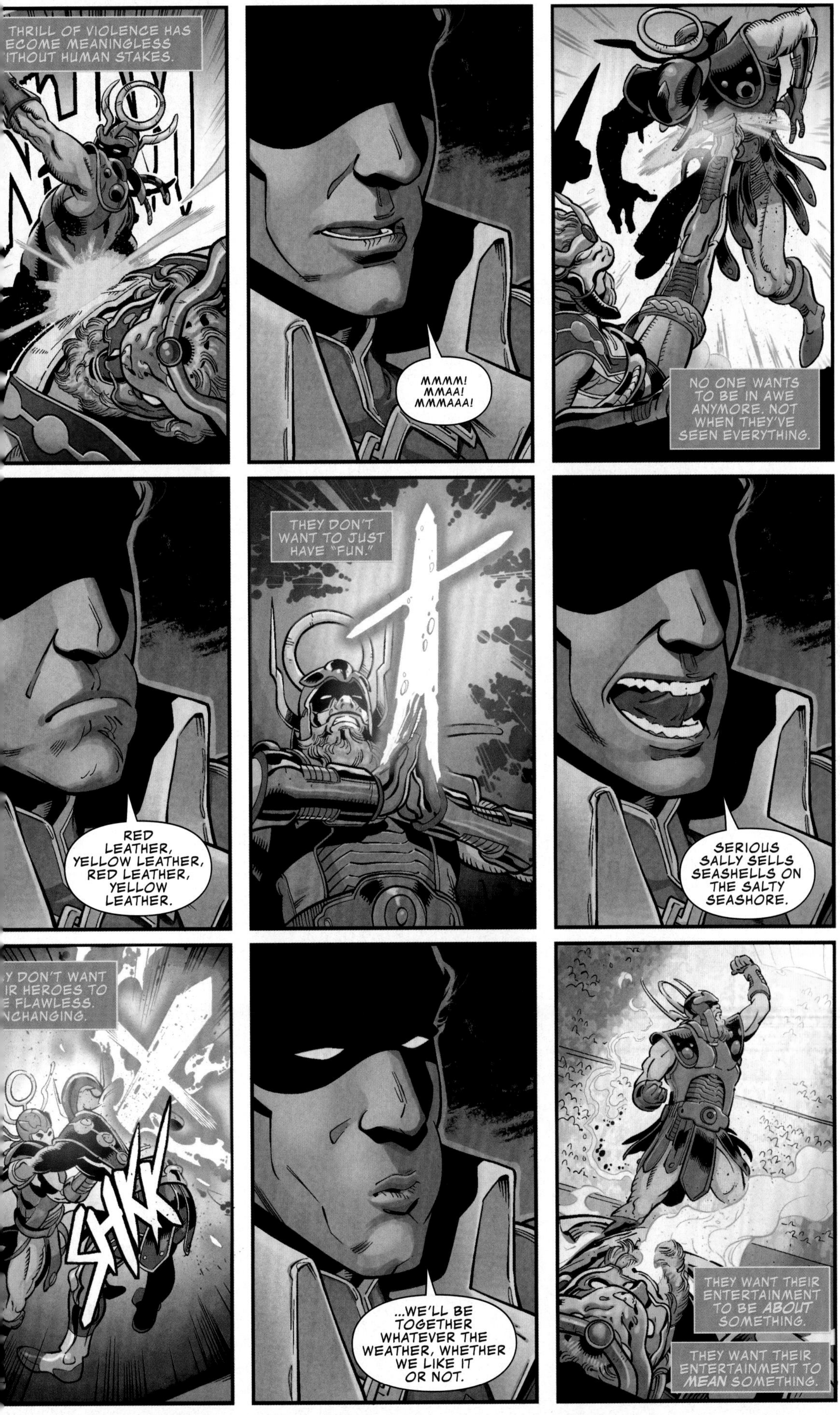
THRILL OF VIOLENCE HAS
ECOME MEANINGLESS
ITHOUT HUMAN STAKES.
MMMM! MMAA! MMMAAA!
NO ONE WANTS TO BE IN AWE ANYMORE. NOT WHEN THEY'VE SEEN EVERYTHING.
RED LEATHER, YELLOW LEATHER, RED LEATHER, YELLOW LEATHER.
THEY DON'T WANT TO JUST HAVE "FUN."
SERIOUS SALLY SELLS SEASHELLS ON THE SALTY SEASHORE.
Y DON'T WANT
IR HEROES TO
E FLAWLESS.
NCHANGING.
SHK
...WE'LL BE TOGETHER WHATEVER THE WEATHER, WHETHER WE LIKE IT OR NOT.
THEY WANT THEIR ENTERTAINMENT TO BE ABOUT SOMETHING.
THEY WANT THEIR ENTERTAINMENT TO MEAN SOMETHING.

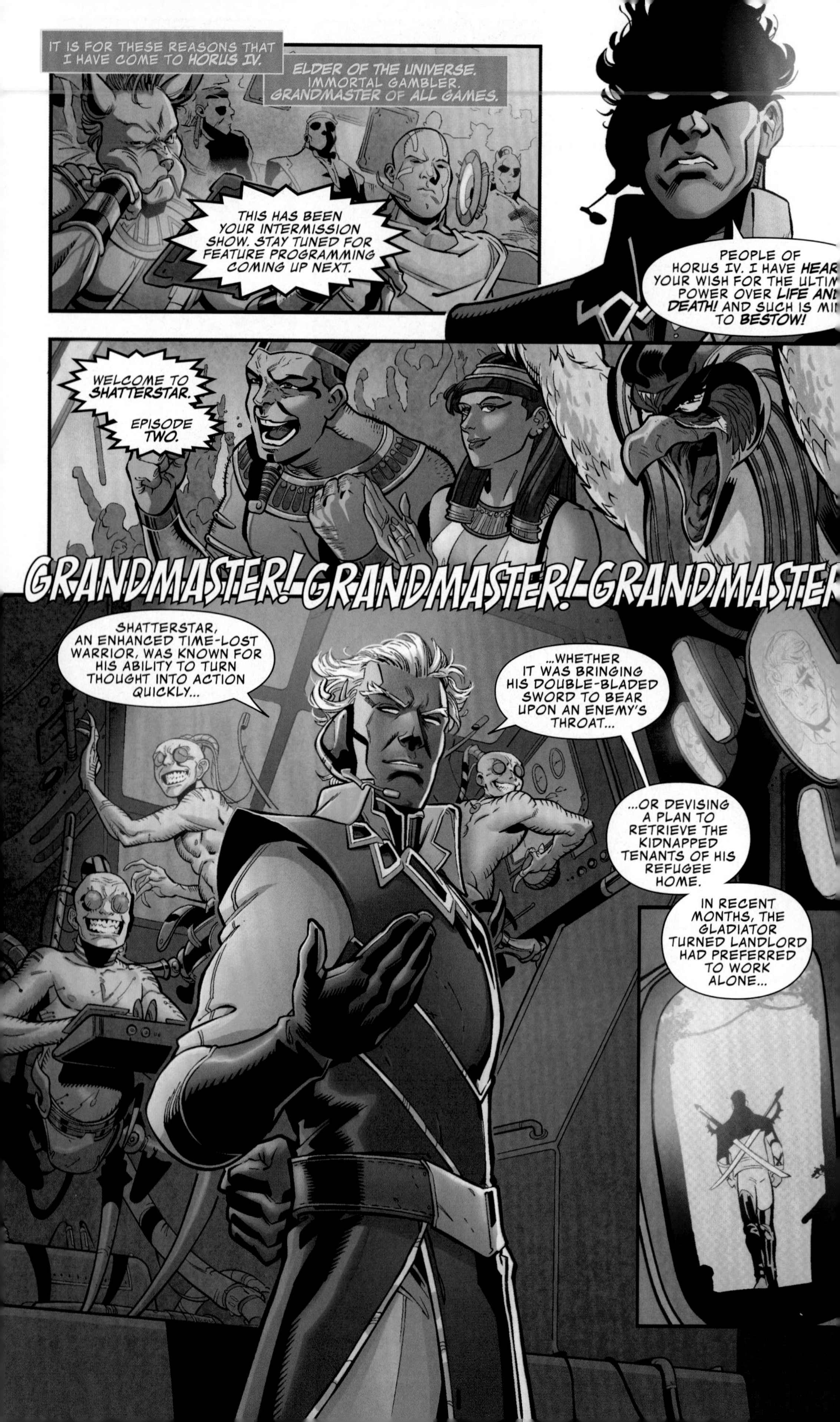
IT IS FOR THESE REASONS THAT I HAVE COME TO HORUS IV.
ELDER OF THE UNIVERSE. IMMORTAL GAMBLER. GRANDMASTER OF ALL GAMES.
THIS HAS BEEN YOUR INTERMISSION SHOW. STAY TUNED FOR FEATURE PROGRAMMING COMING UP NEXT.
PEOPLE OF HORUS IV. I HAVE HEAR YOUR WISH FOR THE ULTIM POWER OVER LIFE AN DEATH! AND SUCH IS MI TO BESTOW!
WELCOME TO SHATTERSTAR.
EPISODE TWO.
GRANDMASTER! GRANDMASTER! GRANDMASTER
SHATTERSTAR, AN ENHANCED TIME-LOST WARRIOR, WAS KNOWN FOR HIS ABILITY TO TURN THOUGHT INTO ACTION QUICKLY...
...WHETHER IT WAS BRINGING HIS DOUBLE-BLADED SWORD TO BEAR UPON AN ENEMY'S THROAT...
...OR DEVISING A PLAN TO RETRIEVE THE KIDNAPPED TENANTS OF HIS REFUGEE HOME.
IN RECENT MONTHS, THE GLADIATOR TURNED LANDLORD HAD PREFERRED TO WORK ALONE...

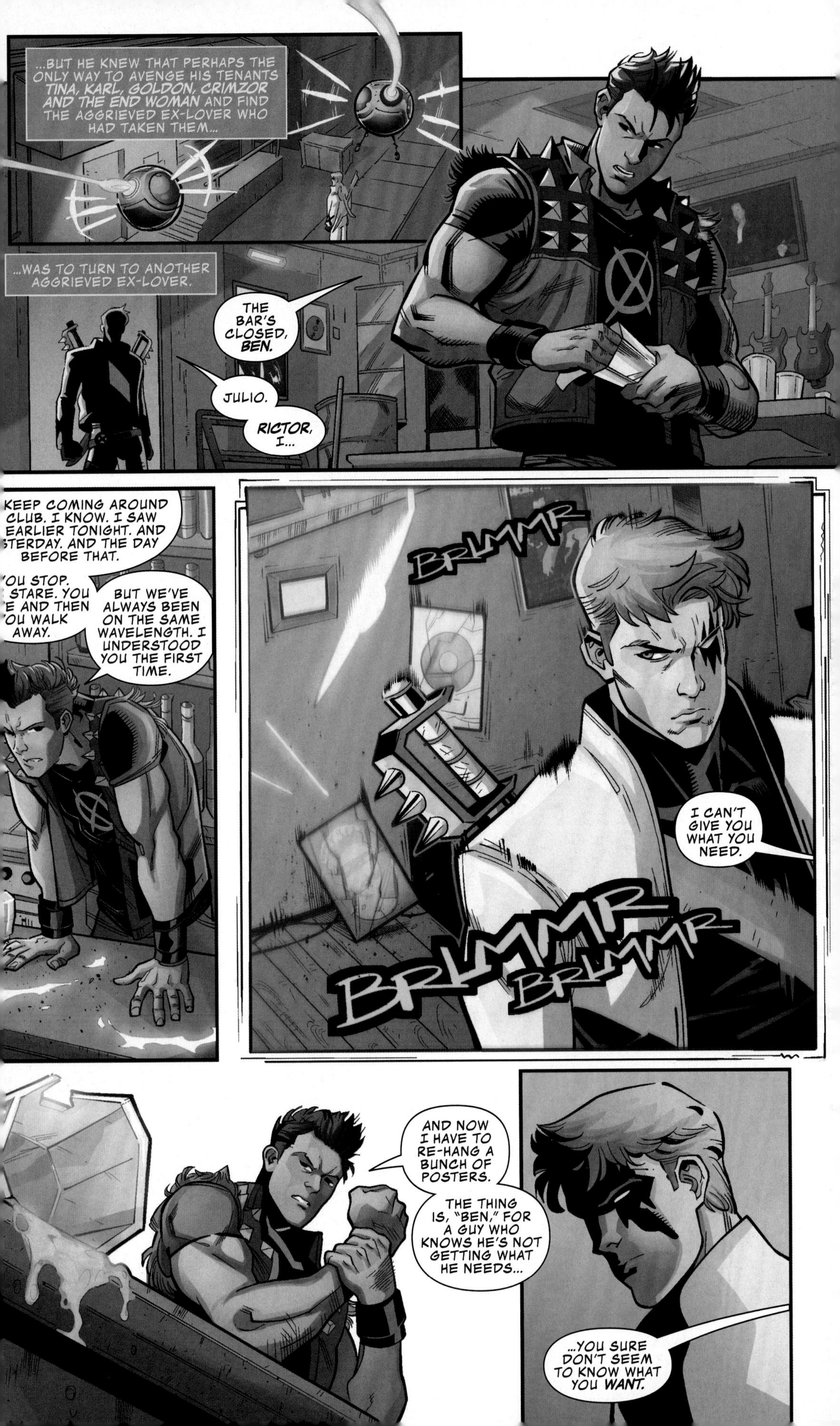

...BUT HE KNEW THAT PERHAPS THE ONLY WAY TO AVENGE HIS TENANTS TINA, KARL, GOLDON, CRIMZOR AND THE END WOMAN AND FIND THE AGGRIEVED EX-LOVER WHO HAD TAKEN THEM...
...WAS TO TURN TO ANOTHER AGGRIEVED EX-LOVER.
THE BAR'S CLOSED, BEN.
JULIO.
RICTOR, I...
KEEP COMING AROUND CLUB. I KNOW. I SAW EARLIER TONIGHT. AND STERDAY. AND THE DAY BEFORE THAT.
YOU STOP. STARE. YOU E AND THEN YOU WALK AWAY.
BUT WE'VE ALWAYS BEEN ON THE SAME WAVELENGTH. I UNDERSTOOD YOU THE FIRST TIME.
BRLMMR
I CAN'T GIVE YOU WHAT YOU NEED.
BRLMMR BRLMMR
AND NOW I HAVE TO RE-HANG A BUNCH OF POSTERS.
THE THING IS, "BEN," FOR A GUY WHO KNOWS HE'S NOT GETTING WHAT HE NEEDS...
...YOU SURE DON'T SEEM TO KNOW WHAT YOU WANT.

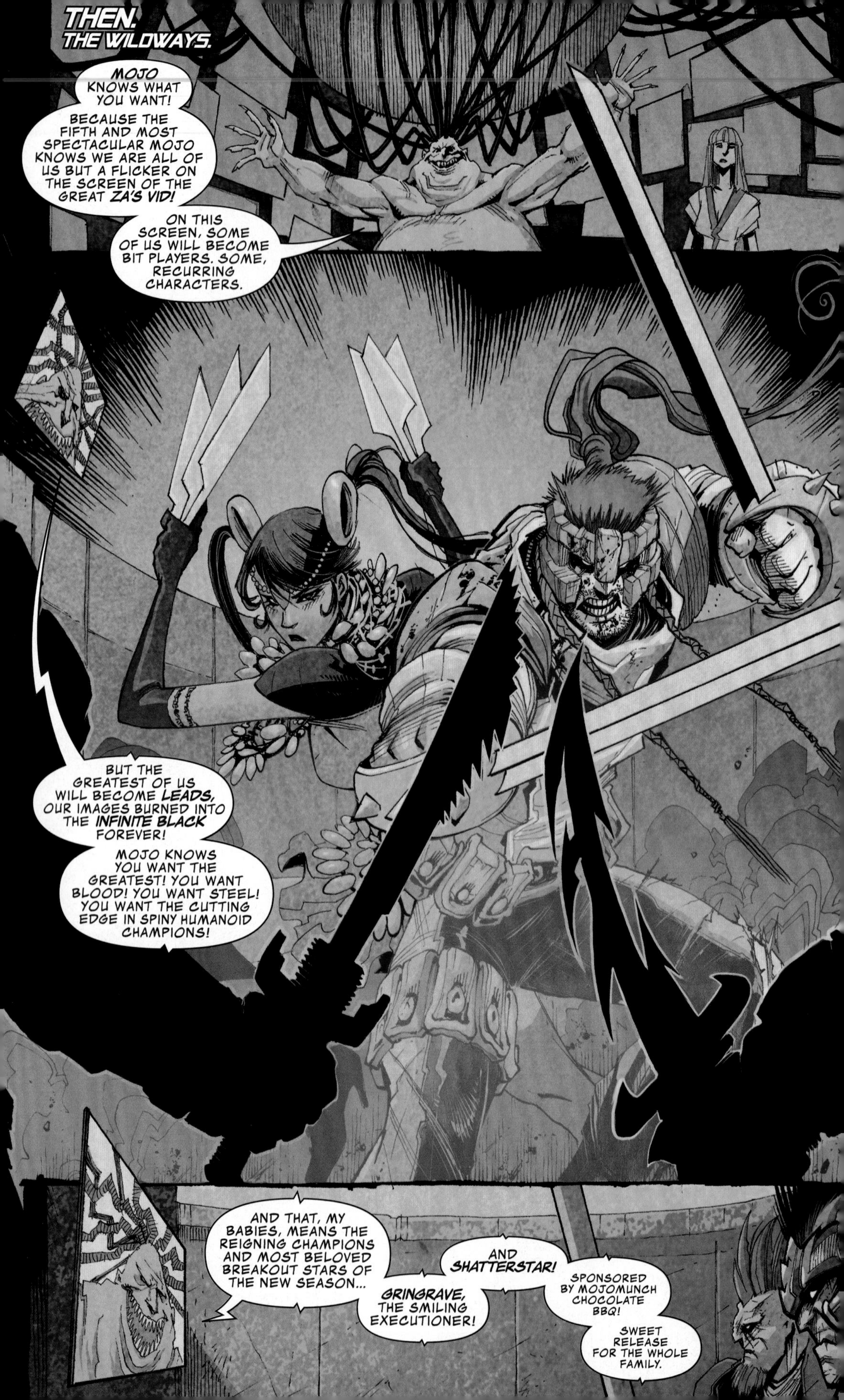
THEN.
THE WILDWAYS.
MOJO KNOWS WHAT YOU WANT!
BECAUSE THE FIFTH AND MOST SPECTACULAR MOJO KNOWS WE ARE ALL OF US BUT A FLICKER ON THE SCREEN OF THE GREAT ZA'S VID!
ON THIS SCREEN, SOME OF US WILL BECOME BIT PLAYERS. SOME, RECURRING CHARACTERS.
BUT THE GREATEST OF US WILL BECOME LEADS, OUR IMAGES BURNED INTO THE INFINITE BLACK FOREVER!
MOJO KNOWS YOU WANT THE GREATEST! YOU WANT BLOOD! YOU WANT STEEL! YOU WANT THE CUTTING EDGE IN SPINY HUMANOID CHAMPIONS!
AND THAT, MY BABIES, MEANS THE REIGNING CHAMPIONS AND MOST BELOVED BREAKOUT STARS OF THE NEW SEASON...
GRINGRAVE, THE SMILING EXECUTIONER!
AND SHATTERSTAR!
SPONSORED BY MOJOMUNCH CHOCOLATE BBQ!
SWEET RELEASE FOR THE WHOLE FAMILY.

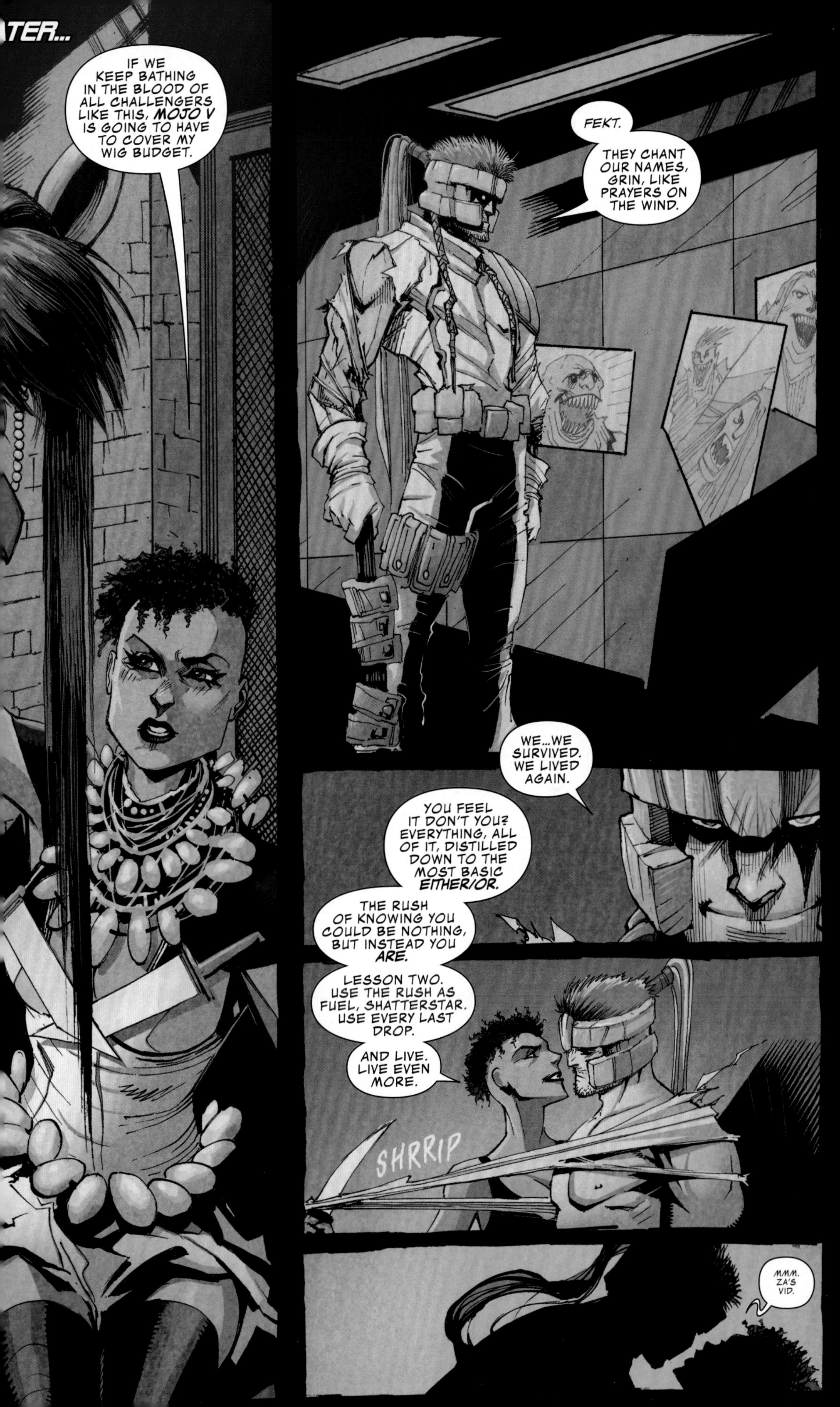

TER...
IF WE KEEP BATHING IN THE BLOOD OF ALL CHALLENGERS LIKE THIS, MOJO V IS GOING TO HAVE TO COVER MY WIG BUDGET.
FEKT.
THEY CHANT OUR NAMES, GRIN, LIKE PRAYERS ON THE WIND.
WE...WE SURVIVED. WE LIVED AGAIN.
YOU FEEL IT DON'T YOU? EVERYTHING, ALL OF IT, DISTILLED DOWN TO THE MOST BASIC EITHER/OR.
THE RUSH OF KNOWING YOU COULD BE NOTHING, BUT INSTEAD YOU ARE.
LESSON TWO. USE THE RUSH AS FUEL, SHATTERSTAR. USE EVERY LAST DROP.
AND LIVE. LIVE EVEN MORE.
SHRRIP
MMM. ZA'S VID.

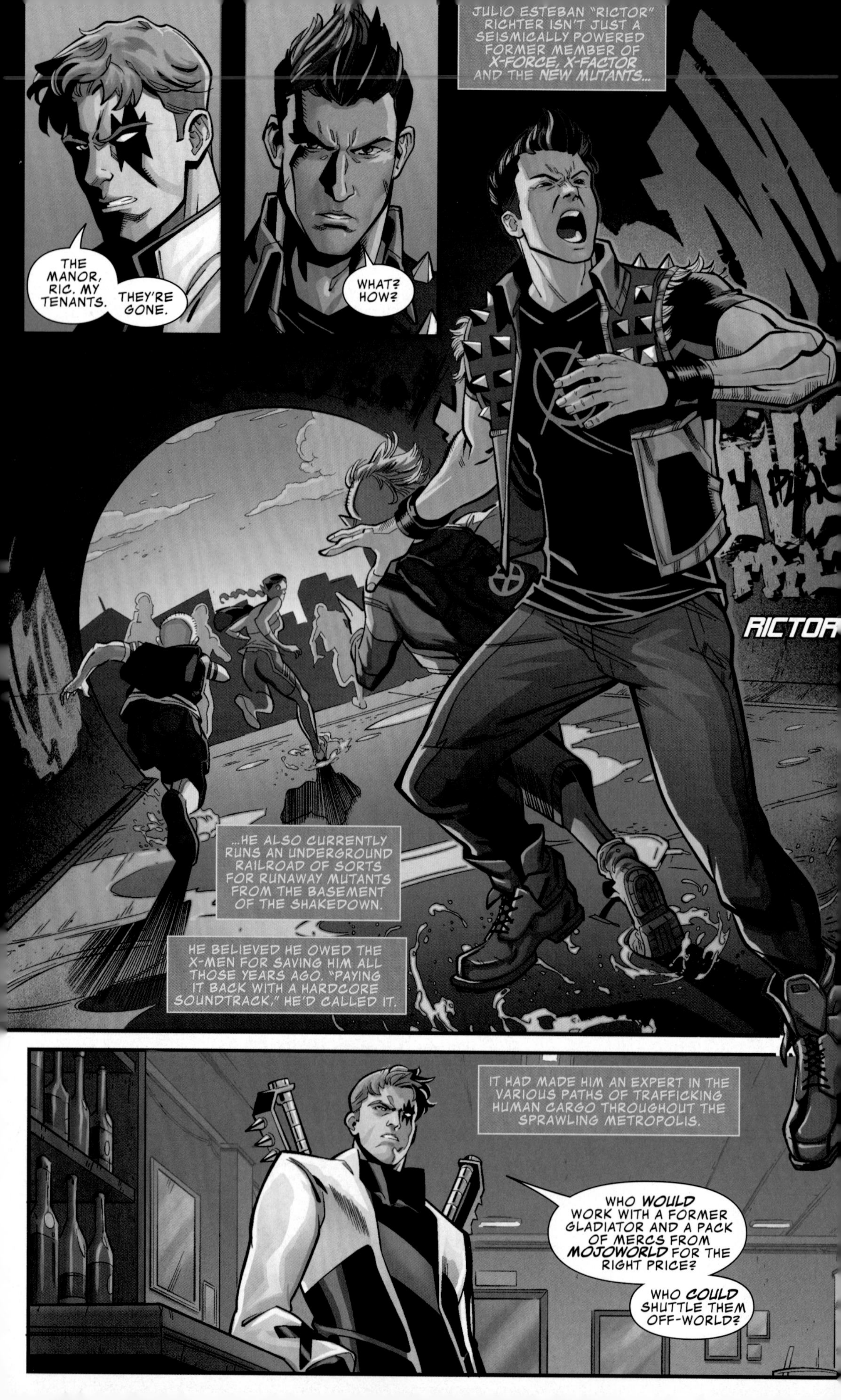

THE MANOR, RIC. MY TENANTS.
THEY'RE GONE.
WHAT? HOW?
JULIO ESTEBAN "RICTOR" RICHTER ISN'T JUST A SEISMICALLY POWERED FORMER MEMBER OF X-FORCE, X-FACTOR AND THE NEW MUTANTS...
RICTOR
...HE ALSO CURRENTLY RUNS AN UNDERGROUND RAILROAD OF SORTS FOR RUNAWAY MUTANTS FROM THE BASEMENT OF THE SHAKEDOWN.
HE BELIEVED HE OWED THE X-MEN FOR SAVING HIM ALL THOSE YEARS AGO. "PAYING IT BACK WITH A HARDCORE SOUNDTRACK," HE'D CALLED IT.
IT HAD MADE HIM AN EXPERT IN THE VARIOUS PATHS OF TRAFFICKING HUMAN CARGO THROUGHOUT THE SPRAWLING METROPOLIS.
WHO WOULD WORK WITH A FORMER GLADIATOR AND A PACK OF MERCS FROM MOJOWORLD FOR THE RIGHT PRICE?
WHO COULD SHUTTLE THEM OFF-WORLD?

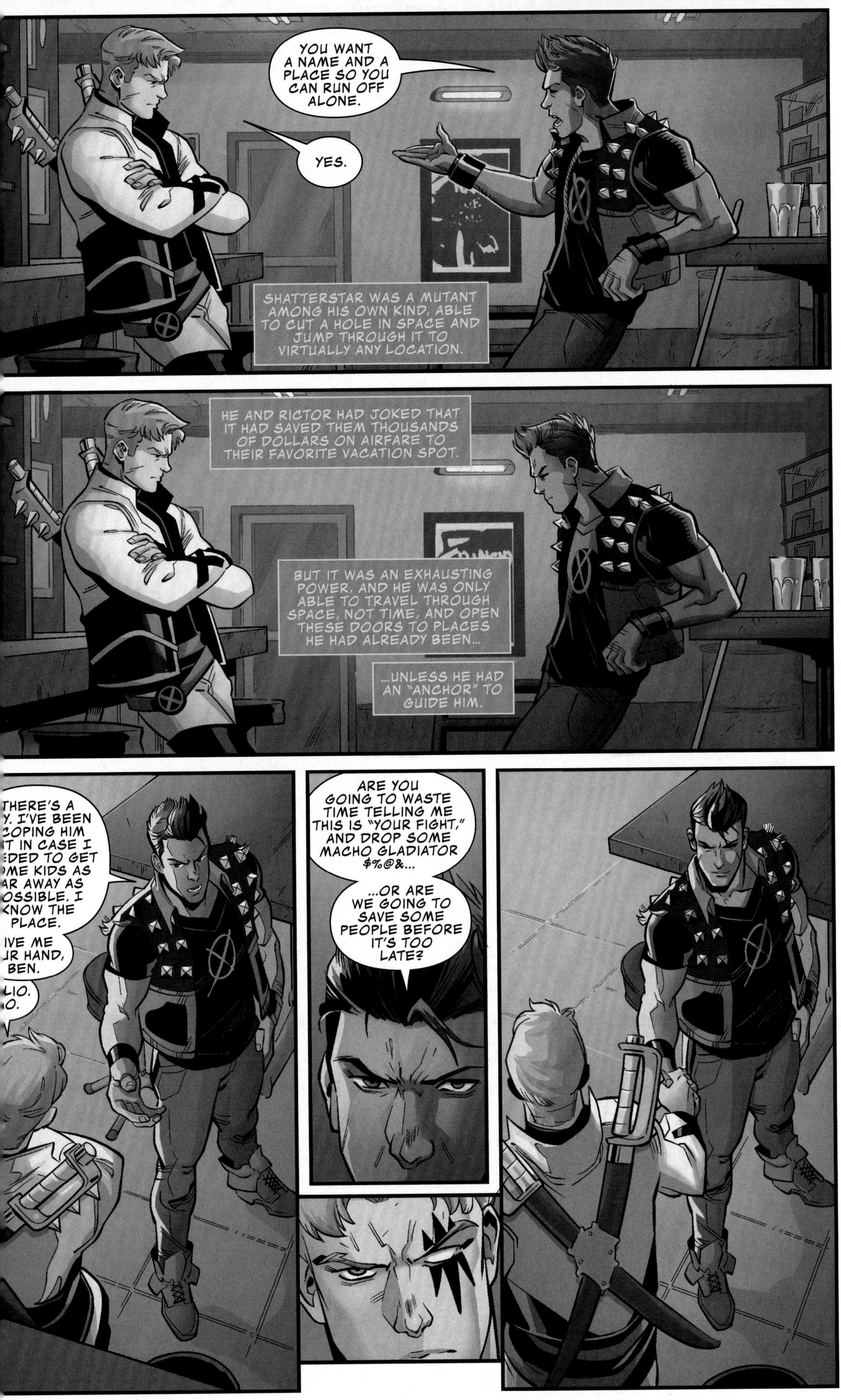

YOU WANT A NAME AND A PLACE SO YOU CAN RUN OFF ALONE.
YES.
SHATTERSTAR WAS A MUTANT AMONG HIS OWN KIND, ABLE TO CUT A HOLE IN SPACE AND JUMP THROUGH IT TO VIRTUALLY ANY LOCATION.
HE AND RICTOR HAD JOKED THAT IT HAD SAVED THEM THOUSANDS OF DOLLARS ON AIRFARE TO THEIR FAVORITE VACATION SPOT.
BUT IT WAS AN EXHAUSTING POWER, AND HE WAS ONLY ABLE TO TRAVEL THROUGH SPACE, NOT TIME, AND OPEN THESE DOORS TO PLACES HE HAD ALREADY BEEN...
...UNLESS HE HAD AN "ANCHOR" TO GUIDE HIM.
THERE'S A Y. I'VE BEEN COPING HIM T IN CASE I EDED TO GET OME KIDS AS AR AWAY AS OSSIBLE. I KNOW THE PLACE.
IVE ME R HAND, BEN.
LIO. O.
ARE YOU GOING TO WASTE TIME TELLING ME THIS IS "YOUR FIGHT," AND DROP SOME MACHO GLADIATOR $%@&...
...OR ARE WE GOING TO SAVE SOME PEOPLE BEFORE IT'S TOO LATE?

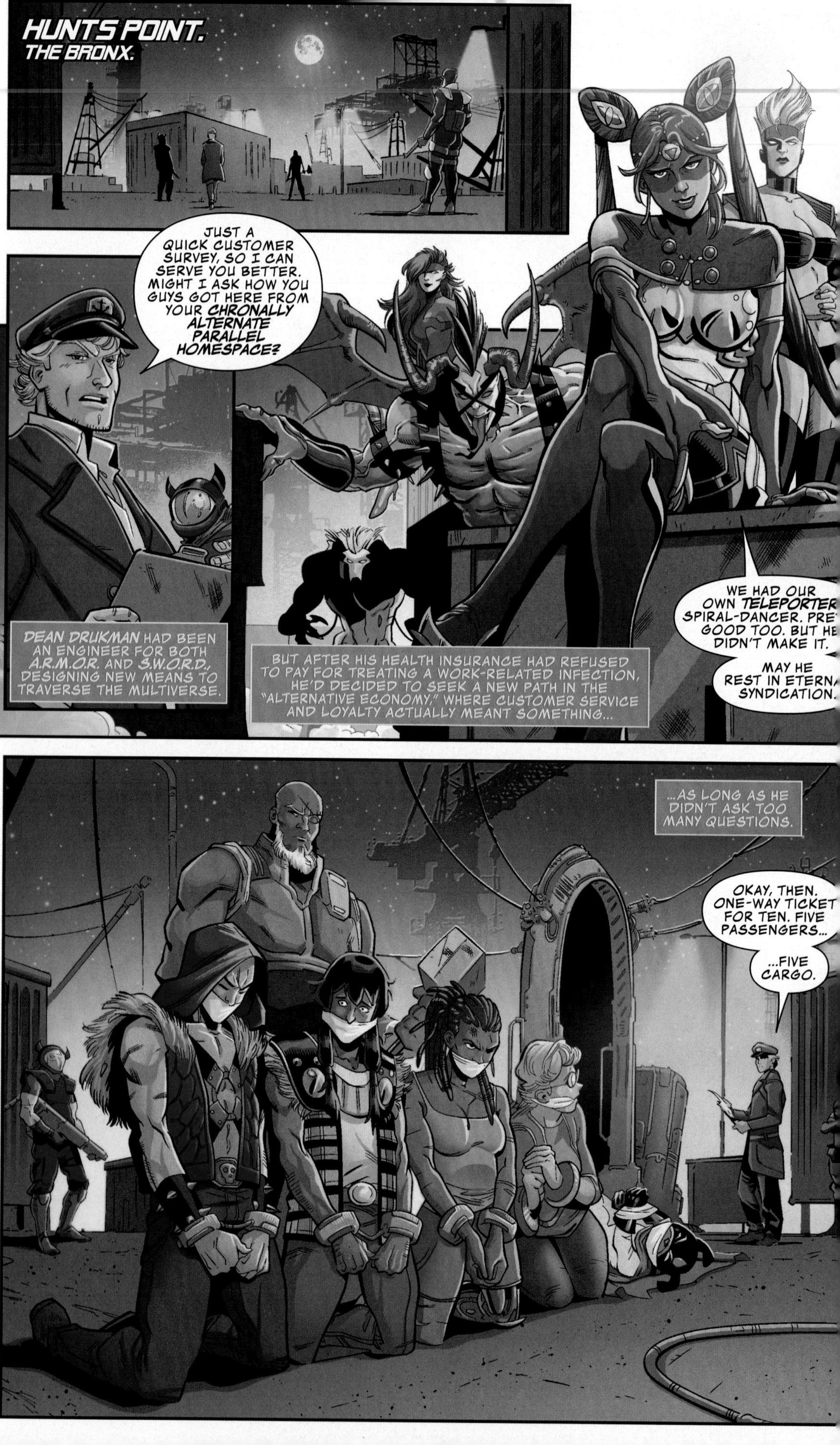
HUNTS POINT.
THE BRONX.
JUST A QUICK CUSTOMER SURVEY, SO I CAN SERVE YOU BETTER. MIGHT I ASK HOW YOU GUYS GOT HERE FROM YOUR CHRONALLY ALTERNATE PARALLEL HOMESPACE?
WE HAD OUR OWN TELEPORTER SPIRAL-DANCER. PRE GOOD TOO. BUT HE DIDN'T MAKE IT.
MAY HE REST IN ETERN SYNDICATION.
DEAN DRUKMAN HAD BEEN AN ENGINEER FOR BOTH A.R.M.O.R. AND S.W.O.R.D., DESIGNING NEW MEANS TO TRAVERSE THE MULTIVERSE.
BUT AFTER HIS HEALTH INSURANCE HAD REFUSED TO PAY FOR TREATING A WORK-RELATED INFECTION, HE'D DECIDED TO SEEK A NEW PATH IN THE "ALTERNATIVE ECONOMY," WHERE CUSTOMER SERVICE AND LOYALTY ACTUALLY MEANT SOMETHING...
...AS LONG AS HE DIDN'T ASK TOO MANY QUESTIONS.
OKAY, THEN. ONE-WAY TICKET FOR TEN. FIVE PASSENGERS...
...FIVE CARGO.

LOOKS LIKE THE FUNDS HAVE CLEARED. THANK YOU AND YOUR DEEP POCKETS FOR DOING BUSINESS WITH *DOCKMASTER* AND THE *LONGSHOREMEN*.

SWZZ

SIT BACK, RELAX AND ENJOY YOUR TRIP. IF THIS IS YOUR *FINAL* DESTINATION...

THE TENANTS OF MANOR CROSSING WATCH THE GATE OPEN WITH FEAR...

WELL, SORRY 'BOUT THAT.

MHRFGK!

...EXCEPT FOR *TINA COOKE* OF *EARTH-1218,* WHO HAS LESS EXPERIENCE WITH SUCH THINGS AND THINKS THE SWIRLING POINT LOOKS A LITTLE LIKE WHAT SHE'S HEARD DESCRIBED IN NEAR-DEATH EXPERIENCES.

HAT E...?

SHVNNN

HEY, I OUGHT YOU SAID YOUR RTER DIDN'T MAKE IT.

THERE'S MY BOY.

ALWAYS ON TIME FOR HIS MATCH.

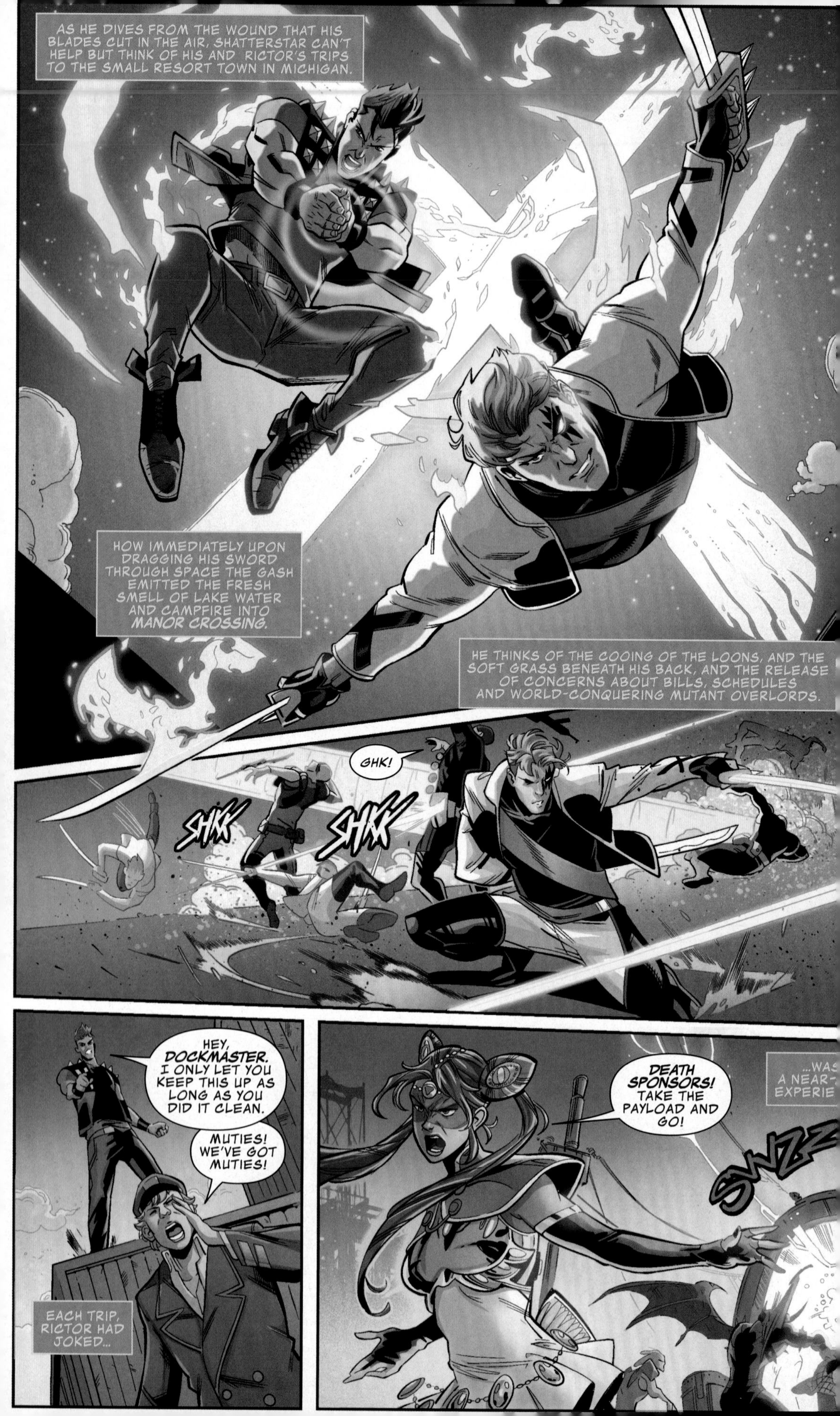

AS HE DIVES FROM THE WOUND THAT HIS BLADES CUT IN THE AIR, SHATTERSTAR CAN'T HELP BUT THINK OF HIS AND RICTOR'S TRIPS TO THE SMALL RESORT TOWN IN MICHIGAN.
HOW IMMEDIATELY UPON DRAGGING HIS SWORD THROUGH SPACE THE GASH EMITTED THE FRESH SMELL OF LAKE WATER AND CAMPFIRE INTO MANOR CROSSING.
HE THINKS OF THE COOING OF THE LOONS, AND THE SOFT GRASS BENEATH HIS BACK, AND THE RELEASE OF CONCERNS ABOUT BILLS, SCHEDULES AND WORLD-CONQUERING MUTANT OVERLORDS.
GHK!
SHKK
SHKK
HEY, DOCKMASTER. I ONLY LET YOU KEEP THIS UP AS LONG AS YOU DID IT CLEAN.
MUTIES! WE'VE GOT MUTIES!
EACH TRIP, RICTOR HAD JOKED...
DEATH SPONSORS! TAKE THE PAYLOAD AND GO!
...WAS A NEAR- EXPERIE

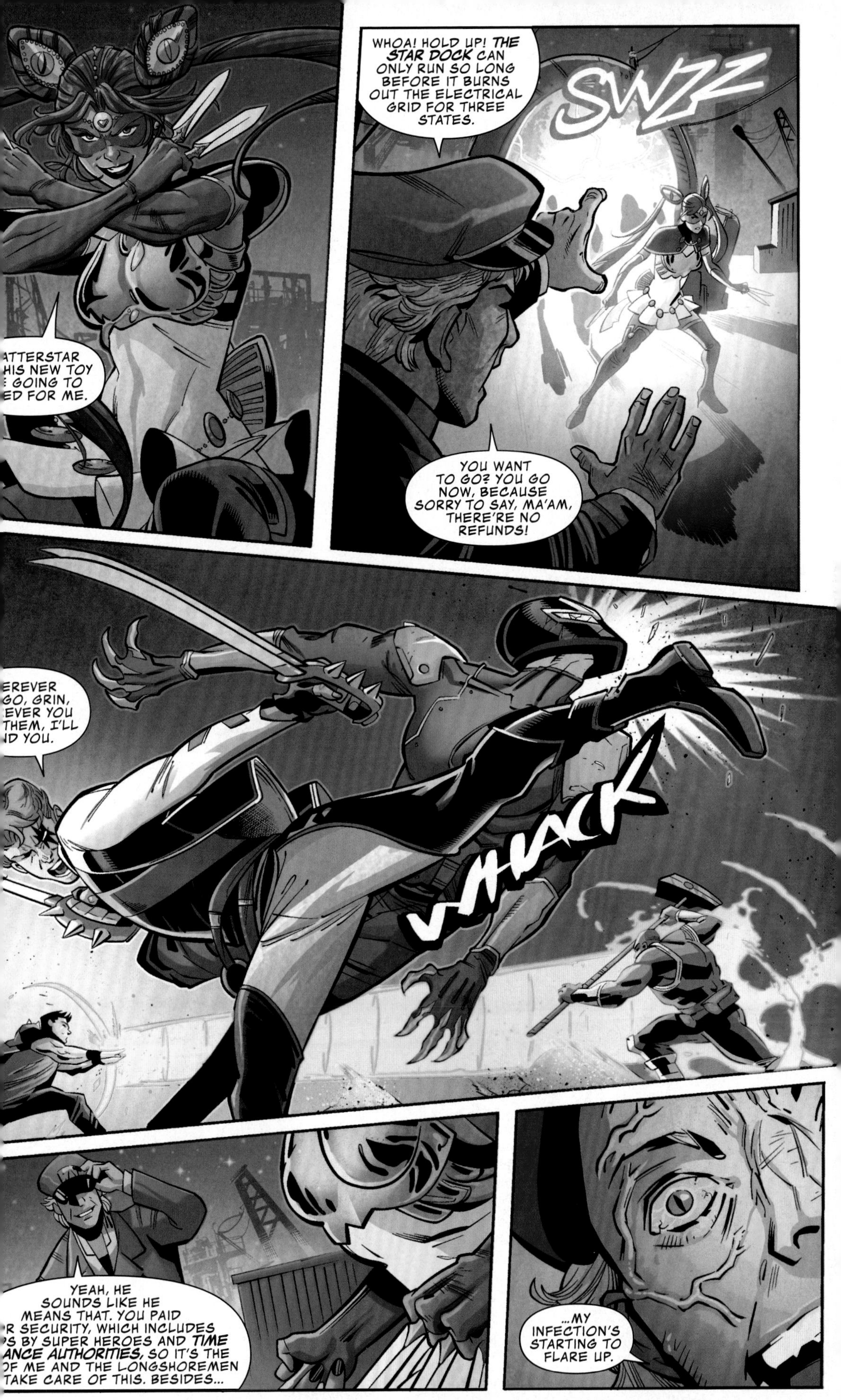
ATTERSTAR
HIS NEW TOY
E GOING TO
ED FOR ME.
WHOA! HOLD UP! THE STAR DOCK CAN ONLY RUN SO LONG BEFORE IT BURNS OUT THE ELECTRICAL GRID FOR THREE STATES.
SWZZ
YOU WANT TO GO? YOU GO NOW, BECAUSE SORRY TO SAY, MA'AM, THERE'RE NO REFUNDS!
EREVER
GO, GRIN,
EVER YOU
THEM, I'LL
ND YOU.
WHACK
YEAH, HE SOUNDS LIKE HE MEANS THAT. YOU PAID
R SECURITY, WHICH INCLUDES
PS BY SUPER HEROES AND TIME
ANCE AUTHORITIES, SO IT'S THE
OF ME AND THE LONGSHOREMEN
TAKE CARE OF THIS. BESIDES...
...MY INFECTION'S STARTING TO FLARE UP.

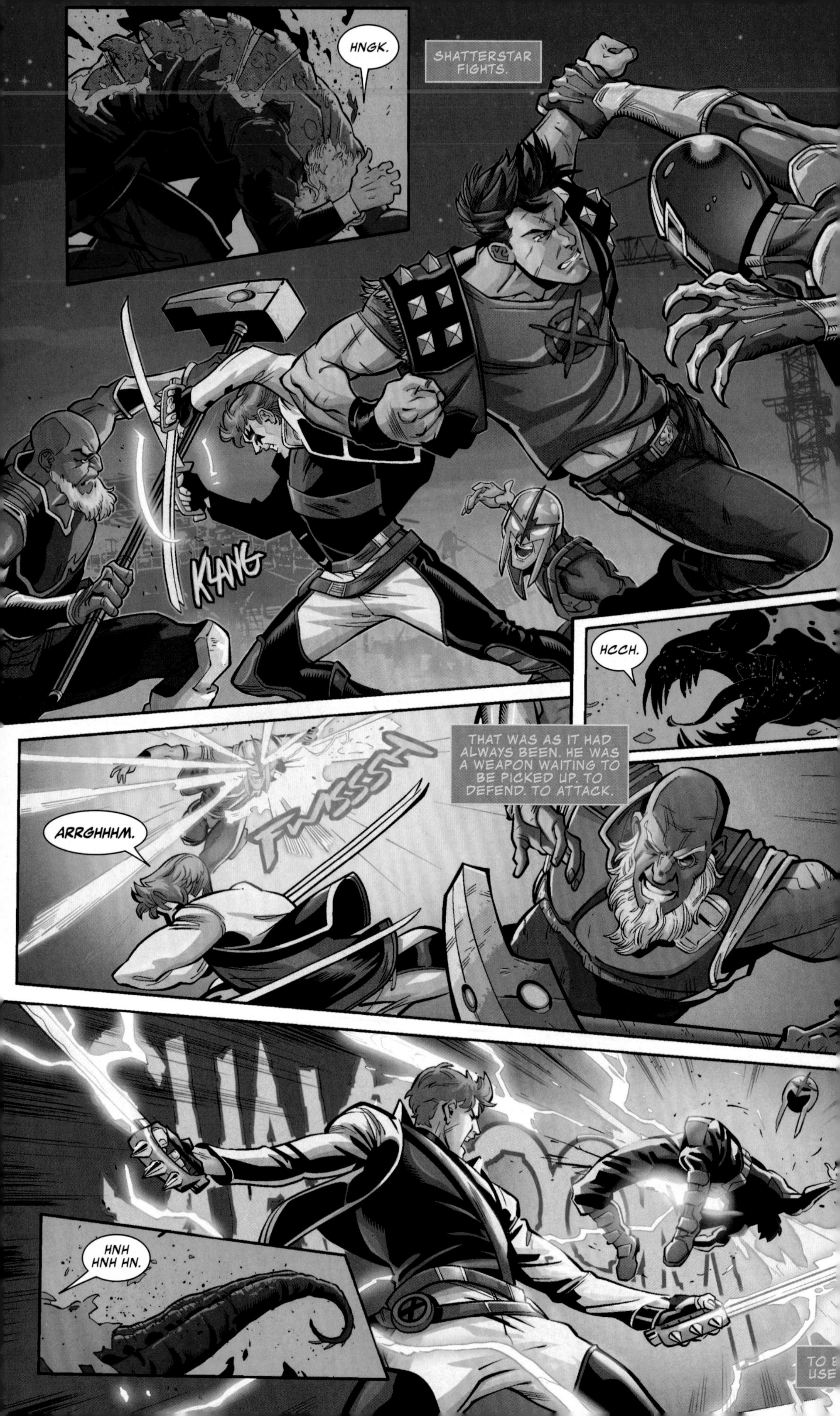
HNGK.
SHATTERSTAR FIGHTS.
KLANG
HCCH.
THAT WAS AS IT HAD ALWAYS BEEN. HE WAS A WEAPON WAITING TO BE PICKED UP. TO DEFEND. TO ATTACK.
FWSSSH
ARRGHHHM.
HNH HNH HN.

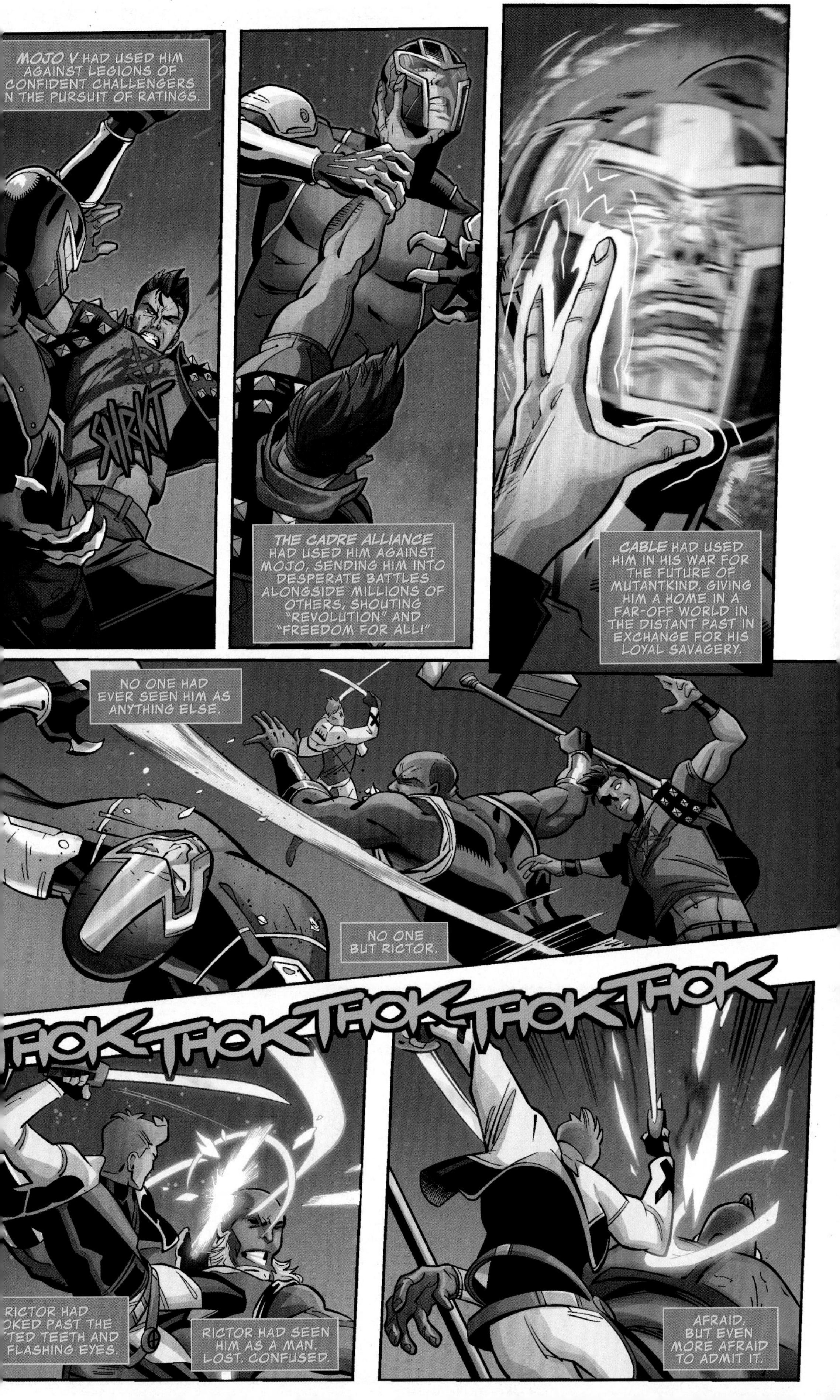
MOJO V HAD USED HIM AGAINST LEGIONS OF CONFIDENT CHALLENGERS N THE PURSUIT OF RATINGS.
SHRKT
THE CADRE ALLIANCE HAD USED HIM AGAINST MOJO, SENDING HIM INTO DESPERATE BATTLES ALONGSIDE MILLIONS OF OTHERS, SHOUTING "REVOLUTION" AND "FREEDOM FOR ALL!"
CABLE HAD USED HIM IN HIS WAR FOR THE FUTURE OF MUTANTKIND, GIVING HIM A HOME IN A FAR-OFF WORLD IN THE DISTANT PAST IN EXCHANGE FOR HIS LOYAL SAVAGERY.
NO ONE HAD EVER SEEN HIM AS ANYTHING ELSE.
NO ONE BUT RICTOR.
HOK THOK THOK THOK THOK
RICTOR HAD OKED PAST THE TED TEETH AND FLASHING EYES.
RICTOR HAD SEEN HIM AS A MAN. LOST. CONFUSED.
AFRAID, BUT EVEN MORE AFRAID TO ADMIT IT.

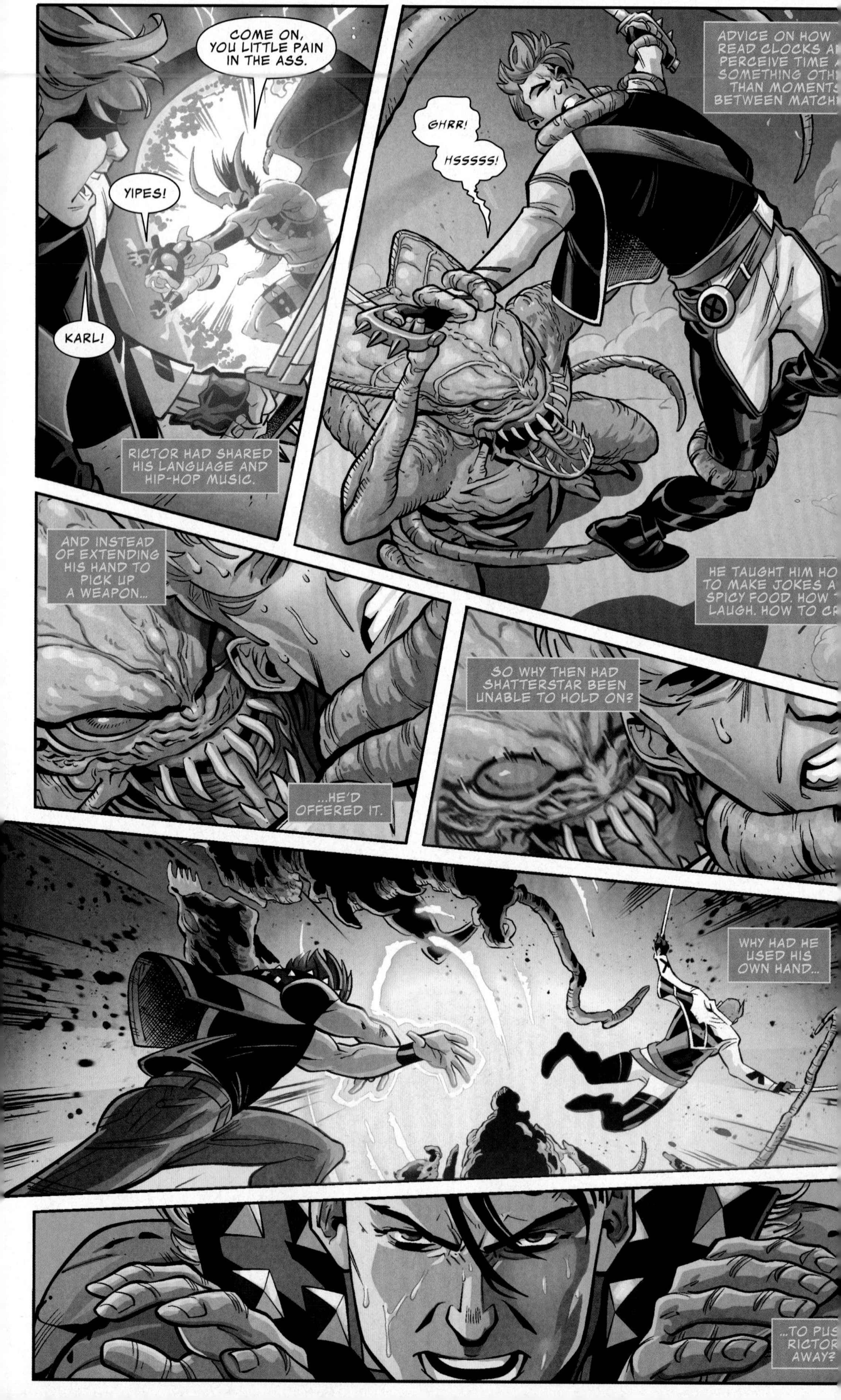
COME ON, YOU LITTLE PAIN IN THE ASS.
YIPES!
KARL!
RICTOR HAD SHARED HIS LANGUAGE AND HIP-HOP MUSIC.
ADVICE ON HOW READ CLOCKS A PERCEIVE TIME SOMETHING OTH THAN MOMENTS BETWEEN MATCH
GHRR!
HSSSSS!
HE TAUGHT HIM HO TO MAKE JOKES A SPICY FOOD. HOW LAUGH. HOW TO CR
AND INSTEAD OF EXTENDING HIS HAND TO PICK UP A WEAPON...
...HE'D OFFERED IT.
SO WHY THEN HAD SHATTERSTAR BEEN UNABLE TO HOLD ON?
WHY HAD HE USED HIS OWN HAND...
...TO PUS RICTOR AWAY?

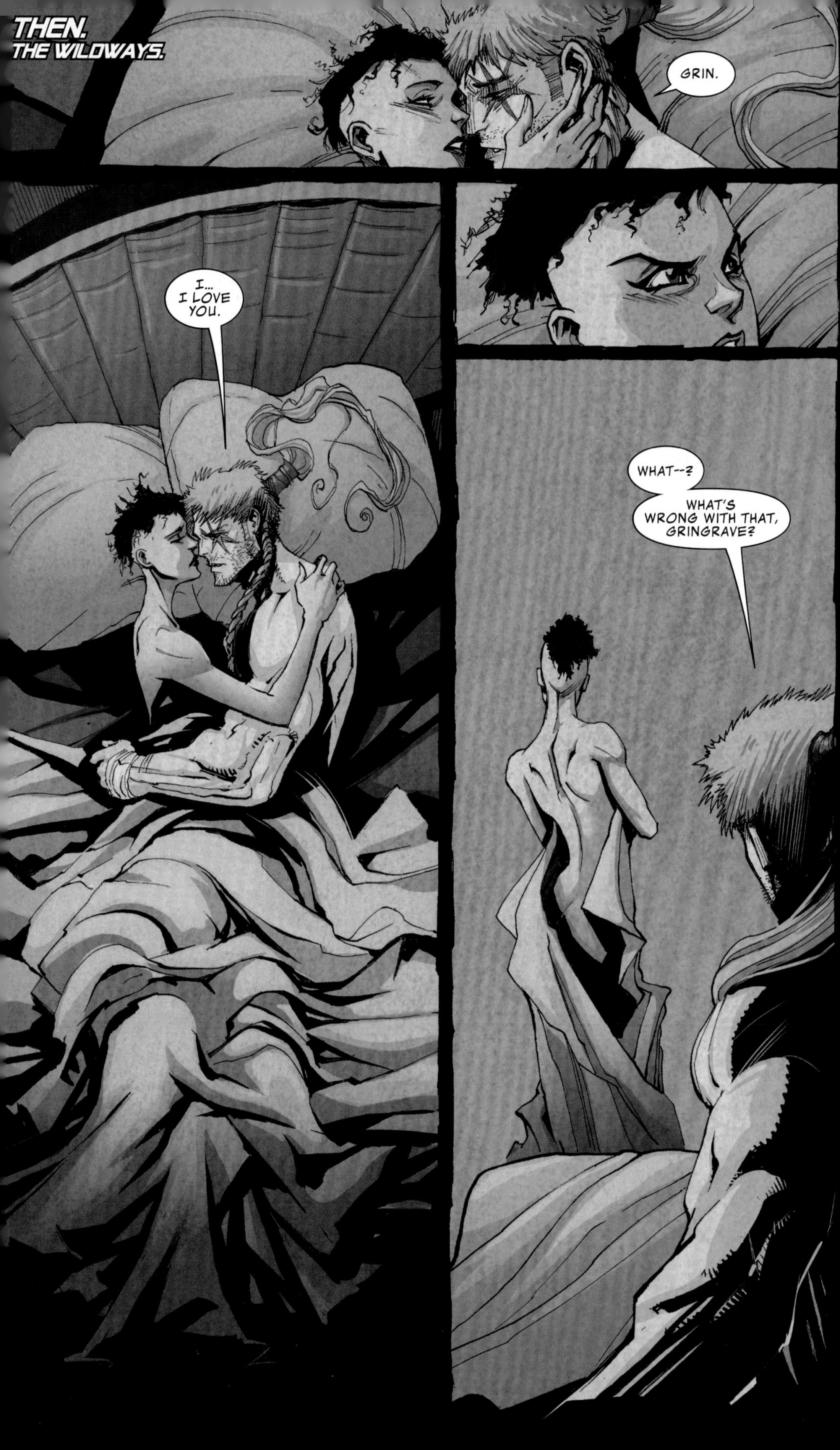
THEN.
THE WILDWAYS.
GRIN.
I... I LOVE YOU.
WHAT--?
WHAT'S WRONG WITH THAT, GRINGRAVE?

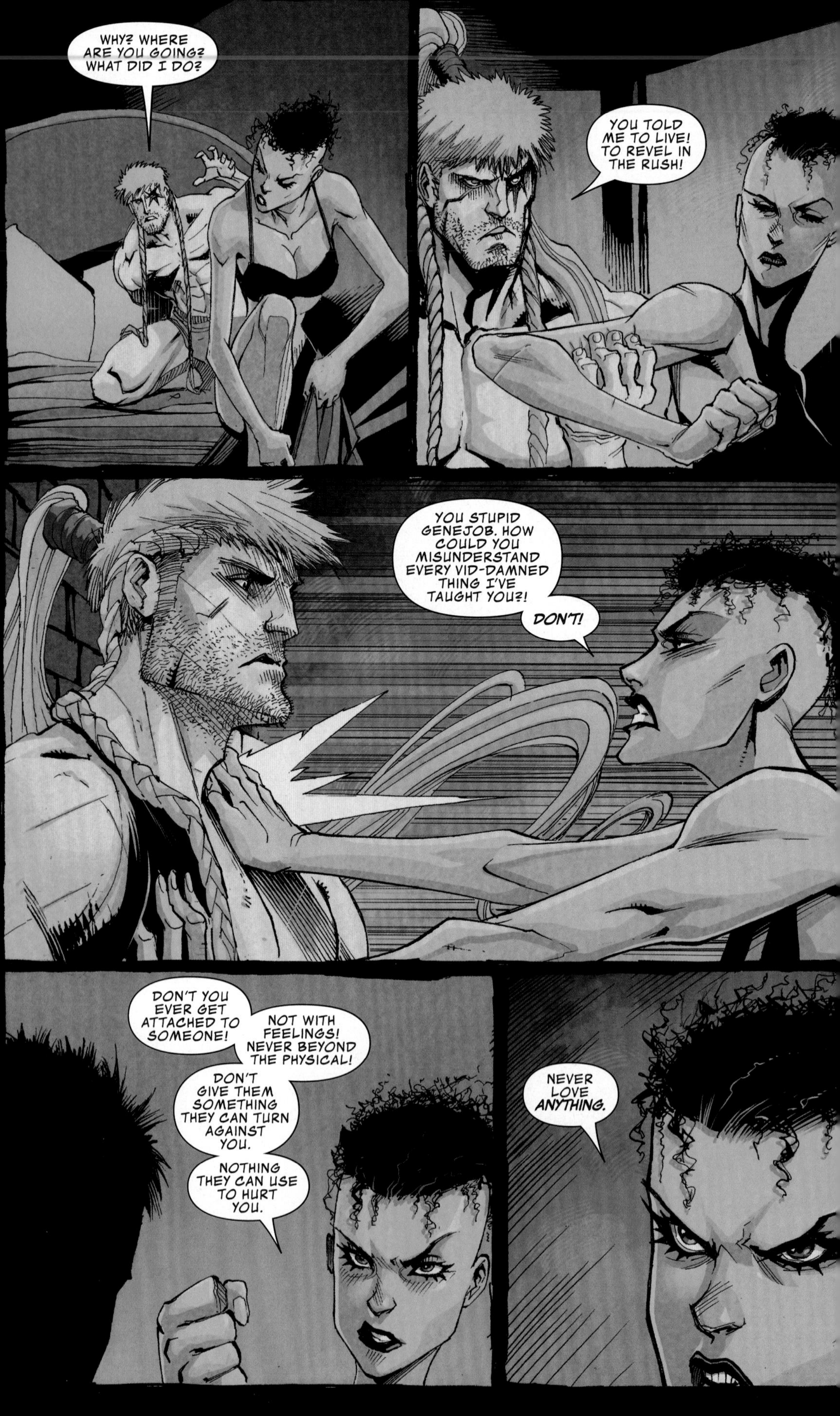
WHY? WHERE ARE YOU GOING? WHAT DID I DO?
YOU TOLD ME TO LIVE! TO REVEL IN THE RUSH!
YOU STUPID GENEJOB. HOW COULD YOU MISUNDERSTAND EVERY VID-DAMNED THING I'VE TAUGHT YOU?!
DON'T!
DON'T YOU EVER GET ATTACHED TO SOMEONE!
NOT WITH FEELINGS! NEVER BEYOND THE PHYSICAL!
DON'T GIVE THEM SOMETHING THEY CAN TURN AGAINST YOU.
NOTHING THEY CAN USE TO HURT YOU.
NEVER LOVE ANYTHING.

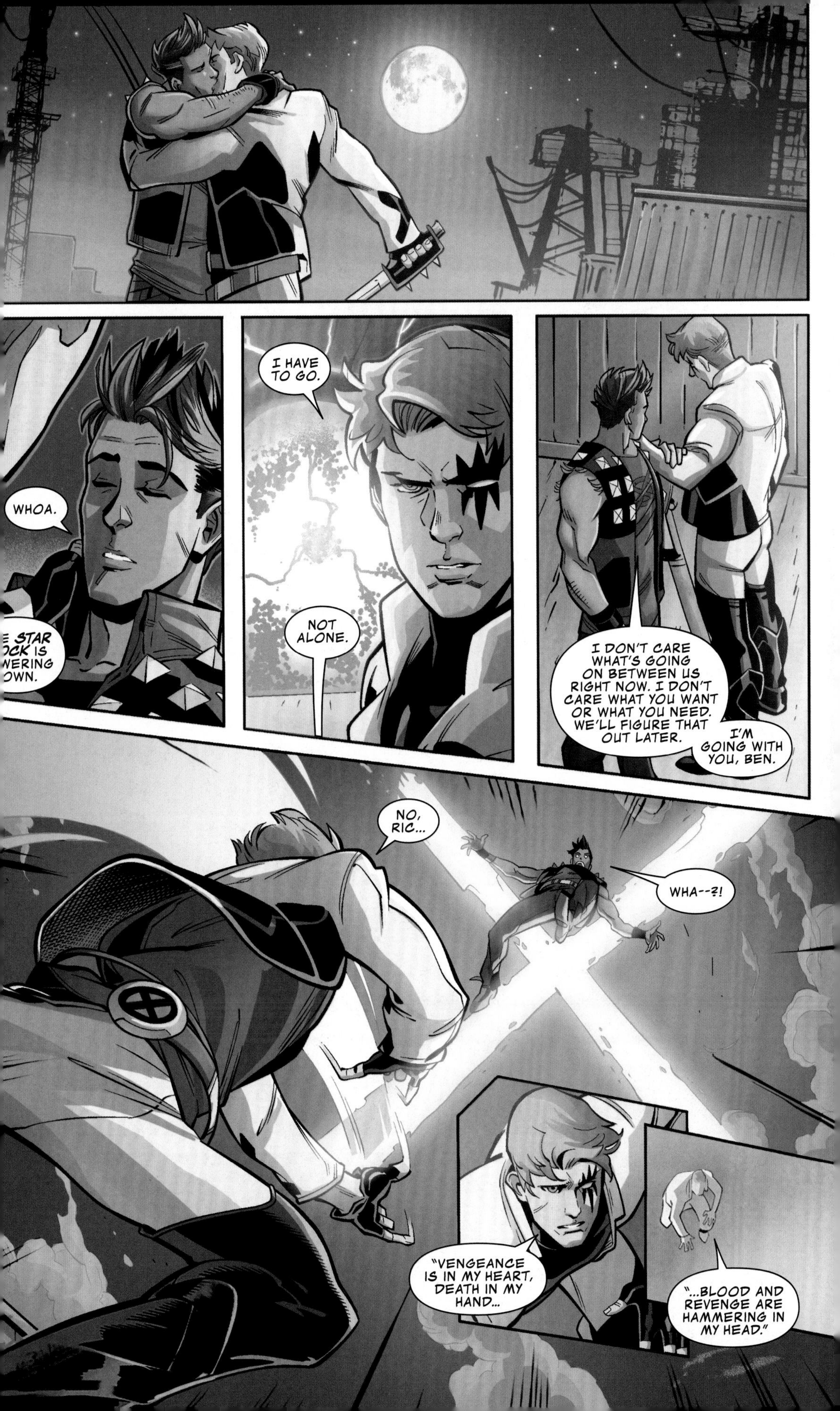

WHOA.
E STAR
OCK IS
WERING
OWN.
I HAVE TO GO.
NOT ALONE.
I DON'T CARE WHAT'S GOING ON BETWEEN US RIGHT NOW. I DON'T CARE WHAT YOU WANT OR WHAT YOU NEED. WE'LL FIGURE THAT OUT LATER.
I'M GOING WITH YOU, BEN.
NO, RIC...
WHA--?!
"VENGEANCE IS IN MY HEART, DEATH IN MY HAND...
"...BLOOD AND REVENGE ARE HAMMERING IN MY HEAD."

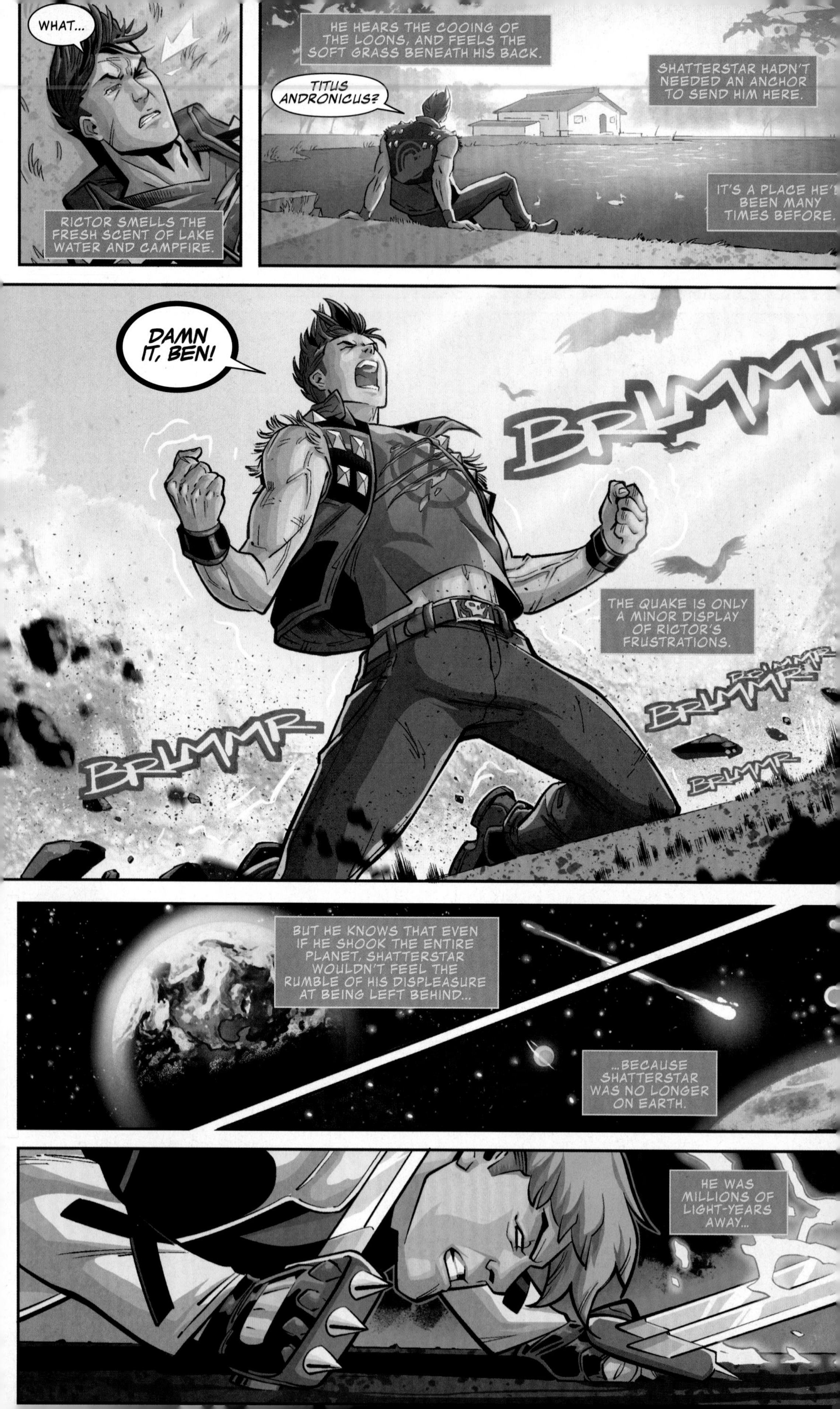

WHAT...
RICTOR SMELLS THE FRESH SCENT OF LAKE WATER AND CAMPFIRE.
HE HEARS THE COOING OF THE LOONS, AND FEELS THE SOFT GRASS BENEATH HIS BACK.
TITUS ANDRONICUS?
SHATTERSTAR HADN'T NEEDED AN ANCHOR TO SEND HIM HERE.
IT'S A PLACE HE'S BEEN MANY TIMES BEFORE.
DAMN IT, BEN!
BRLMMR
THE QUAKE IS ONLY A MINOR DISPLAY OF RICTOR'S FRUSTRATIONS.
BRLMMR
BRLMMR
BRLMMR
BRLMMR
BRLMMR
BUT HE KNOWS THAT EVEN IF HE SHOOK THE ENTIRE PLANET, SHATTERSTAR WOULDN'T FEEL THE RUMBLE OF HIS DISPLEASURE AT BEING LEFT BEHIND...
...BECAUSE SHATTERSTAR WAS NO LONGER ON EARTH.
HE WAS MILLIONS OF LIGHT-YEARS AWAY...

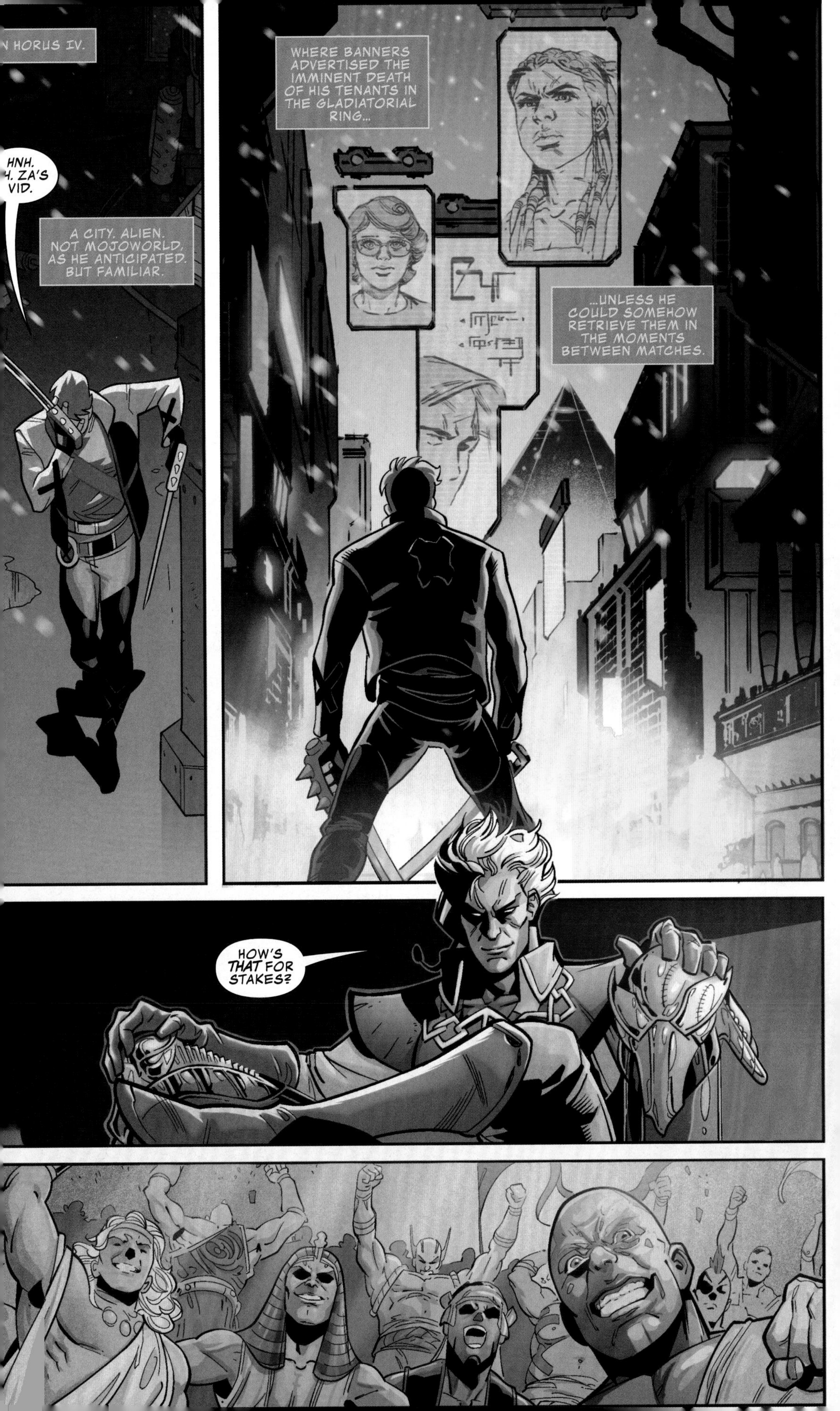
N HORUS IV.
HNH.
H. ZA'S
VID.
A CITY. ALIEN. NOT MOJOWORLD, AS HE ANTICIPATED. BUT FAMILIAR.
WHERE BANNERS ADVERTISED THE IMMINENT DEATH OF HIS TENANTS IN THE GLADIATORIAL RING...
...UNLESS HE COULD SOMEHOW RETRIEVE THEM IN THE MOMENTS BETWEEN MATCHES.
HOW'S *THAT* FOR STAKES?

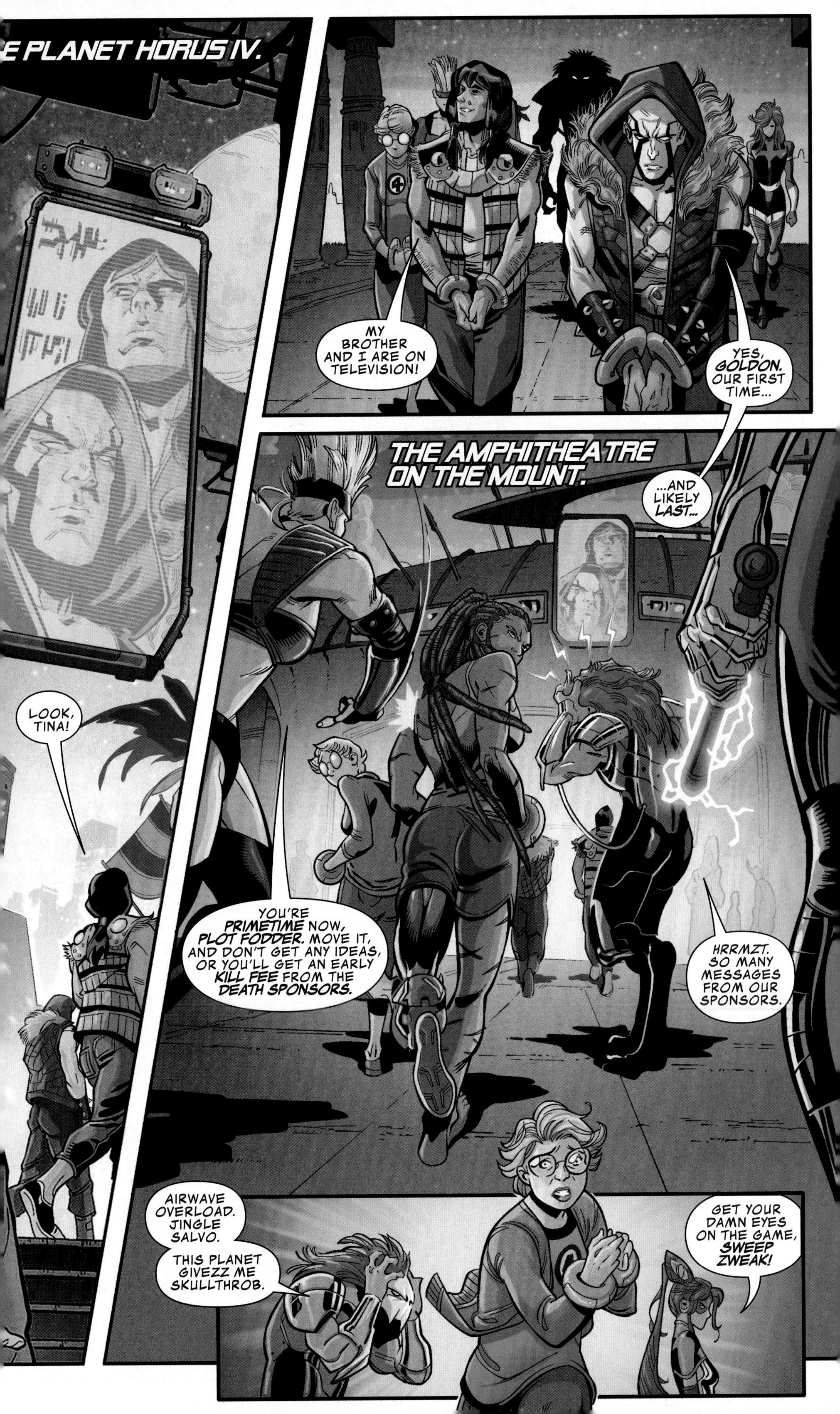

E PLANET HORUS IV.
MY BROTHER AND I ARE ON TELEVISION!
YES, GOLDON. OUR FIRST TIME...
THE AMPHITHEATRE ON THE MOUNT.
...AND LIKELY LAST...
LOOK, TINA!
YOU'RE PRIMETIME NOW, PLOT FODDER. MOVE IT, AND DON'T GET ANY IDEAS, OR YOU'LL GET AN EARLY KILL FEE FROM THE DEATH SPONSORS.
HRRMZT. SO MANY MESSAGES FROM OUR SPONSORS.
AIRWAVE OVERLOAD. JINGLE SALVO.
THIS PLANET GIVEZZ ME SKULLTHROB.
GET YOUR DAMN EYES ON THE GAME, SWEEP ZWEAK!

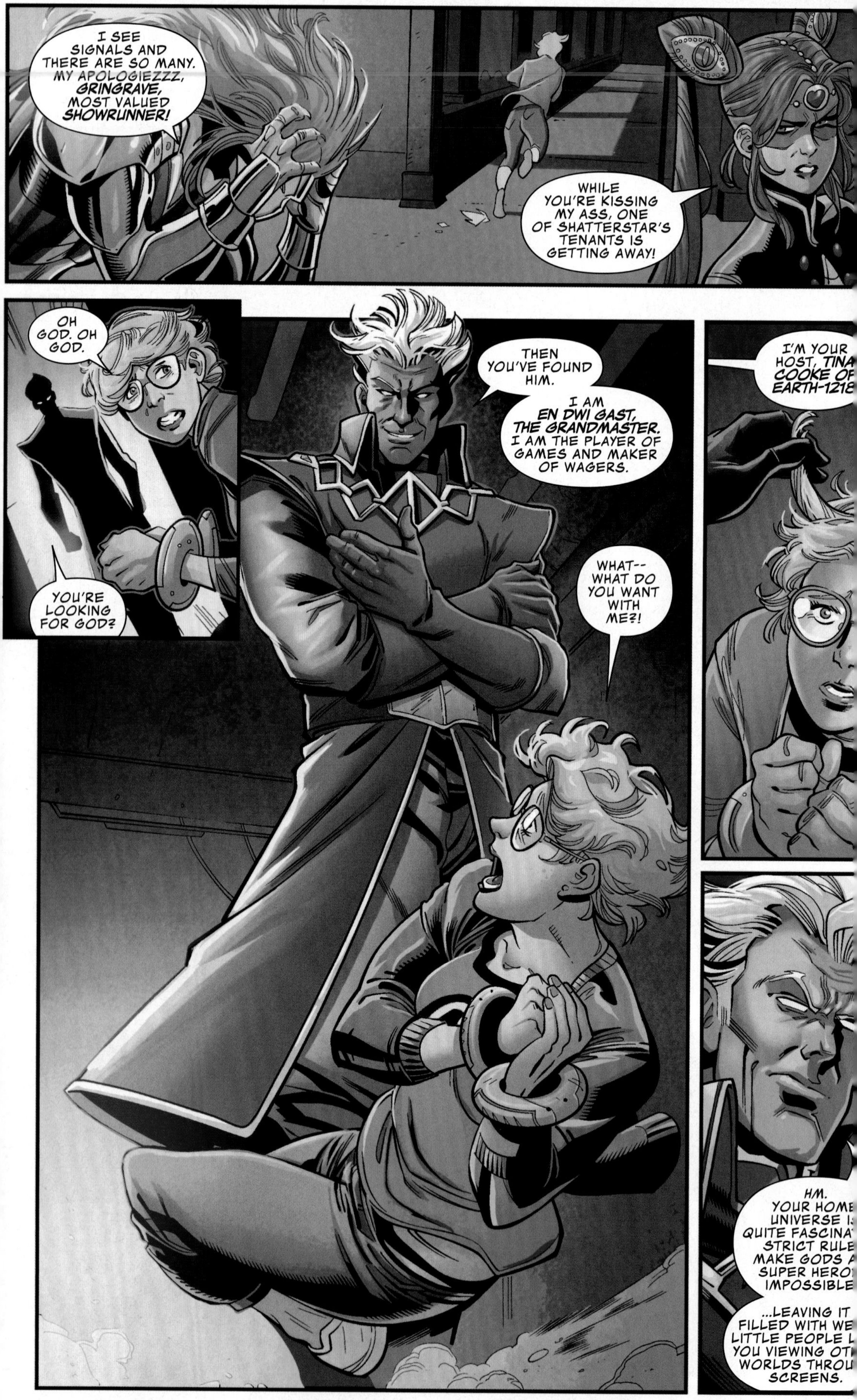
I SEE SIGNALS AND THERE ARE SO MANY. MY APOLOGIEZZZ, GRINGRAVE, MOST VALUED SHOWRUNNER!
WHILE YOU'RE KISSING MY ASS, ONE OF SHATTERSTAR'S TENANTS IS GETTING AWAY!
OH GOD. OH GOD.
YOU'RE LOOKING FOR GOD?
THEN YOU'VE FOUND HIM.
I AM EN DWI GAST, THE GRANDMASTER. I AM THE PLAYER OF GAMES AND MAKER OF WAGERS.
WHAT-- WHAT DO YOU WANT WITH ME?!
I'M YOUR HOST, TINA COOKE OF EARTH-1218
HM. YOUR HOME UNIVERSE IS QUITE FASCINAT STRICT RULE MAKE GODS A SUPER HERO IMPOSSIBLE
...LEAVING IT FILLED WITH WE LITTLE PEOPLE L YOU VIEWING OT WORLDS THROU SCREENS.

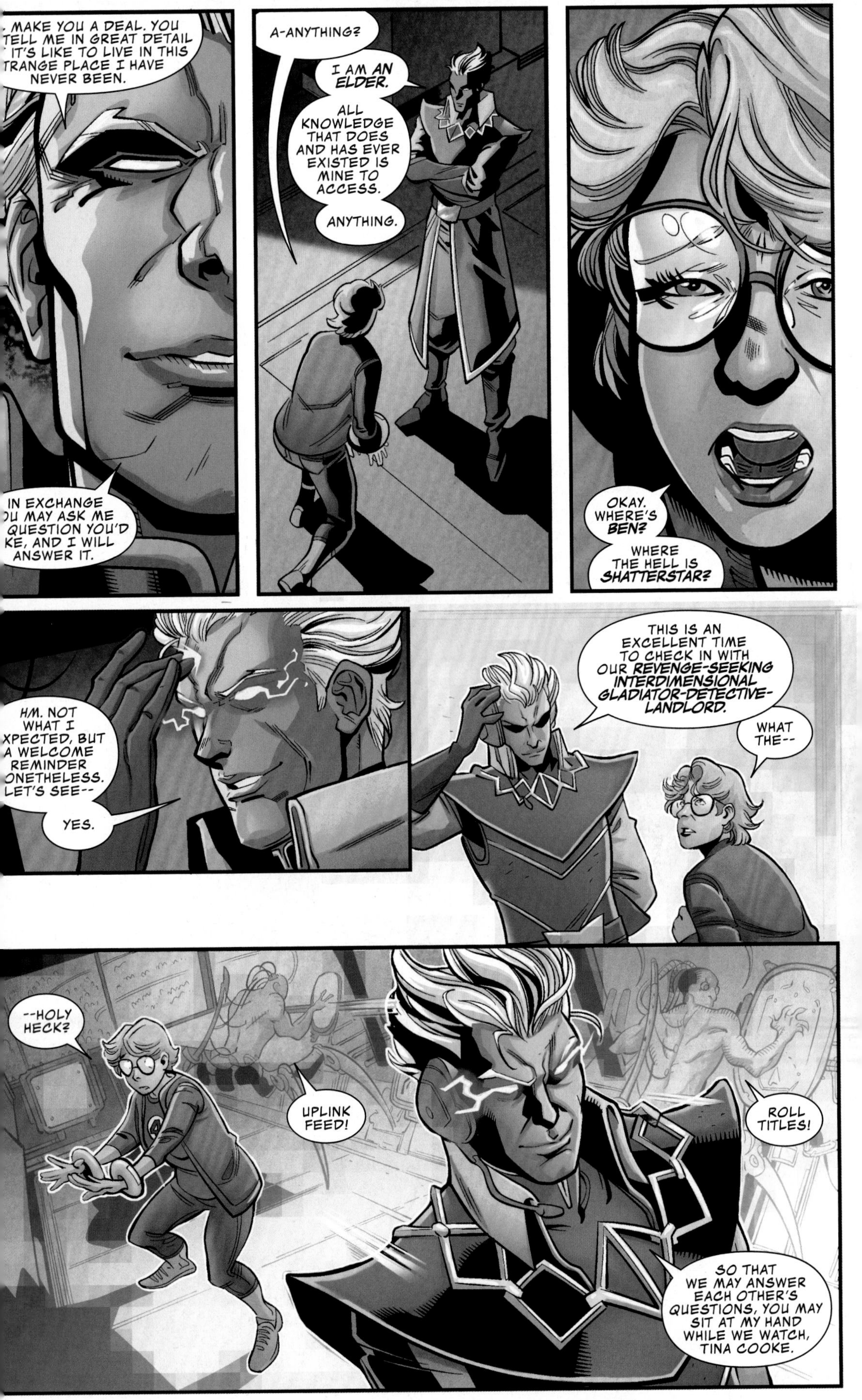
MAKE YOU A DEAL. YOU TELL ME IN GREAT DETAIL IT'S LIKE TO LIVE IN THIS TRANGE PLACE I HAVE NEVER BEEN.
IN EXCHANGE OU MAY ASK ME QUESTION YOU'D KE, AND I WILL ANSWER IT.
A-ANYTHING?
I AM AN ELDER.
ALL KNOWLEDGE THAT DOES AND HAS EVER EXISTED IS MINE TO ACCESS.
ANYTHING.
OKAY. WHERE'S BEN?
WHERE THE HELL IS SHATTERSTAR?
HM. NOT WHAT I XPECTED, BUT A WELCOME REMINDER ONETHELESS. LET'S SEE--
YES.
THIS IS AN EXCELLENT TIME TO CHECK IN WITH OUR REVENGE-SEEKING INTERDIMENSIONAL GLADIATOR-DETECTIVE-LANDLORD.
WHAT THE--
--HOLY HECK?
UPLINK FEED!
ROLL TITLES!
SO THAT WE MAY ANSWER EACH OTHER'S QUESTIONS, YOU MAY SIT AT MY HAND WHILE WE WATCH, TINA COOKE.

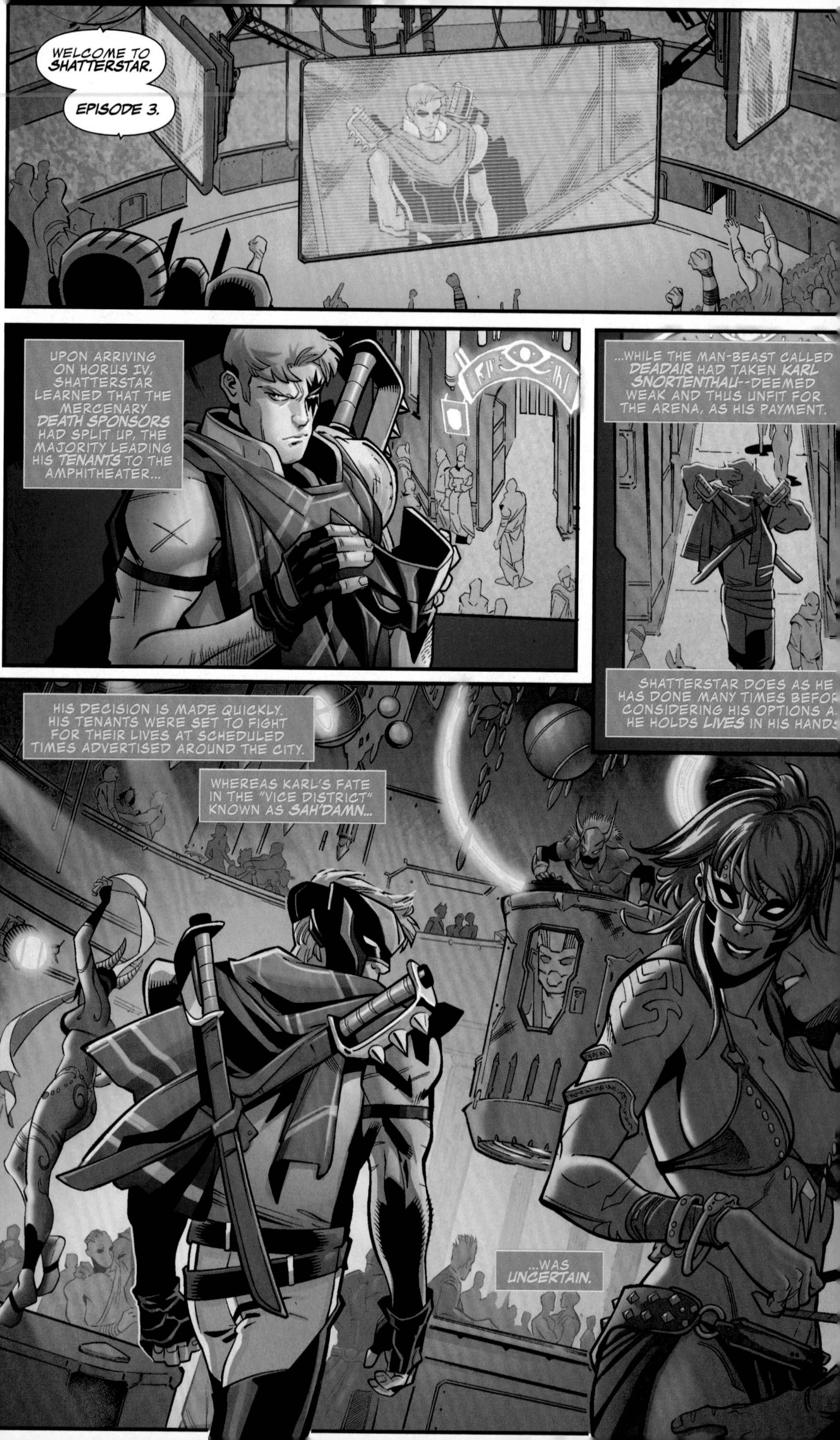
WELCOME TO SHATTERSTAR.
EPISODE 3.
UPON ARRIVING ON HORUS IV, SHATTERSTAR LEARNED THAT THE MERCENARY DEATH SPONSORS HAD SPLIT UP, THE MAJORITY LEADING HIS TENANTS TO THE AMPHITHEATER...
...WHILE THE MAN-BEAST CALLED DEADAIR HAD TAKEN KARL SNORTENTHAU--DEEMED WEAK AND THUS UNFIT FOR THE ARENA, AS HIS PAYMENT.
SHATTERSTAR DOES AS HE HAS DONE MANY TIMES BEFOR CONSIDERING HIS OPTIONS A HE HOLDS LIVES IN HIS HAND
HIS DECISION IS MADE QUICKLY. HIS TENANTS WERE SET TO FIGHT FOR THEIR LIVES AT SCHEDULED TIMES ADVERTISED AROUND THE CITY.
WHEREAS KARL'S FATE IN THE "VICE DISTRICT" KNOWN AS SAH'DAMN...
...WAS UNCERTAIN.

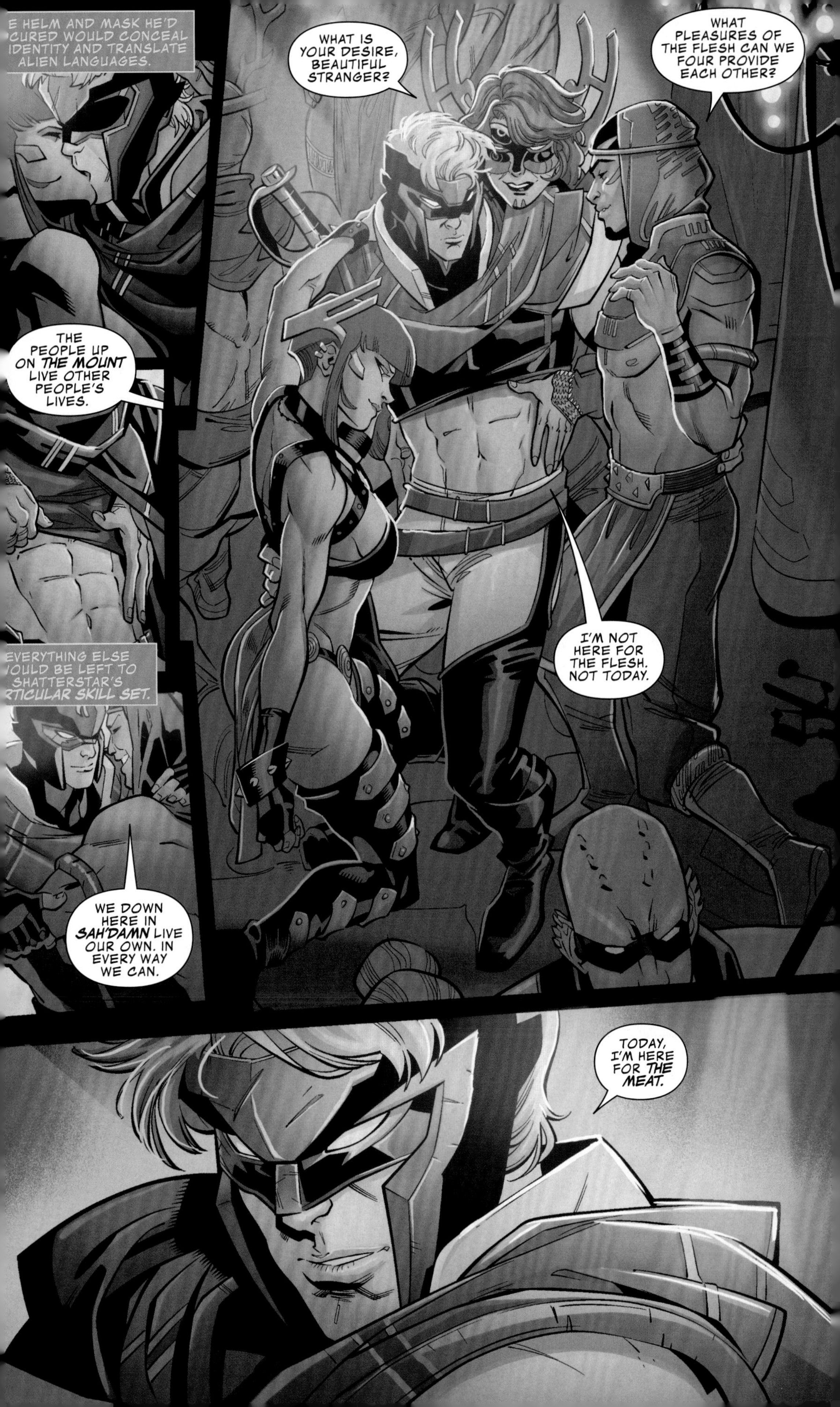

E HELM AND MASK HE'D CURED WOULD CONCEAL IDENTITY AND TRANSLATE ALIEN LANGUAGES.
WHAT IS YOUR DESIRE, BEAUTIFUL STRANGER?
WHAT PLEASURES OF THE FLESH CAN WE FOUR PROVIDE EACH OTHER?
THE PEOPLE UP ON THE MOUNT LIVE OTHER PEOPLE'S LIVES.
I'M NOT HERE FOR THE FLESH. NOT TODAY.
EVERYTHING ELSE OULD BE LEFT TO SHATTERSTAR'S RTICULAR SKILL SET.
WE DOWN HERE IN SAH'DAMN LIVE OUR OWN. IN EVERY WAY WE CAN.
TODAY, I'M HERE FOR THE MEAT.

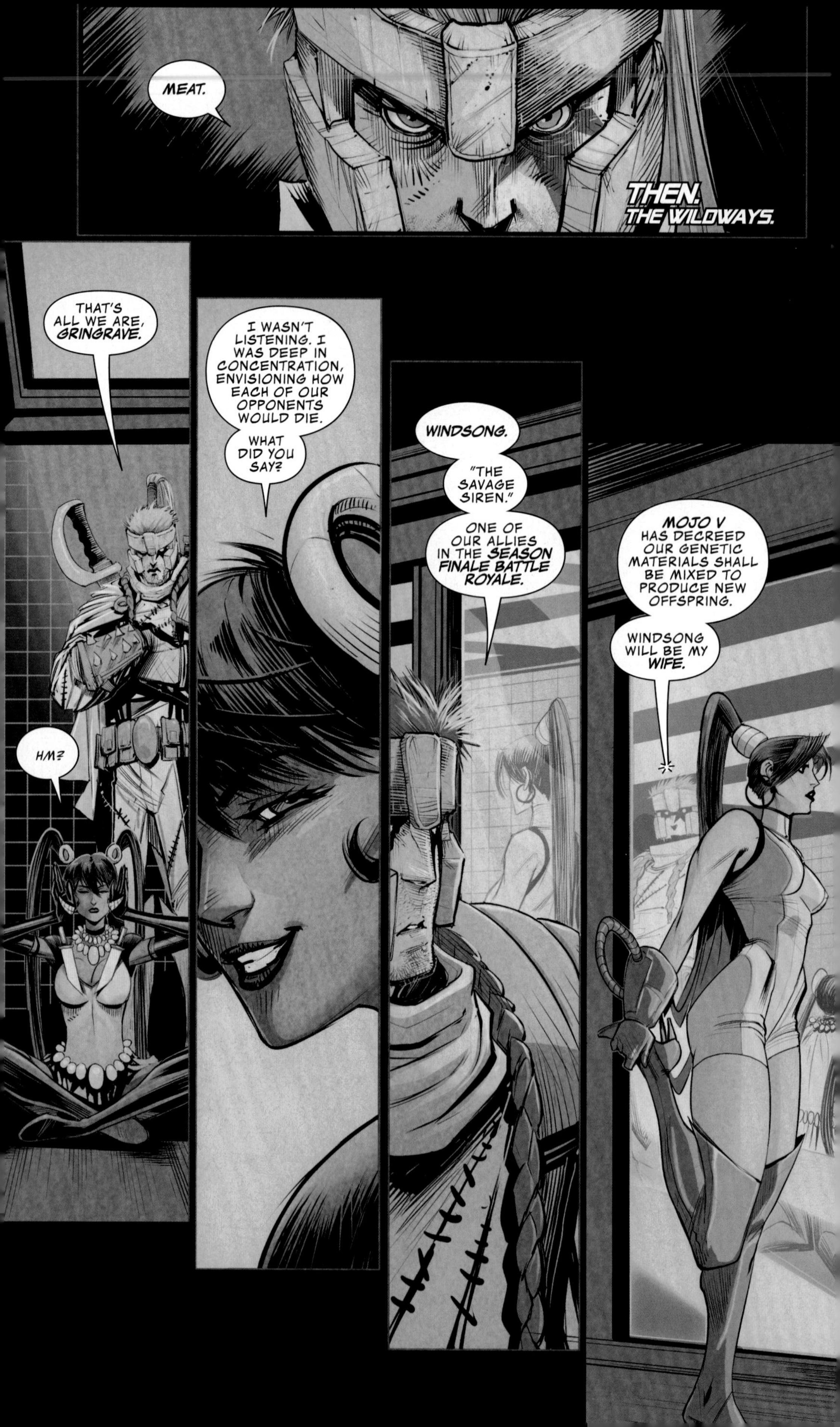
MEAT.
THEN.
THE WILDWAYS.
THAT'S ALL WE ARE, GRINGRAVE.
HM?
I WASN'T LISTENING. I WAS DEEP IN CONCENTRATION, ENVISIONING HOW EACH OF OUR OPPONENTS WOULD DIE.
WHAT DID YOU SAY?
WINDSONG.
"THE SAVAGE SIREN."
ONE OF OUR ALLIES IN THE SEASON FINALE BATTLE ROYALE.
MOJO V HAS DECREED OUR GENETIC MATERIALS SHALL BE MIXED TO PRODUCE NEW OFFSPRING.
WINDSONG WILL BE MY WIFE.

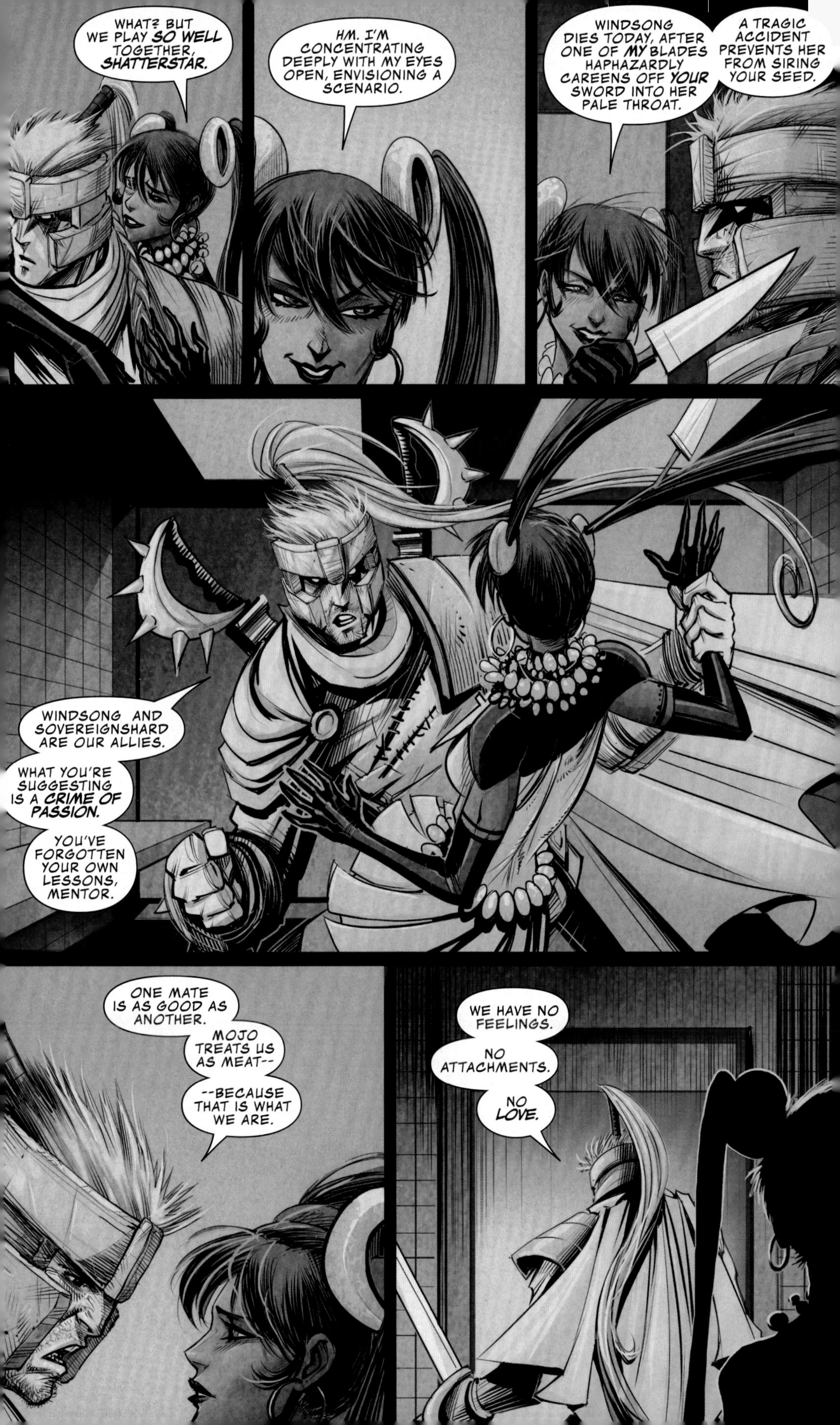
WHAT? BUT WE PLAY SO WELL TOGETHER, SHATTERSTAR.
HM. I'M CONCENTRATING DEEPLY WITH MY EYES OPEN, ENVISIONING A SCENARIO.
WINDSONG DIES TODAY, AFTER ONE OF MY BLADES HAPHAZARDLY CAREENS OFF YOUR SWORD INTO HER PALE THROAT.
A TRAGIC ACCIDENT PREVENTS HER FROM SIRING YOUR SEED.
WINDSONG AND SOVEREIGNSHARD ARE OUR ALLIES.
WHAT YOU'RE SUGGESTING IS A CRIME OF PASSION.
YOU'VE FORGOTTEN YOUR OWN LESSONS, MENTOR.
ONE MATE IS AS GOOD AS ANOTHER.
MOJO TREATS US AS MEAT--
--BECAUSE THAT IS WHAT WE ARE.
WE HAVE NO FEELINGS.
NO ATTACHMENTS.
NO LOVE.

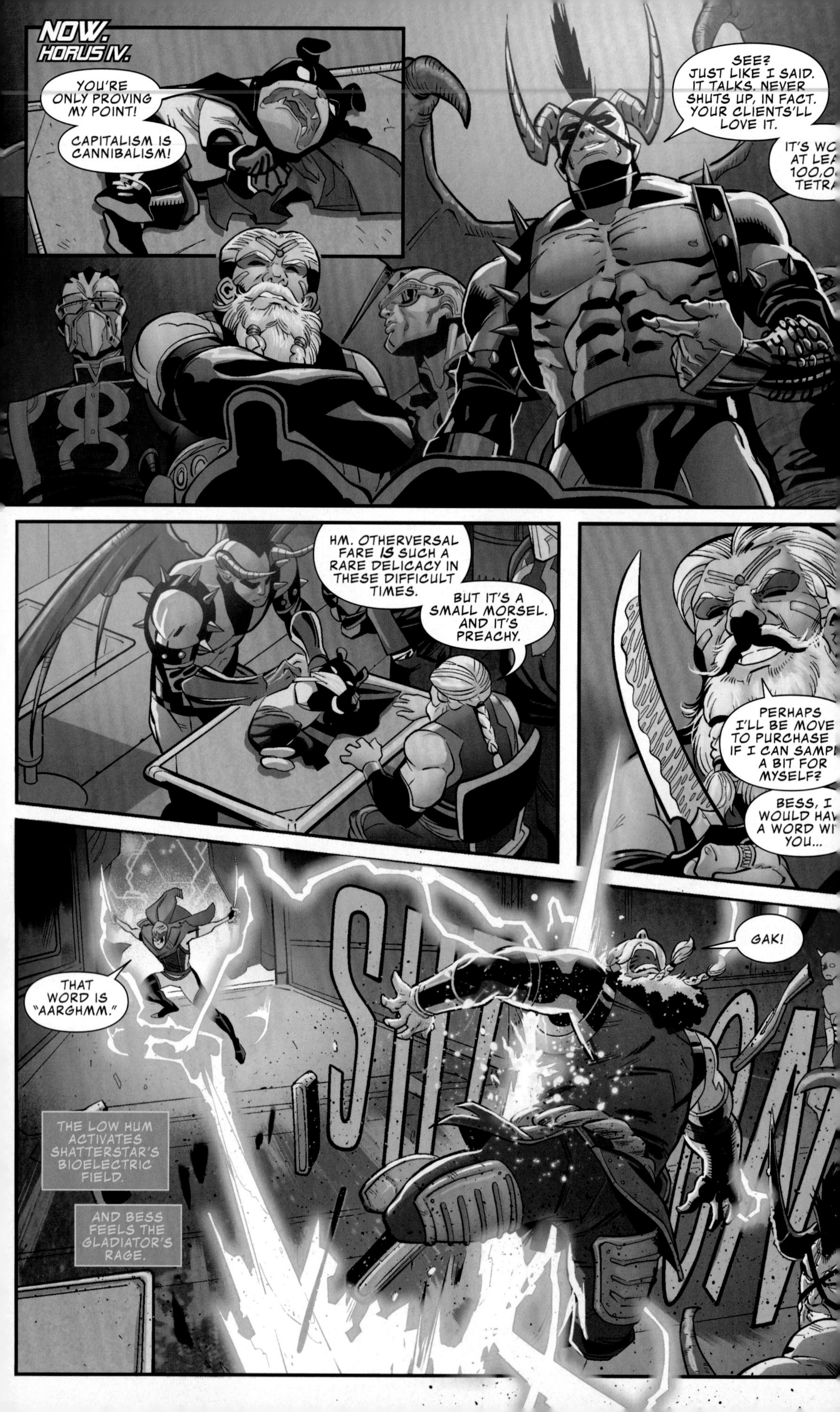
NOW.
HORUS IV.
YOU'RE ONLY PROVING MY POINT!
CAPITALISM IS CANNIBALISM!
SEE? JUST LIKE I SAID. IT TALKS. NEVER SHUTS UP, IN FACT. YOUR CLIENTS'LL LOVE IT.
IT'S WO AT LEA 100,0 TETR
HM. OTHERVERSAL FARE IS SUCH A RARE DELICACY IN THESE DIFFICULT TIMES.
BUT IT'S A SMALL MORSEL. AND IT'S PREACHY.
PERHAPS I'LL BE MOVE TO PURCHASE IF I CAN SAMP A BIT FOR MYSELF?
BESS, I WOULD HAV A WORD WI YOU...
GAK!
THAT WORD IS "AARGHMM."
THE LOW HUM ACTIVATES SHATTERSTAR'S BIOELECTRIC FIELD.
AND BESS FEELS THE GLADIATOR'S RAGE.

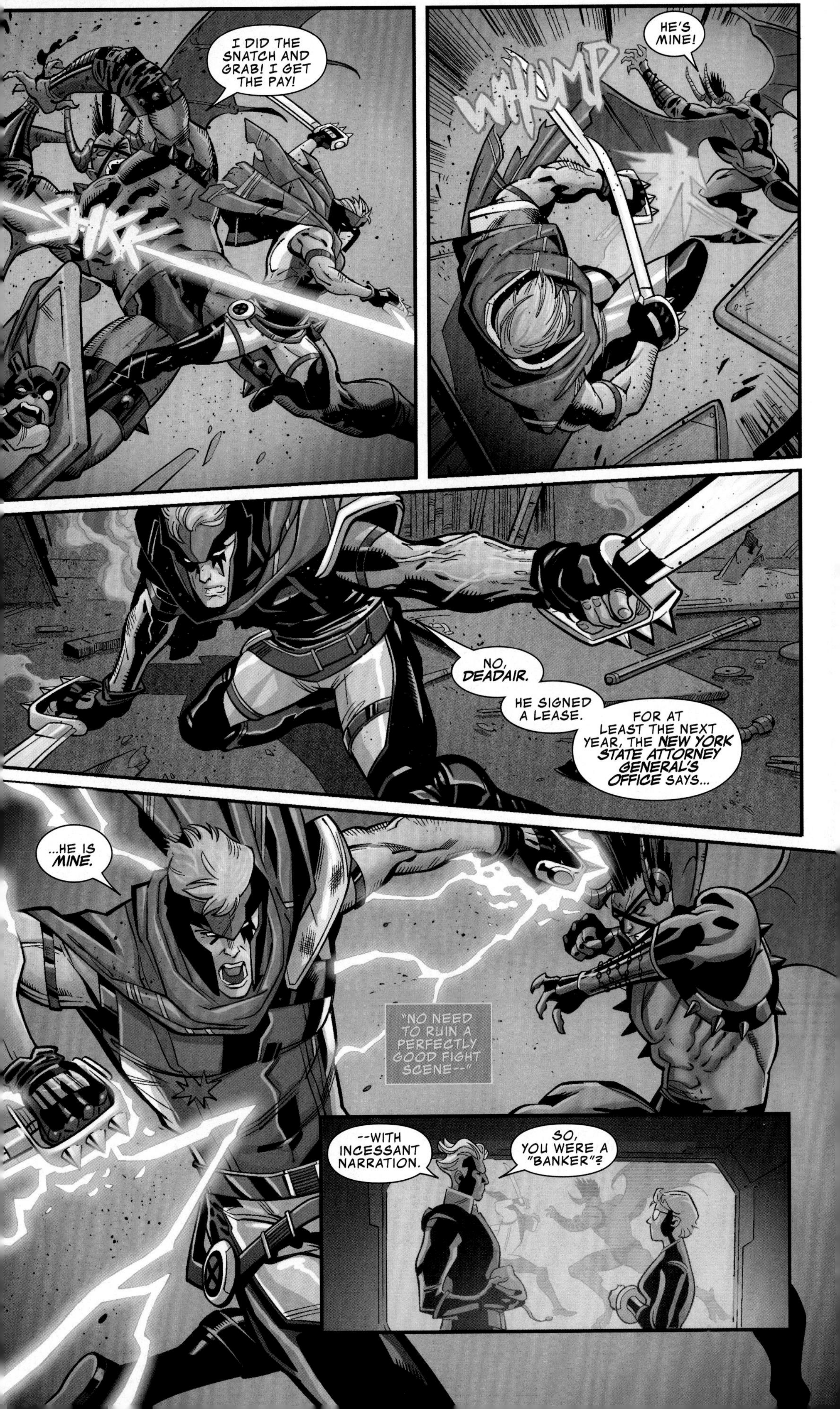
I DID THE SNATCH AND GRAB! I GET THE PAY!
SHKK
HE'S MINE!
WHUMP
NO, DEADAIR.
HE SIGNED A LEASE.
FOR AT LEAST THE NEXT YEAR, THE NEW YORK STATE ATTORNEY GENERAL'S OFFICE SAYS...
...HE IS MINE.
"NO NEED TO RUIN A PERFECTLY GOOD FIGHT SCENE--"
--WITH INCESSANT NARRATION.
SO, YOU WERE A "BANKER"?

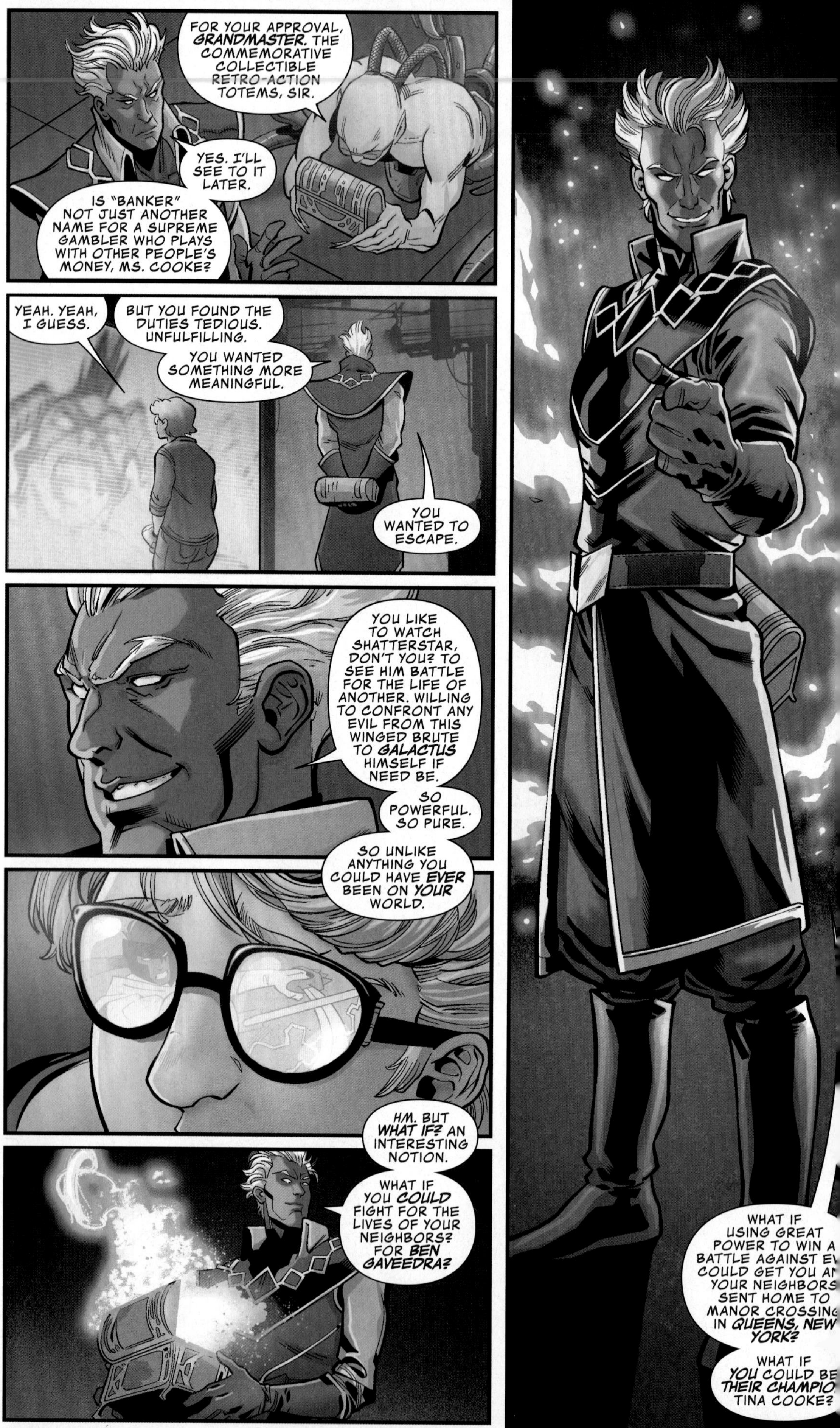

FOR YOUR APPROVAL, **GRANDMASTER.** THE COMMEMORATIVE COLLECTIBLE RETRO-ACTION TOTEMS, SIR.
YES. I'LL SEE TO IT LATER.
IS "BANKER" NOT JUST ANOTHER NAME FOR A SUPREME GAMBLER WHO PLAYS WITH OTHER PEOPLE'S MONEY, MS. COOKE?
YEAH. YEAH, I GUESS.
BUT YOU FOUND THE DUTIES TEDIOUS. UNFULFILLING.
YOU WANTED SOMETHING MORE MEANINGFUL.
YOU WANTED TO ESCAPE.
YOU LIKE TO WATCH SHATTERSTAR, DON'T YOU? TO SEE HIM BATTLE FOR THE LIFE OF ANOTHER. WILLING TO CONFRONT ANY EVIL FROM THIS WINGED BRUTE TO **GALACTUS** HIMSELF IF NEED BE.
SO POWERFUL. SO PURE.
SO UNLIKE ANYTHING YOU COULD HAVE **EVER** BEEN ON **YOUR** WORLD.
HM. BUT **WHAT IF?** AN INTERESTING NOTION.
WHAT IF YOU **COULD** FIGHT FOR THE LIVES OF YOUR NEIGHBORS? FOR **BEN GAVEEDRA?**
WHAT IF USING GREAT POWER TO WIN A BATTLE AGAINST E COULD GET YOU A YOUR NEIGHBORS SENT HOME TO MANOR CROSSIN IN **QUEENS, NEW YORK?**
WHAT IF **YOU** COULD BE **THEIR CHAMPIO** TINA COOKE?

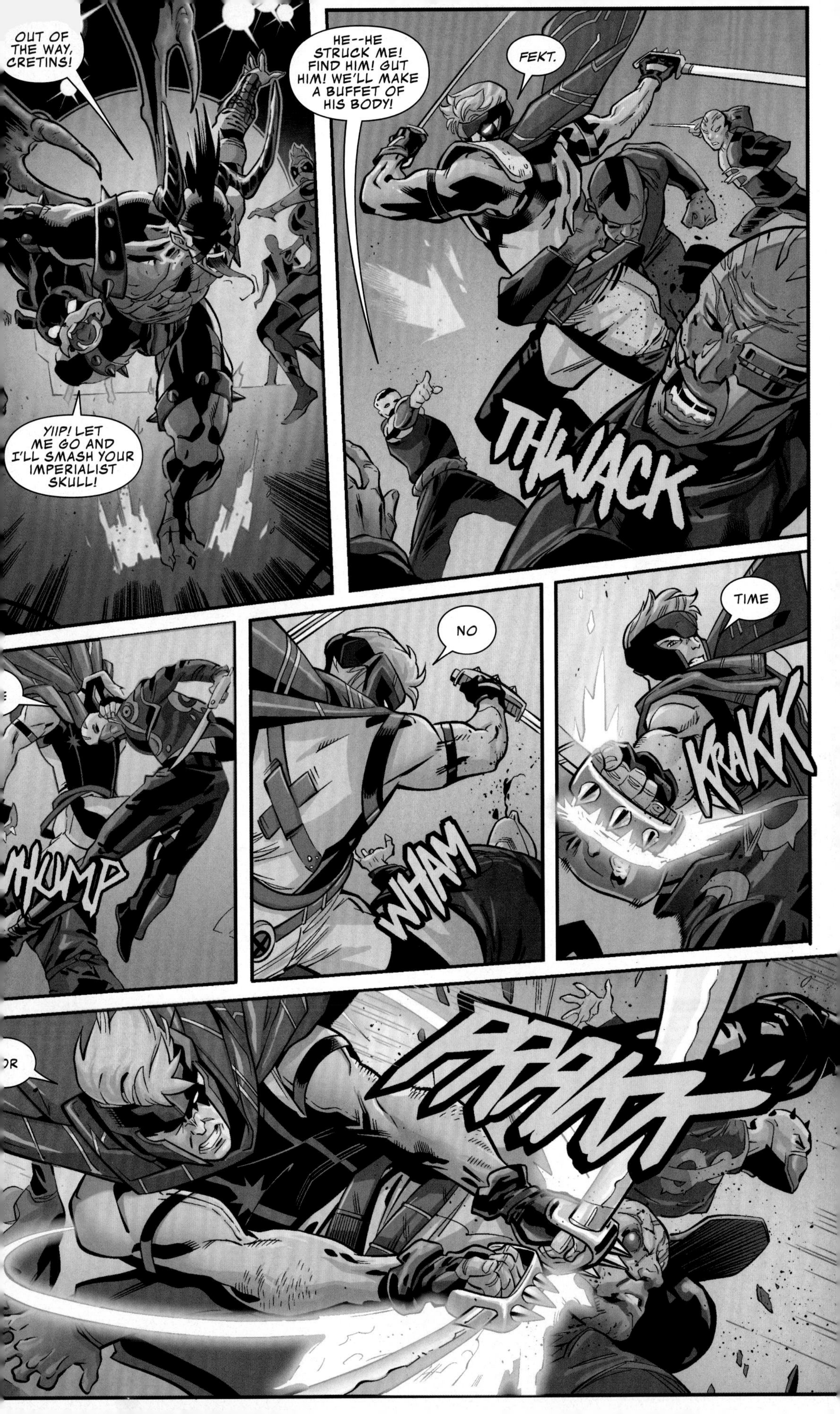
OUT OF THE WAY, CRETINS!
YIIP! LET ME GO AND I'LL SMASH YOUR IMPERIALIST SKULL!
HE--HE STRUCK ME! FIND HIM! GUT HIM! WE'LL MAKE A BUFFET OF HIS BODY!
FEKT.
THWACK
HUMP
NO
WHAM
TIME
KRAKK

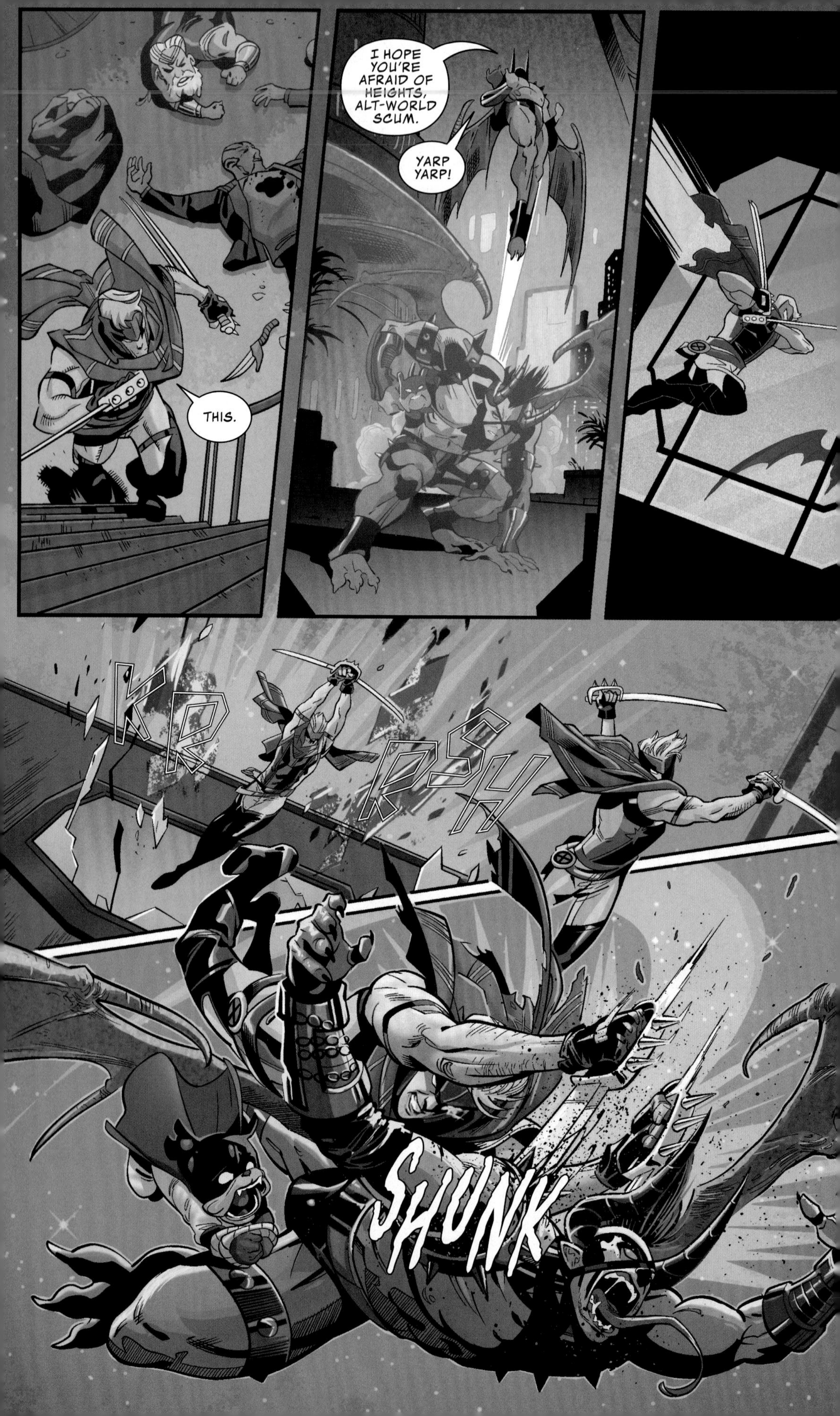
THIS.
I HOPE YOU'RE AFRAID OF HEIGHTS, ALT-WORLD SCUM.
YARP YARP!
KRRSH
SHUNK

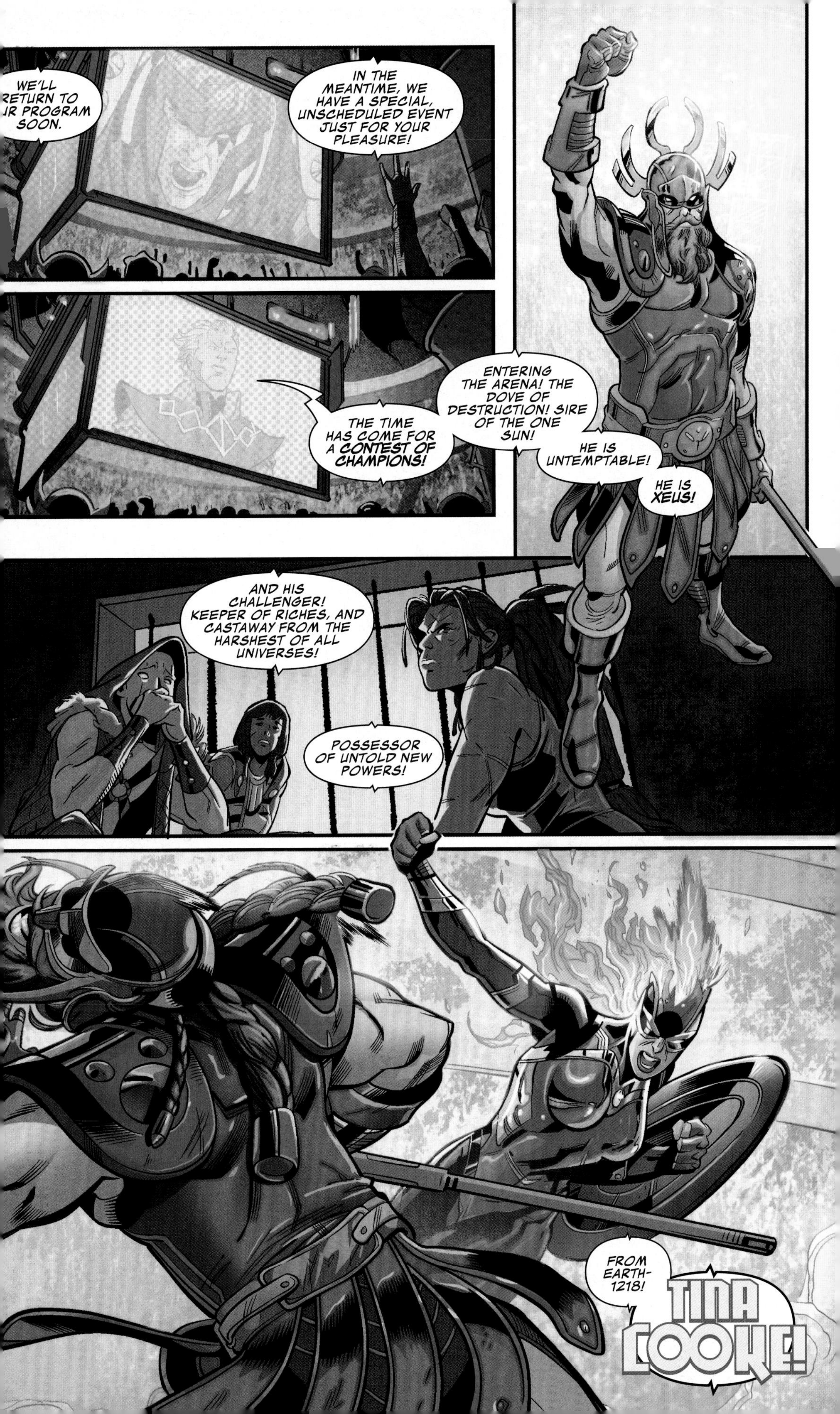

WE'LL RETURN TO UR PROGRAM SOON.
IN THE MEANTIME, WE HAVE A SPECIAL, UNSCHEDULED EVENT JUST FOR YOUR PLEASURE!
THE TIME HAS COME FOR A CONTEST OF CHAMPIONS!
ENTERING THE ARENA! THE DOVE OF DESTRUCTION! SIRE OF THE ONE SUN!
HE IS UNTEMPTABLE!
HE IS XEUS!
AND HIS CHALLENGER! KEEPER OF RICHES, AND CASTAWAY FROM THE HARSHEST OF ALL UNIVERSES!
POSSESSOR OF UNTOLD NEW POWERS!
FROM EARTH-1218!
TINA COOKE!

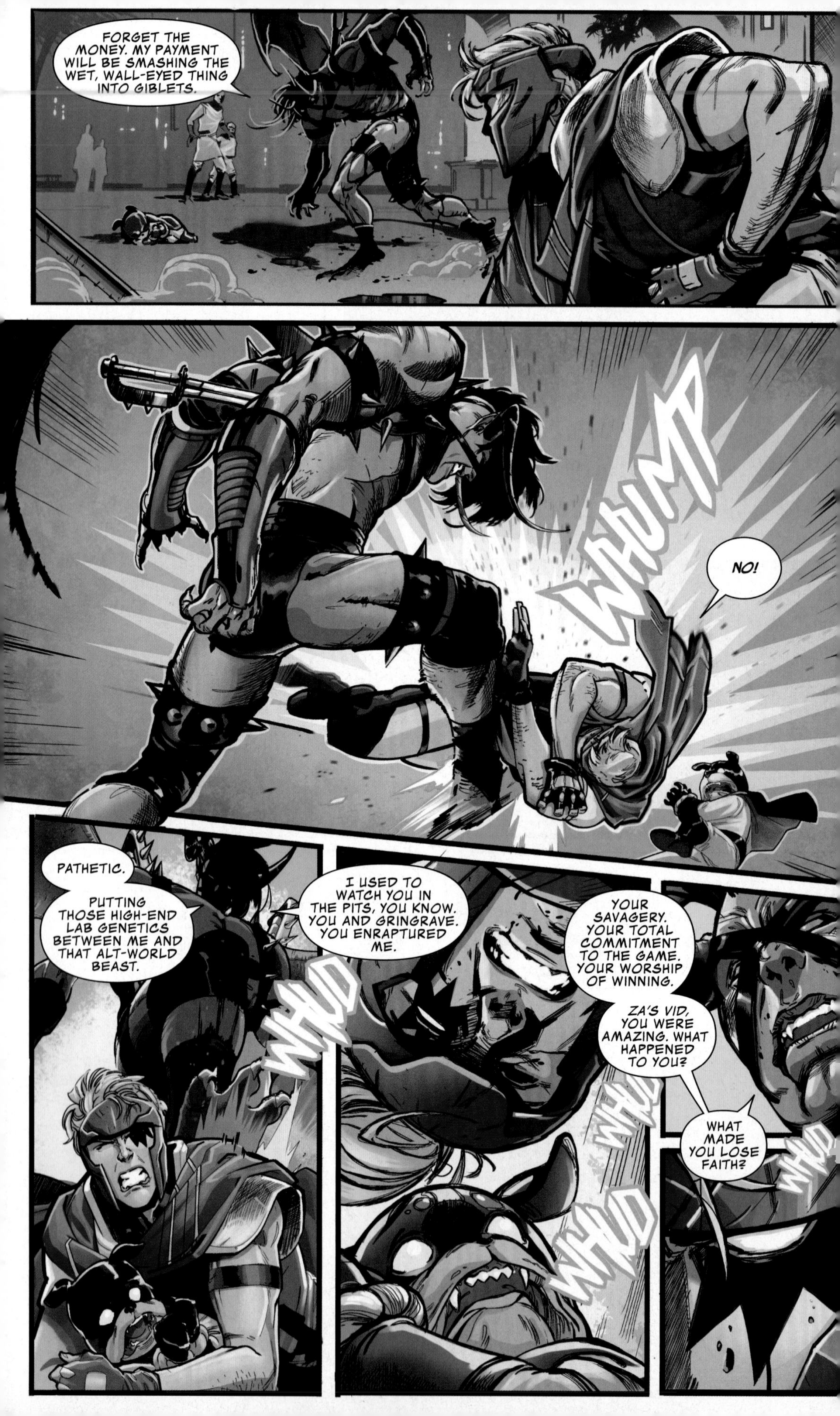
FORGET THE MONEY. MY PAYMENT WILL BE SMASHING THE WET, WALL-EYED THING INTO GIBLETS.
WHUMP
NO!
PATHETIC.
PUTTING THOSE HIGH-END LAB GENETICS BETWEEN ME AND THAT ALT-WORLD BEAST.
WHUD
I USED TO WATCH YOU IN THE PITS, YOU KNOW. YOU AND GRINGRAVE. YOU ENRAPTURED ME.
YOUR SAVAGERY. YOUR TOTAL COMMITMENT TO THE GAME. YOUR WORSHIP OF WINNING.
ZA'S VID, YOU WERE AMAZING. WHAT HAPPENED TO YOU?
WHUD
WHUD
WHAT MADE YOU LOSE FAITH?
WHUD

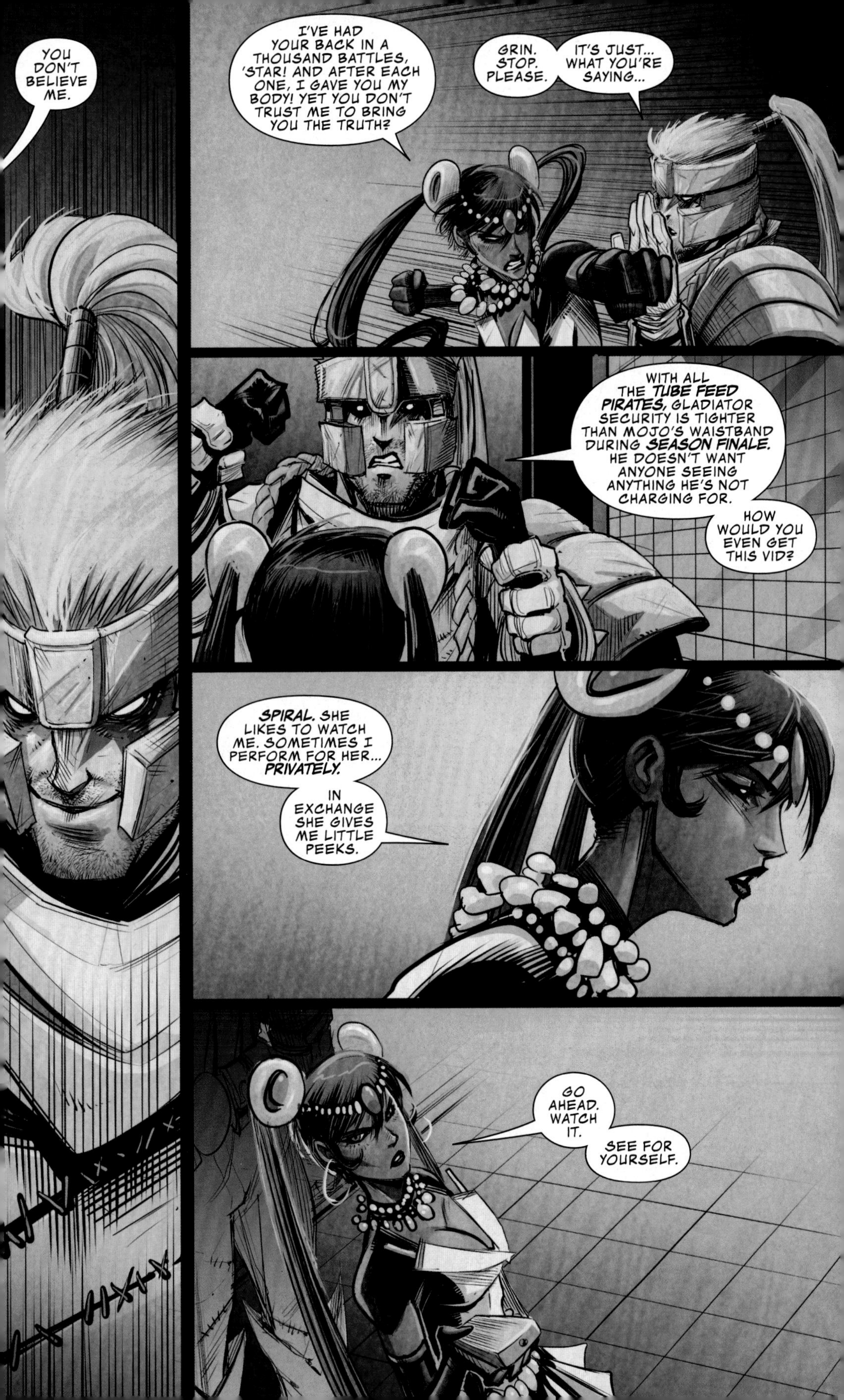

YOU DON'T BELIEVE ME.
I'VE HAD YOUR BACK IN A THOUSAND BATTLES, 'STAR! AND AFTER EACH ONE, I GAVE YOU MY BODY! YET YOU DON'T TRUST ME TO BRING YOU THE TRUTH?
GRIN. STOP. PLEASE.
IT'S JUST... WHAT YOU'RE SAYING...
WITH ALL THE TUBE FEED PIRATES, GLADIATOR SECURITY IS TIGHTER THAN MOJO'S WAISTBAND DURING SEASON FINALE. HE DOESN'T WANT ANYONE SEEING ANYTHING HE'S NOT CHARGING FOR.
HOW WOULD YOU EVEN GET THIS VID?
SPIRAL. SHE LIKES TO WATCH ME. SOMETIMES I PERFORM FOR HER... PRIVATELY.
IN EXCHANGE SHE GIVES ME LITTLE PEEKS.
GO AHEAD. WATCH IT.
SEE FOR YOURSELF.

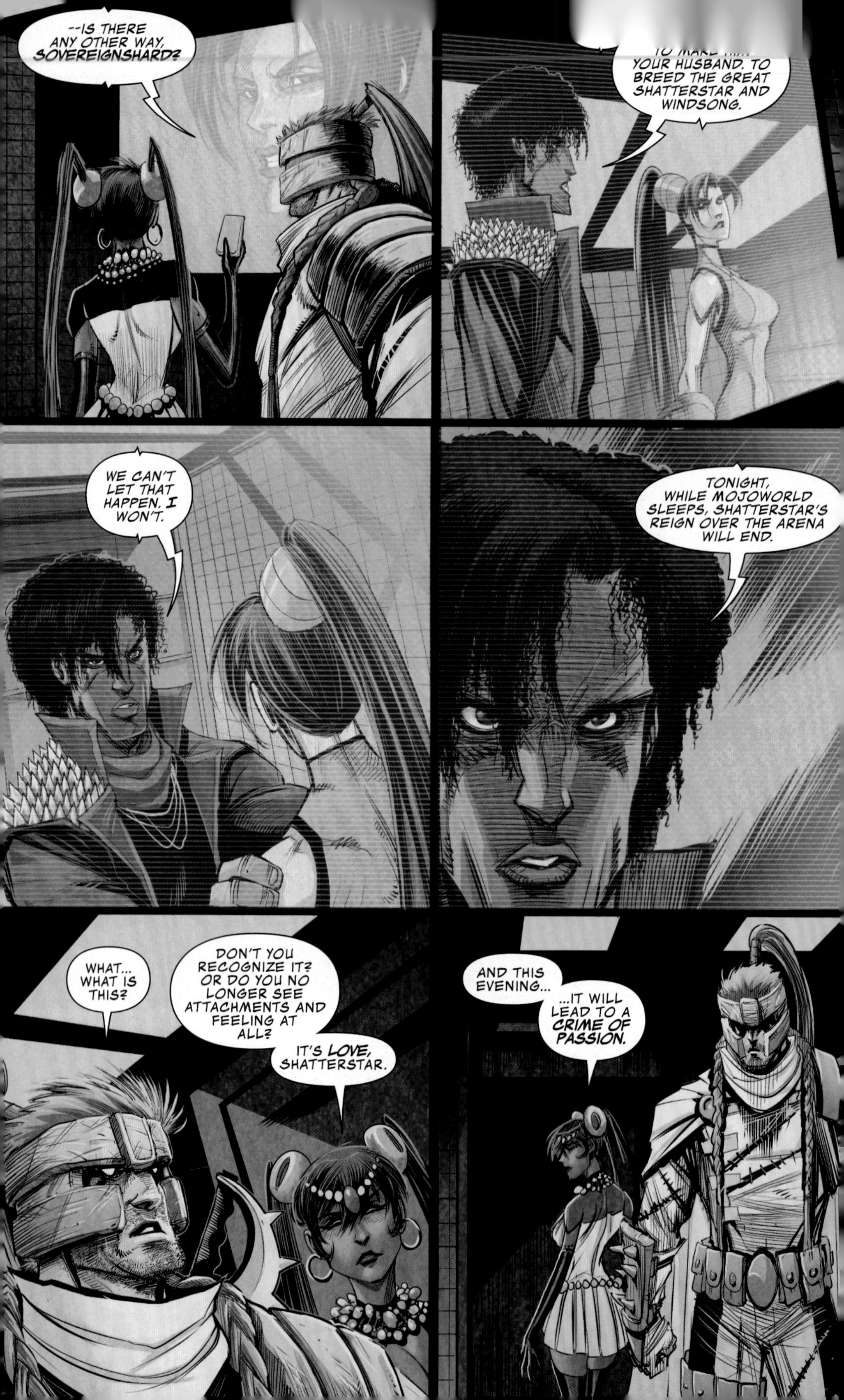
--IS THERE ANY OTHER WAY, SOVEREIGNSHARD?
YOUR HUSBAND. TO BREED THE GREAT SHATTERSTAR AND WINDSONG.
WE CAN'T LET THAT HAPPEN. I WON'T.
TONIGHT, WHILE MOJOWORLD SLEEPS, SHATTERSTAR'S REIGN OVER THE ARENA WILL END.
WHAT... WHAT IS THIS?
DON'T YOU RECOGNIZE IT? OR DO YOU NO LONGER SEE ATTACHMENTS AND FEELING AT ALL?
IT'S LOVE, SHATTERSTAR.
AND THIS EVENING...
...IT WILL LEAD TO A CRIME OF PASSION.

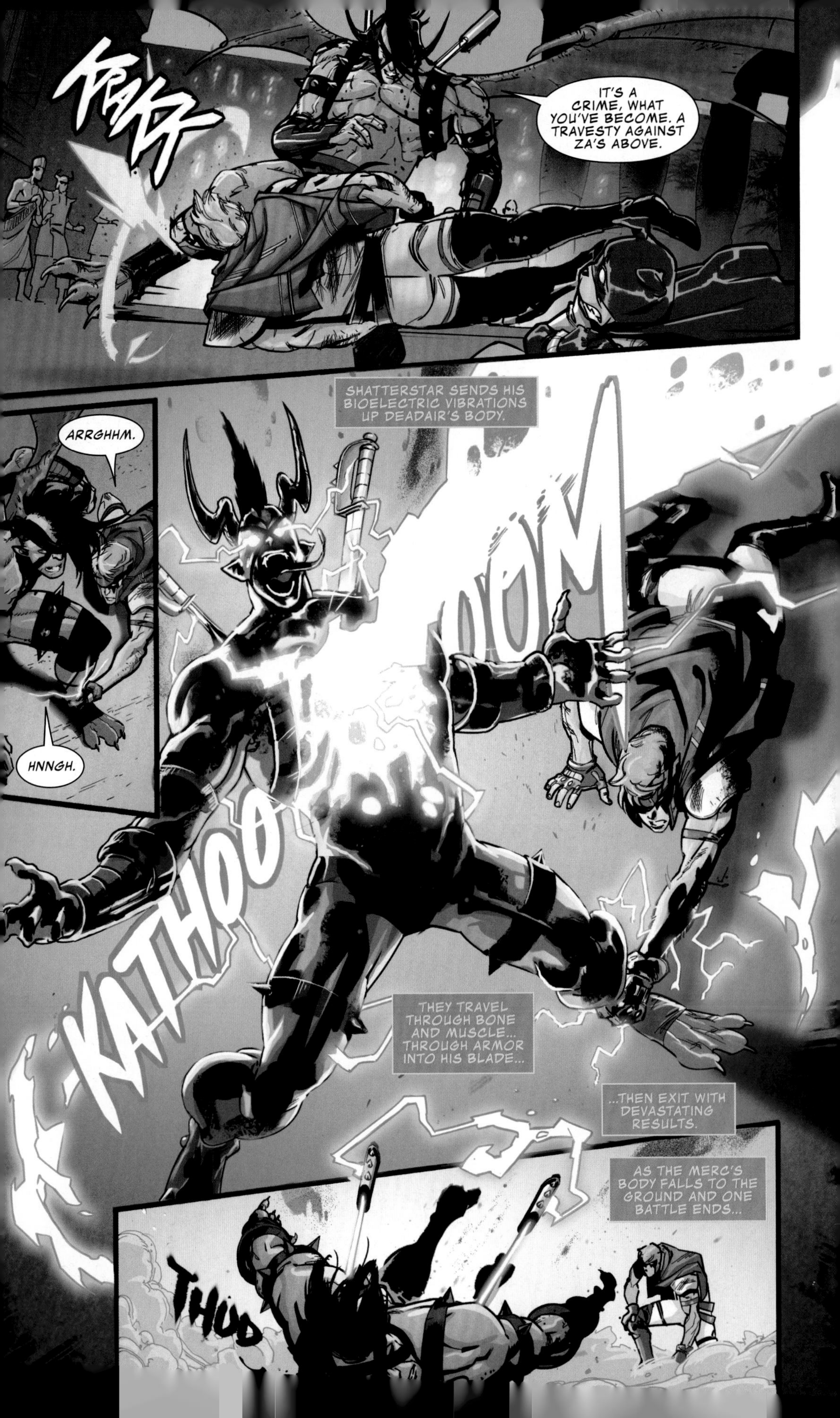
KRAK
IT'S A CRIME, WHAT YOU'VE BECOME. A TRAVESTY AGAINST ZA'S ABOVE.
SHATTERSTAR SENDS HIS BIOELECTRIC VIBRATIONS UP DEADAIR'S BODY.
ARRGHHM.
HNNGH.
KATHOOOOOM
THEY TRAVEL THROUGH BONE AND MUSCLE... THROUGH ARMOR INTO HIS BLADE...
...THEN EXIT WITH DEVASTATING RESULTS.
AS THE MERC'S BODY FALLS TO THE GROUND AND ONE BATTLE ENDS...
THUD

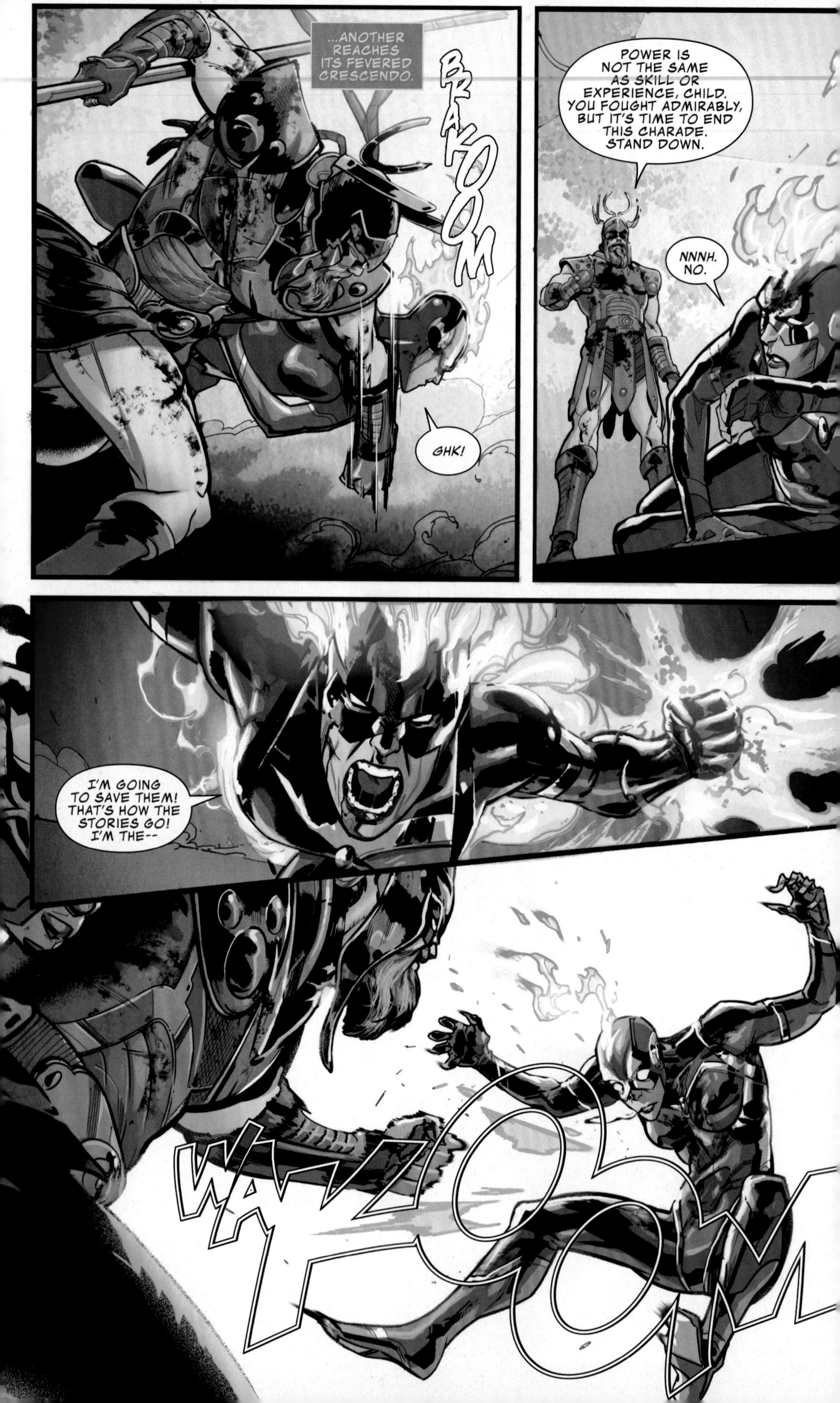
...ANOTHER REACHES ITS FEVERED CRESCENDO.
BRAKOOM
GHK!
POWER IS NOT THE SAME AS SKILL OR EXPERIENCE, CHILD. YOU FOUGHT ADMIRABLY, BUT IT'S TIME TO END THIS CHARADE. STAND DOWN.
NNNH. NO.
I'M GOING TO SAVE THEM! THAT'S HOW THE STORIES GO! I'M THE--
WAKOOM

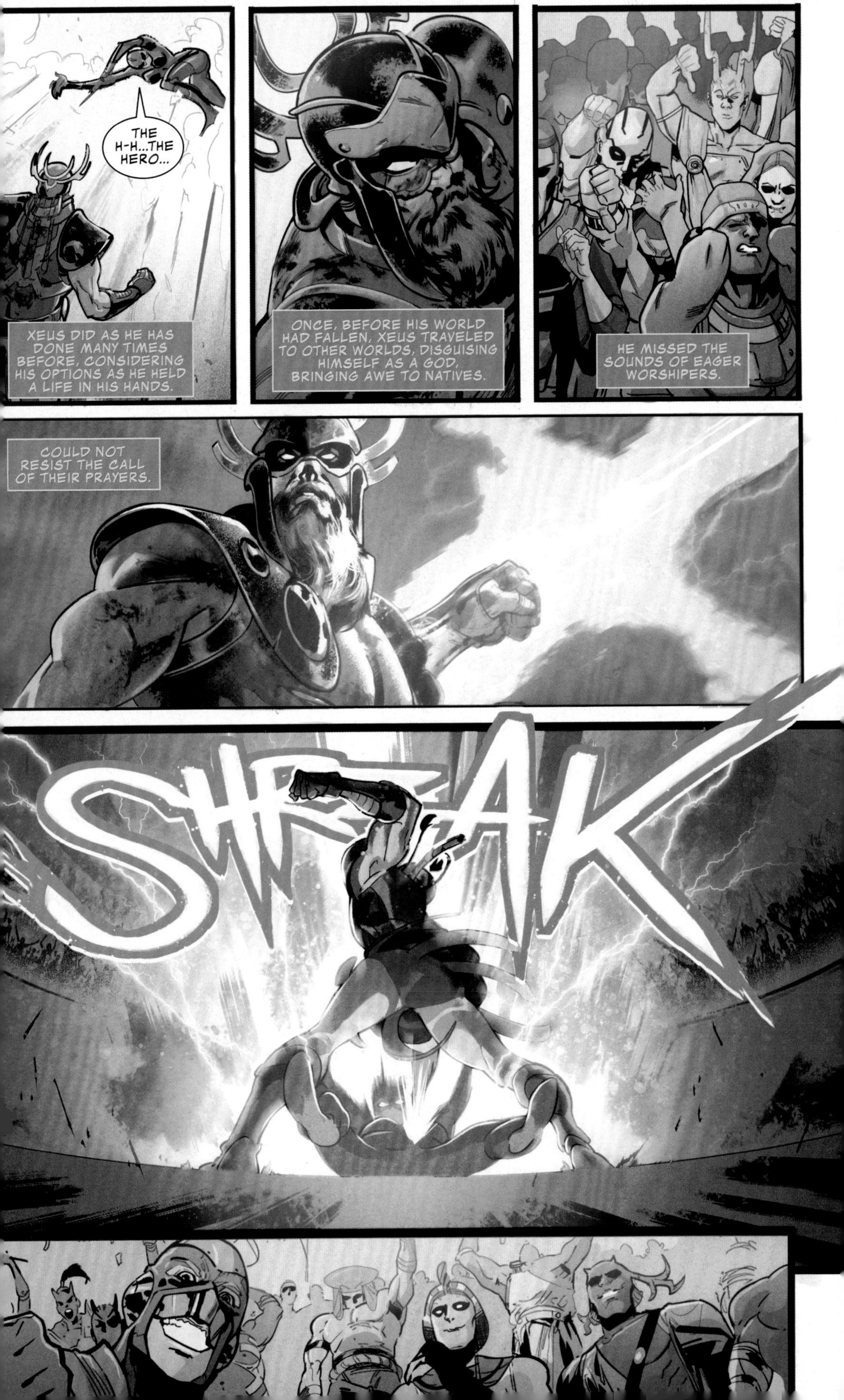
THE H-H...THE HERO...
XEUS DID AS HE HAS DONE MANY TIMES BEFORE, CONSIDERING HIS OPTIONS AS HE HELD A LIFE IN HIS HANDS.
ONCE, BEFORE HIS WORLD HAD FALLEN, XEUS TRAVELED TO OTHER WORLDS, DISGUISING HIMSELF AS A GOD, BRINGING AWE TO NATIVES.
HE MISSED THE SOUNDS OF EAGER WORSHIPERS.
COULD NOT RESIST THE CALL OF THEIR PRAYERS.
SHRAK

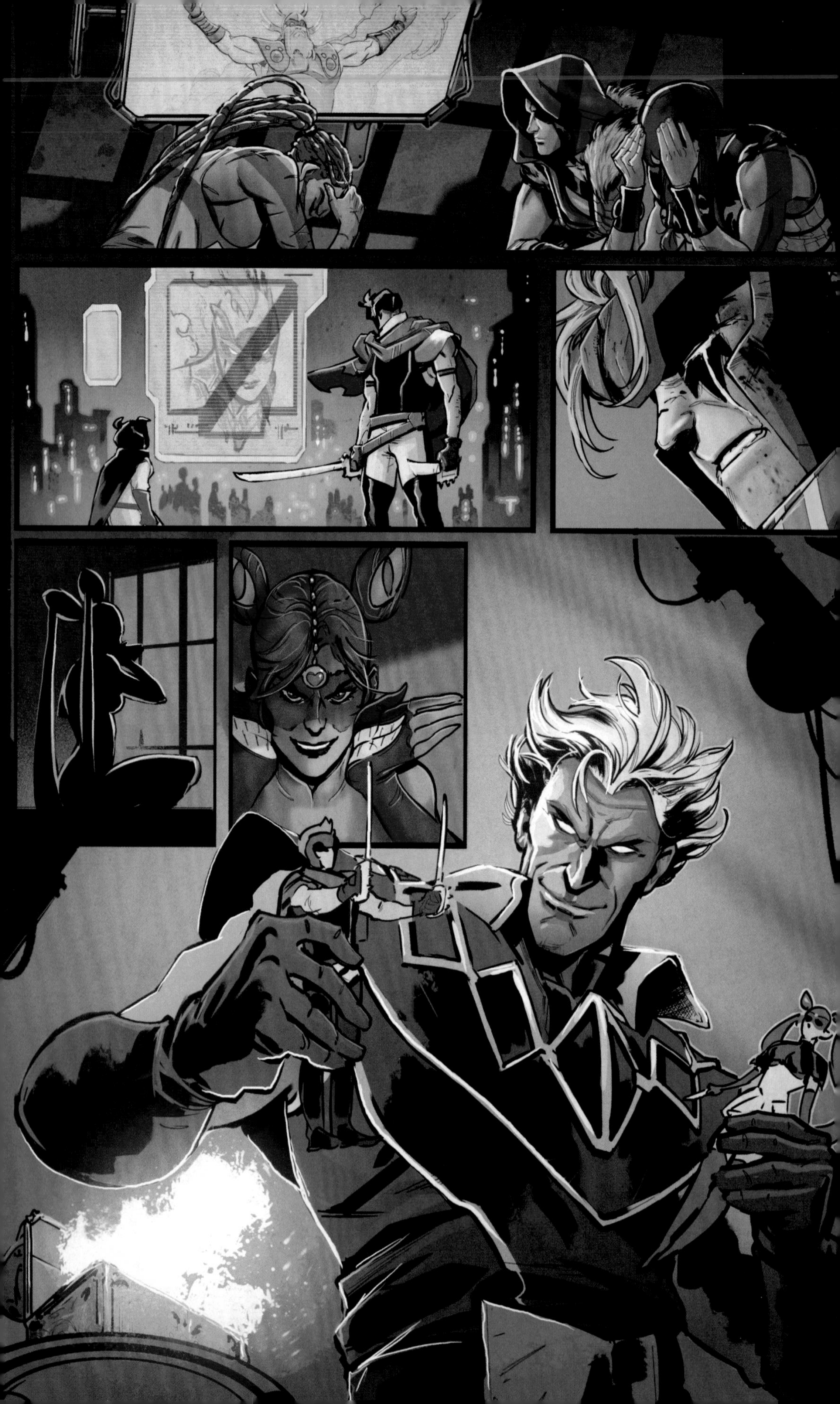

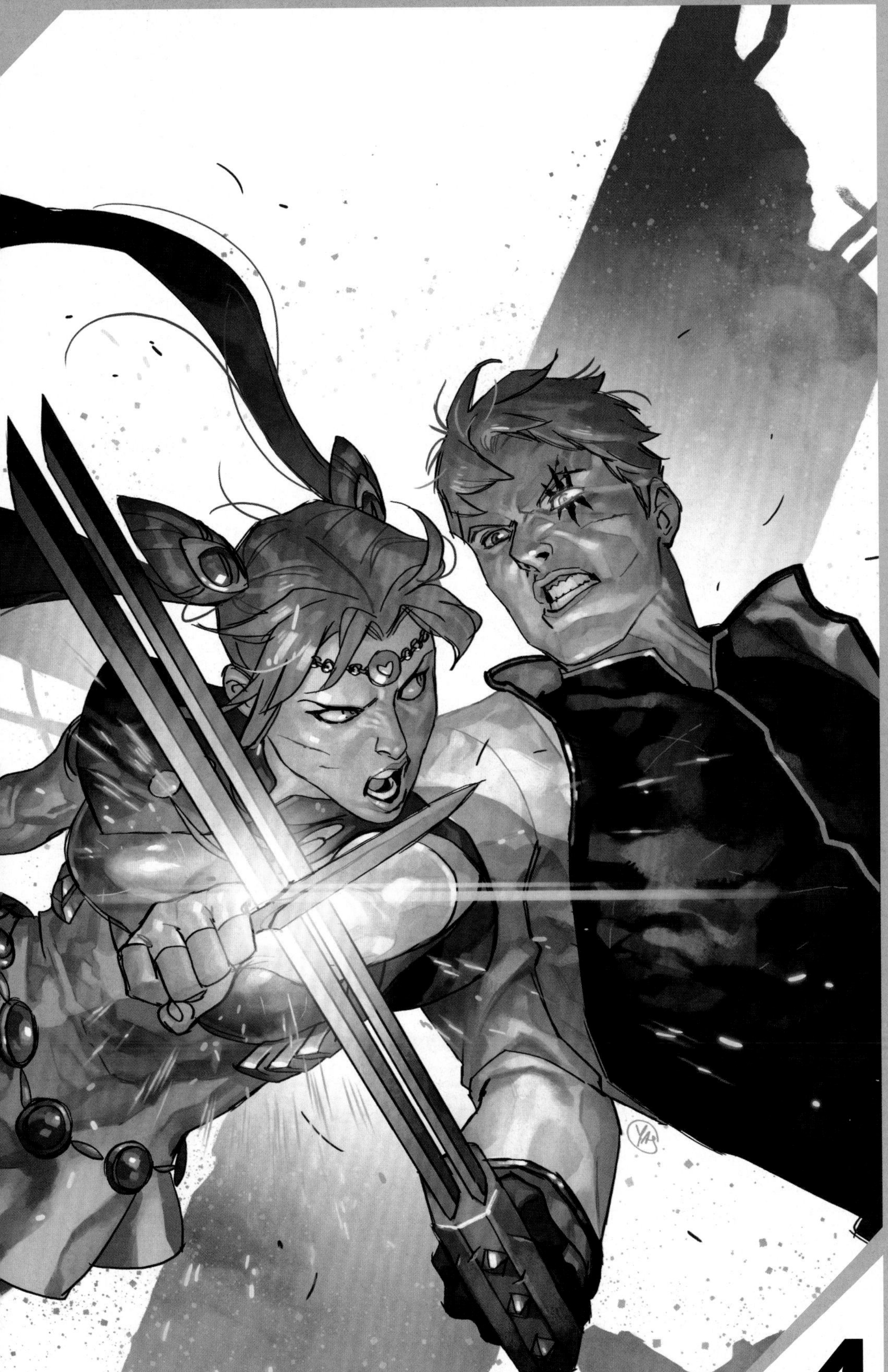
4

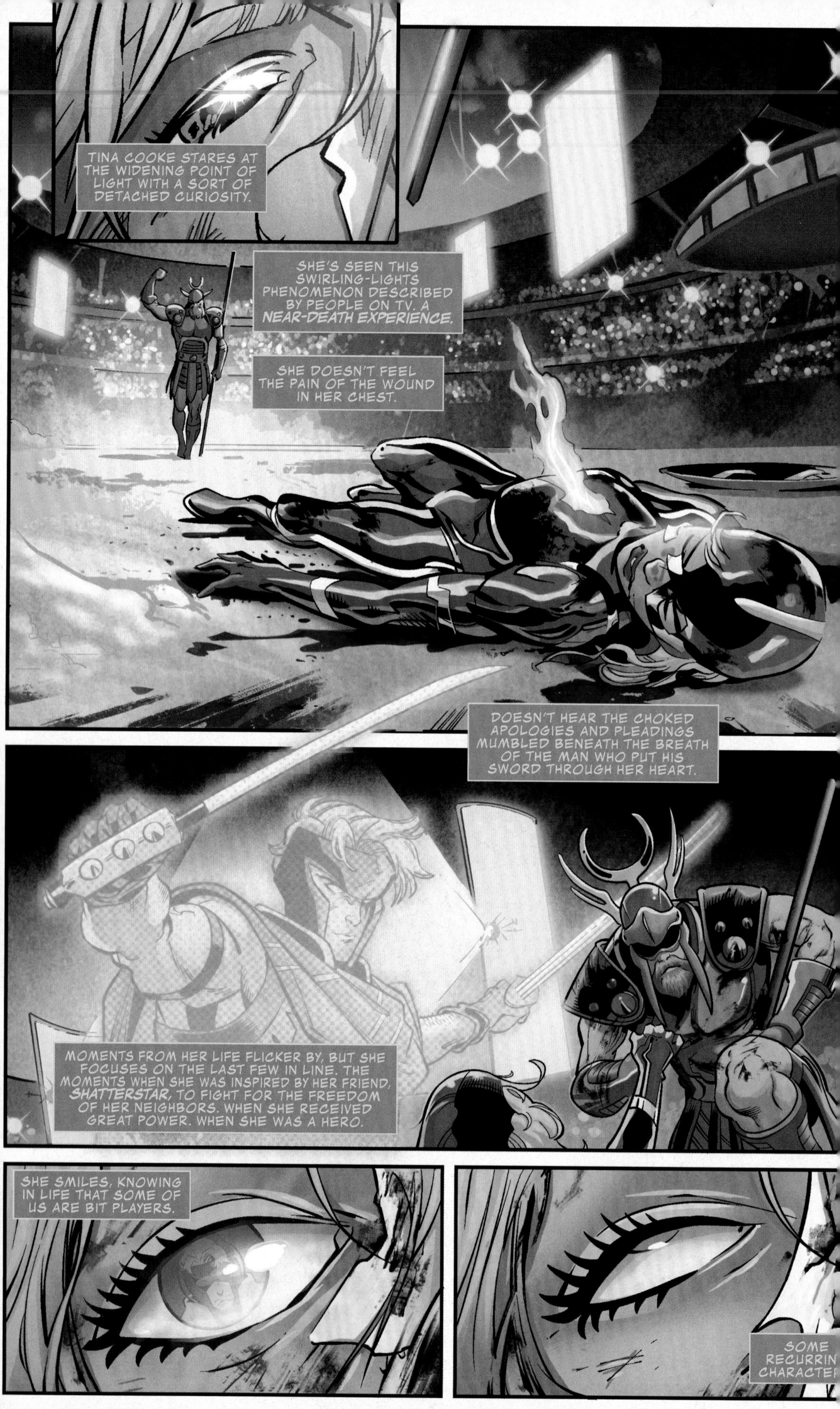

TINA COOKE STARES AT THE WIDENING POINT OF LIGHT WITH A SORT OF DETACHED CURIOSITY.
SHE'S SEEN THIS SWIRLING-LIGHTS PHENOMENON DESCRIBED BY PEOPLE ON TV. A *NEAR-DEATH EXPERIENCE.*
SHE DOESN'T FEEL THE PAIN OF THE WOUND IN HER CHEST.
DOESN'T HEAR THE CHOKED APOLOGIES AND PLEADINGS MUMBLED BENEATH THE BREATH OF THE MAN WHO PUT HIS SWORD THROUGH HER HEART.
MOMENTS FROM HER LIFE FLICKER BY, BUT SHE FOCUSES ON THE LAST FEW IN LINE. THE MOMENTS WHEN SHE WAS INSPIRED BY HER FRIEND, ***SHATTERSTAR,*** TO FIGHT FOR THE FREEDOM OF HER NEIGHBORS. WHEN SHE RECEIVED GREAT POWER. WHEN SHE WAS A HERO.
SHE SMILES, KNOWING IN LIFE THAT SOME OF US ARE BIT PLAYERS.
SOME RECURRIN CHARACTE

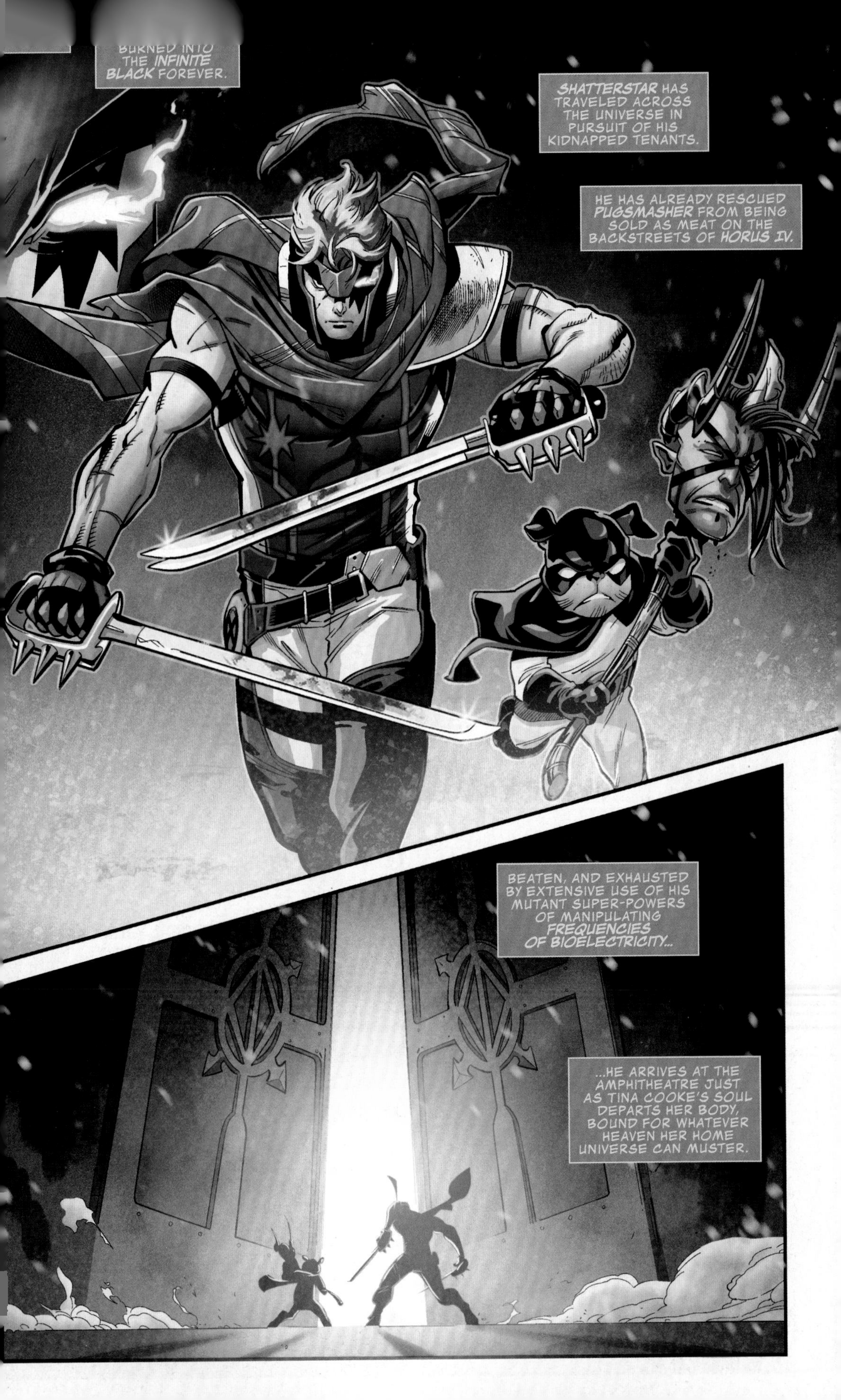
BURNED INTO THE INFINITE BLACK FOREVER.
SHATTERSTAR HAS TRAVELED ACROSS THE UNIVERSE IN PURSUIT OF HIS KIDNAPPED TENANTS.
HE HAS ALREADY RESCUED PUGSMASHER FROM BEING SOLD AS MEAT ON THE BACKSTREETS OF HORUS IV.
BEATEN, AND EXHAUSTED BY EXTENSIVE USE OF HIS MUTANT SUPER-POWERS OF MANIPULATING FREQUENCIES OF BIOELECTRICITY...
...HE ARRIVES AT THE AMPHITHEATRE JUST AS TINA COOKE'S SOUL DEPARTS HER BODY, BOUND FOR WHATEVER HEAVEN HER HOME UNIVERSE CAN MUSTER.

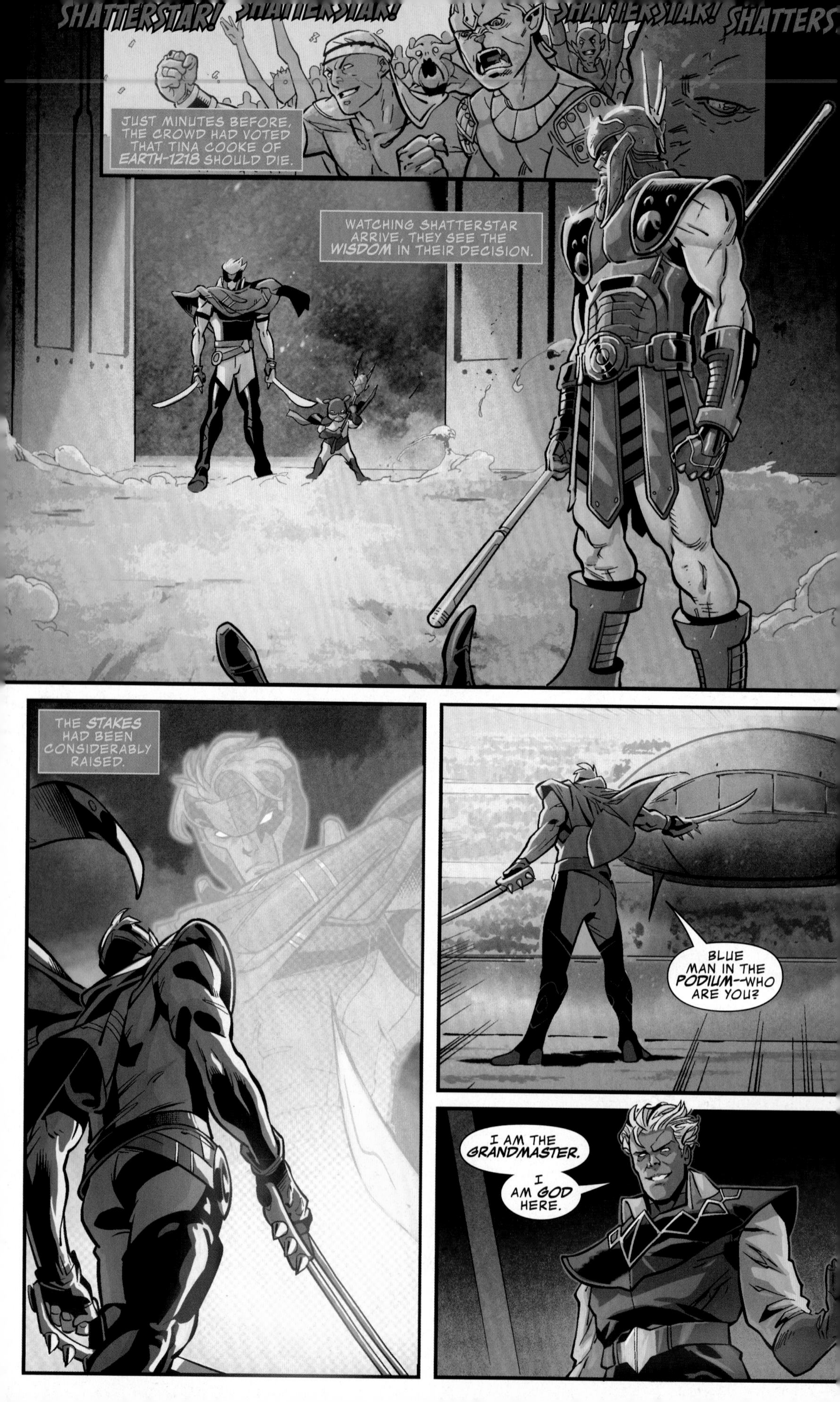
SHATTERSTAR! SHATTERSTAR! SHATTERSTAR! SHATTERS
JUST MINUTES BEFORE, THE CROWD HAD VOTED THAT TINA COOKE OF EARTH-1218 SHOULD DIE.
WATCHING SHATTERSTAR ARRIVE, THEY SEE THE WISDOM IN THEIR DECISION.
THE STAKES HAD BEEN CONSIDERABLY RAISED.
BLUE MAN IN THE PODIUM--WHO ARE YOU?
I AM THE GRANDMASTER.
I AM GOD HERE.

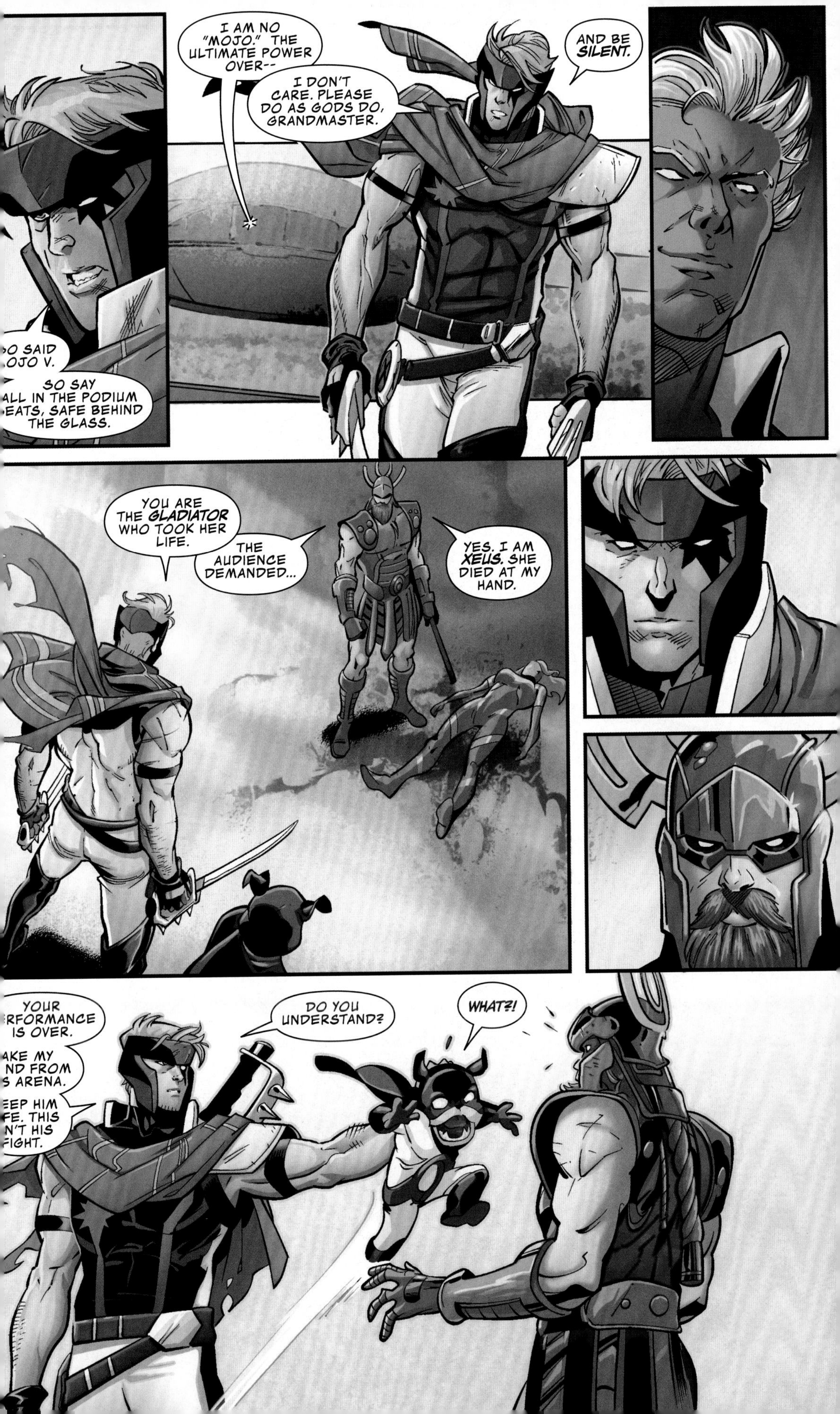
I AM NO "MOJO." THE ULTIMATE POWER OVER--
I DON'T CARE. PLEASE DO AS GODS DO, GRANDMASTER.
AND BE SILENT.
O SAID OJO V.
SO SAY ALL IN THE PODIUM EATS, SAFE BEHIND THE GLASS.
YOU ARE THE GLADIATOR WHO TOOK HER LIFE.
THE AUDIENCE DEMANDED...
YES. I AM XEUS. SHE DIED AT MY HAND.
YOUR RFORMANCE IS OVER.
AKE MY ND FROM S ARENA.
EEP HIM FE. THIS N'T HIS FIGHT.
DO YOU UNDERSTAND?
WHAT?!

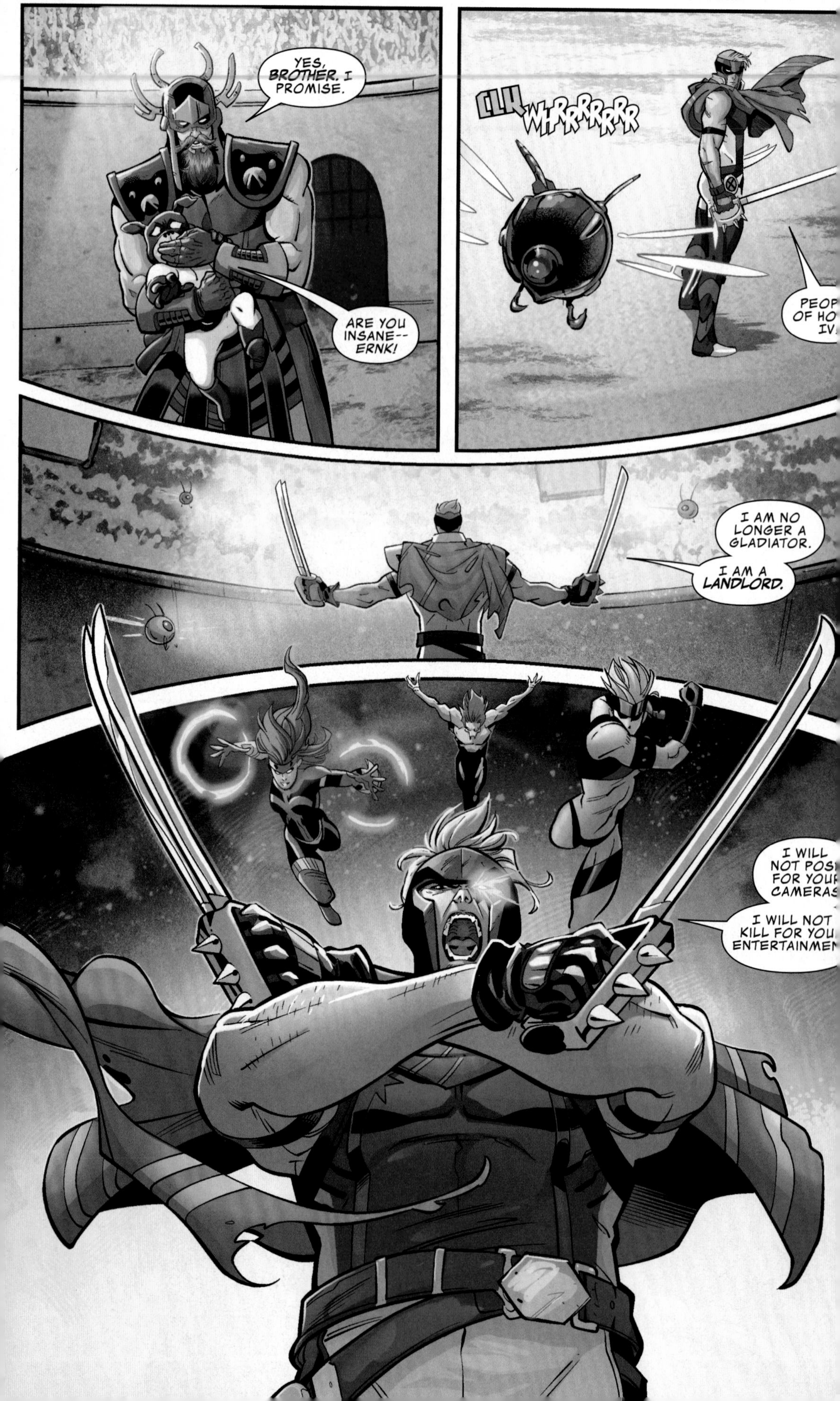
YES, BROTHER. I PROMISE.
ARE YOU INSANE-- ERNK!
CLIK WHRRRRRRR
PEOP OF HO IV.
I AM NO LONGER A GLADIATOR.
I AM A LANDLORD.
I WILL NOT POS FOR YOUR CAMERAS
I WILL NOT KILL FOR YOU ENTERTAINMEN

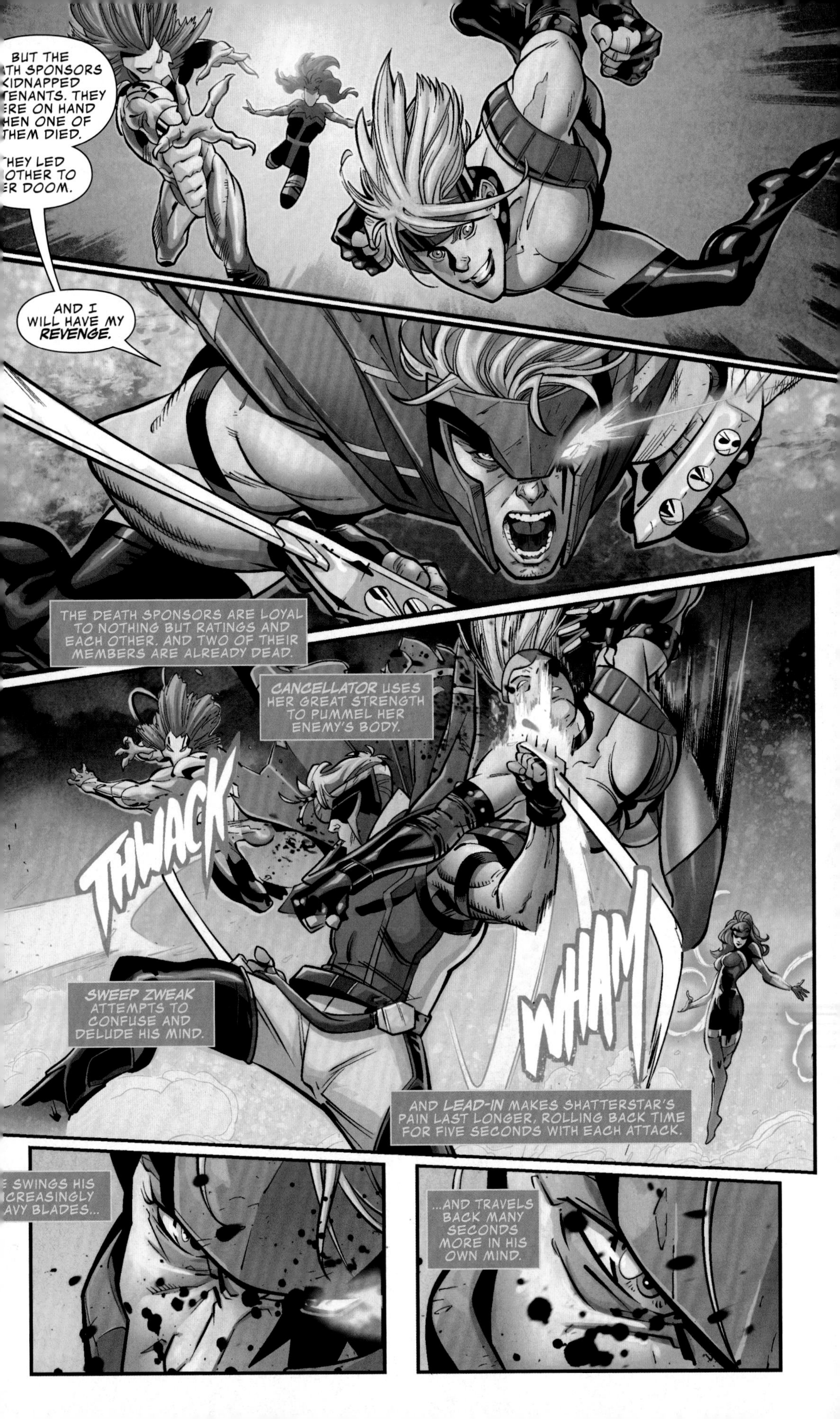
BUT THE
ATH SPONSORS
KIDNAPPED
TENANTS. THEY
ERE ON HAND
HEN ONE OF
THEM DIED.
THEY LED
OTHER TO
ER DOOM.
AND I WILL HAVE MY REVENGE.
THE DEATH SPONSORS ARE LOYAL TO NOTHING BUT RATINGS AND EACH OTHER. AND TWO OF THEIR MEMBERS ARE ALREADY DEAD.
CANCELLATOR USES HER GREAT STRENGTH TO PUMMEL HER ENEMY'S BODY.
THWACK
SWEEP ZWEAK ATTEMPTS TO CONFUSE AND DELUDE HIS MIND.
WHAM
AND LEAD-IN MAKES SHATTERSTAR'S PAIN LAST LONGER, ROLLING BACK TIME FOR FIVE SECONDS WITH EACH ATTACK.
E SWINGS HIS
CREASINGLY
AVY BLADES...
...AND TRAVELS BACK MANY SECONDS MORE IN HIS OWN MIND.

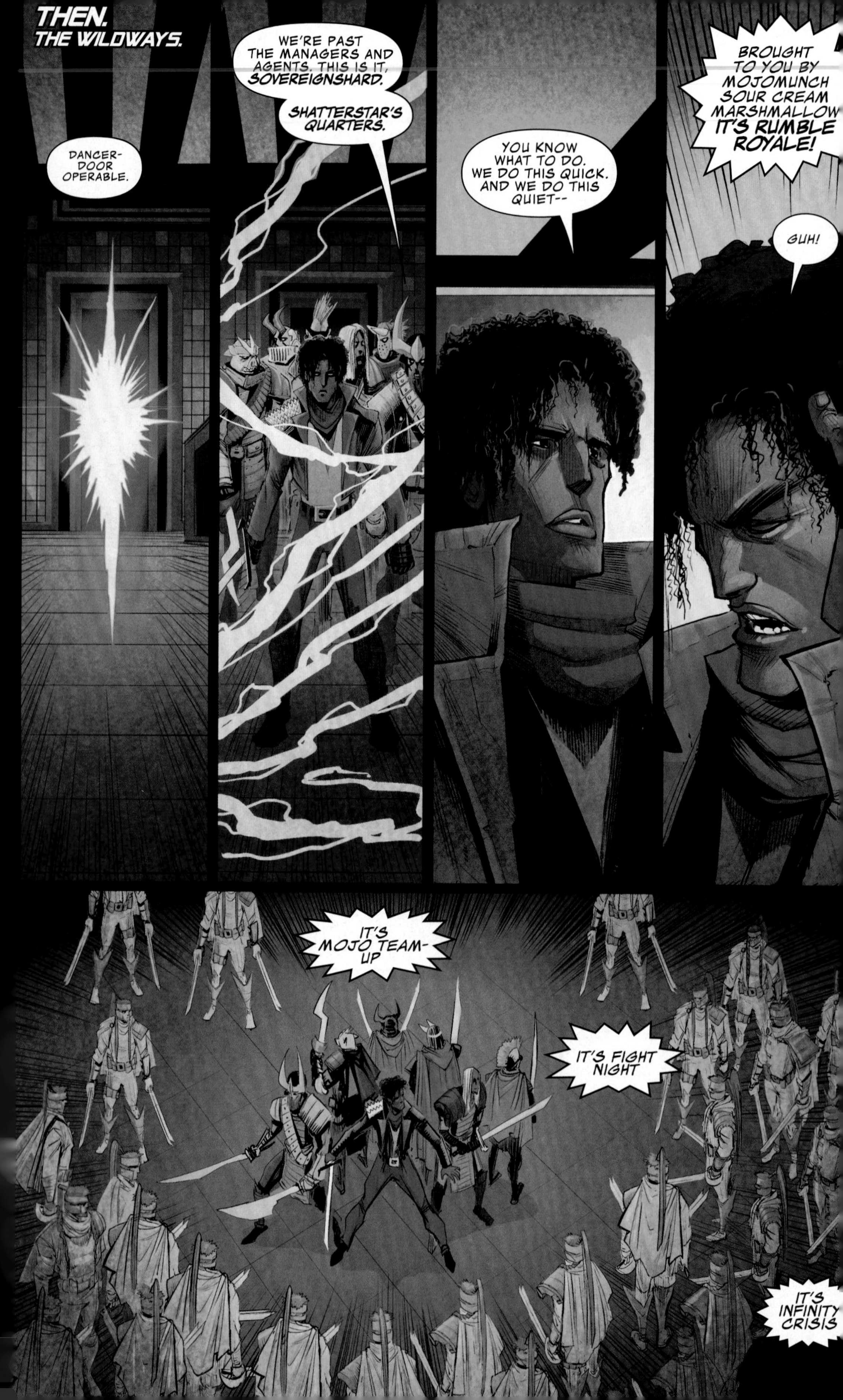
THEN.
THE WILDWAYS.
DANCER-DOOR OPERABLE.
WE'RE PAST THE MANAGERS AND AGENTS. THIS IS IT, SOVEREIGNSHARD.
SHATTERSTAR'S QUARTERS.
YOU KNOW WHAT TO DO. WE DO THIS QUICK. AND WE DO THIS QUIET--
BROUGHT TO YOU BY MOJOMUNCH SOUR CREAM MARSHMALLOW IT'S RUMBLE ROYALE!
GUH!
IT'S MOJO TEAM-UP
IT'S FIGHT NIGHT
IT'S INFINITY CRISIS

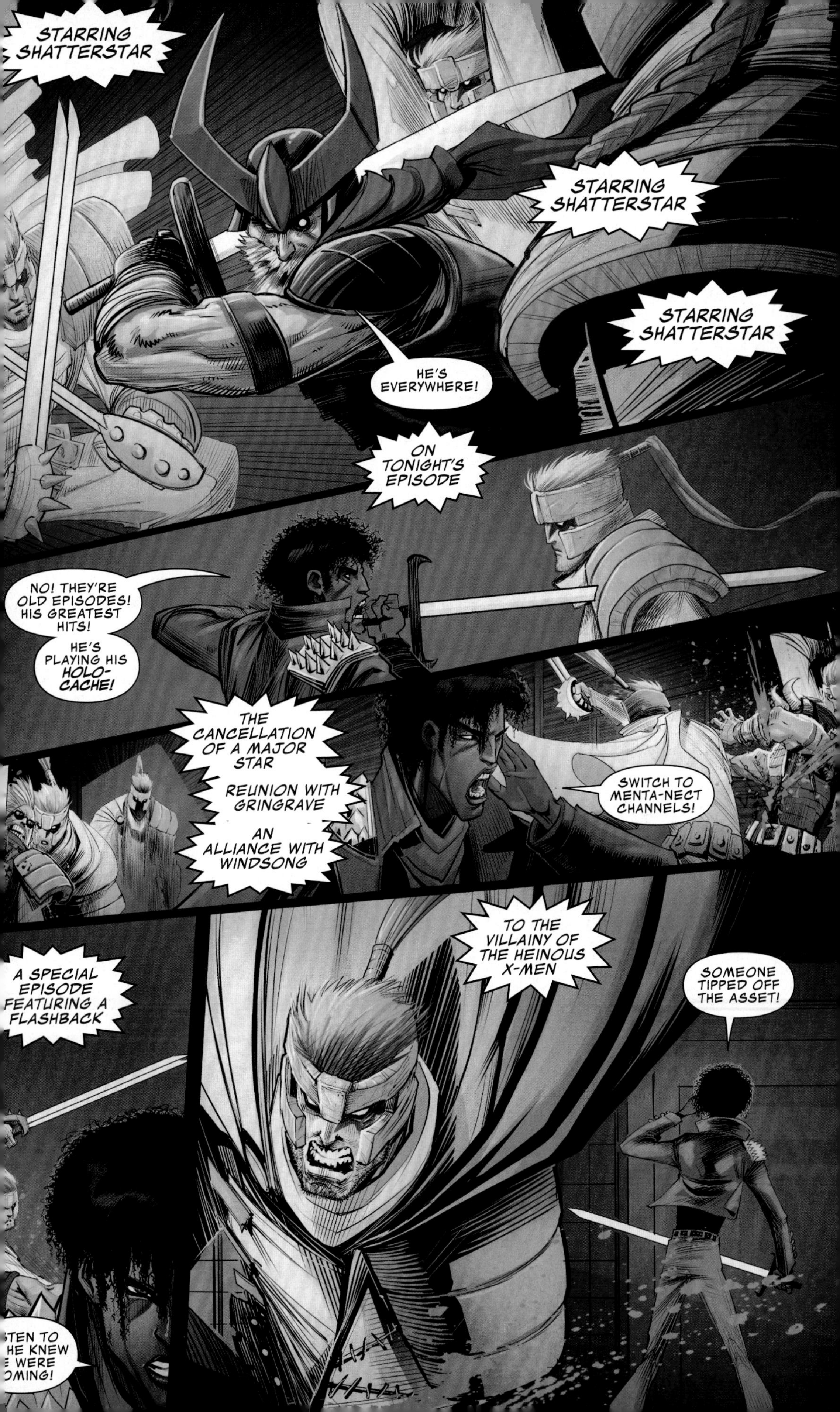
STARRING SHATTERSTAR
STARRING SHATTERSTAR
STARRING SHATTERSTAR
HE'S EVERYWHERE!
ON TONIGHT'S EPISODE
NO! THEY'RE OLD EPISODES! HIS GREATEST HITS!
HE'S PLAYING HIS HOLO-CACHE!
THE CANCELLATION OF A MAJOR STAR
REUNION WITH GRINGRAVE
AN ALLIANCE WITH WINDSONG
SWITCH TO MENTA-NECT CHANNELS!
A SPECIAL EPISODE FEATURING A FLASHBACK
TO THE VILLAINY OF THE HEINOUS X-MEN
SOMEONE TIPPED OFF THE ASSET!
STEN TO HE KNEW E WERE OMING!

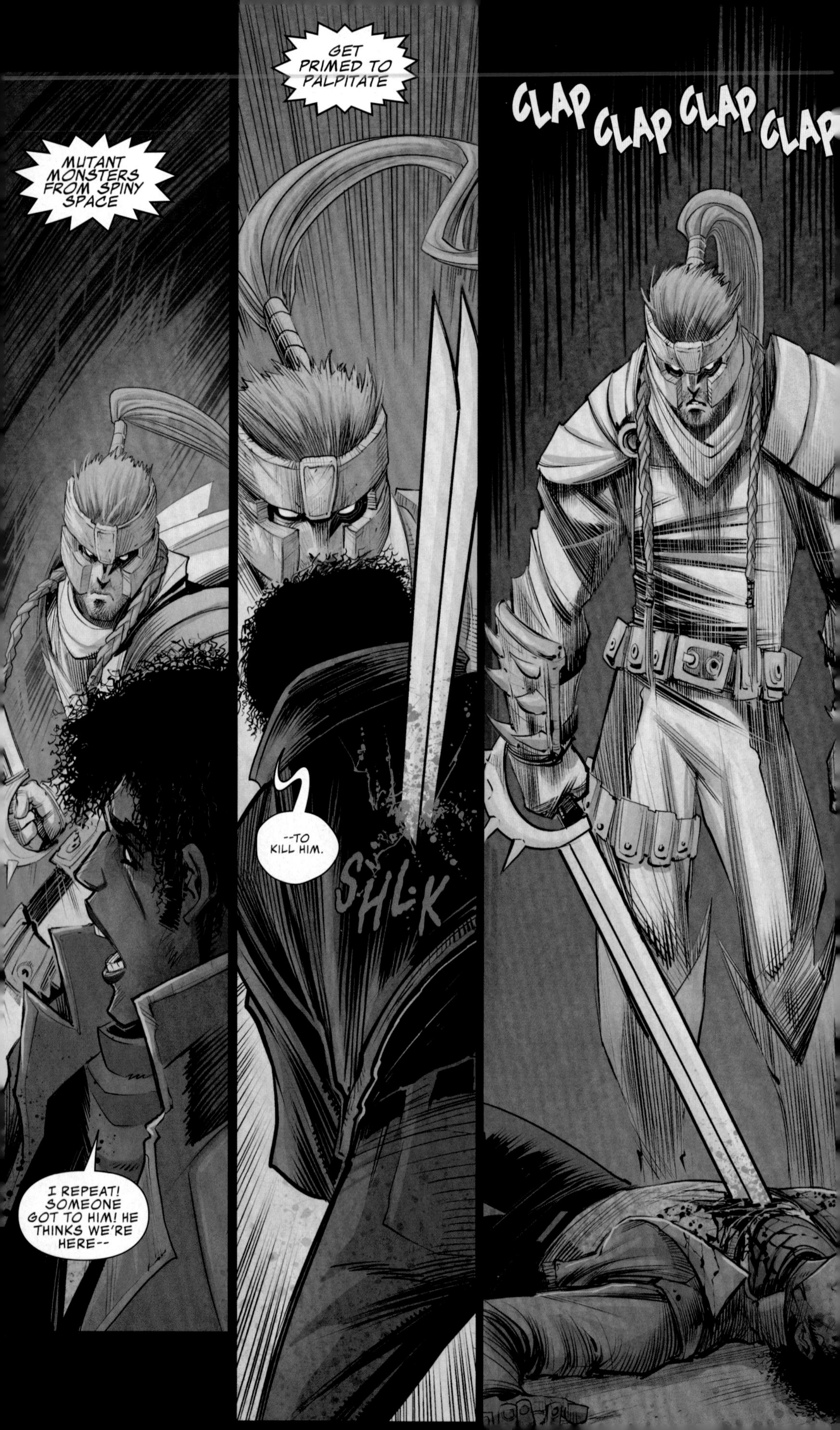
MUTANT MONSTERS FROM SPINY SPACE
I REPEAT! SOMEONE GOT TO HIM! HE THINKS WE'RE HERE--
GET PRIMED TO PALPITATE
--TO KILL HIM.
SHLK
CLAP CLAP CLAP CLAP

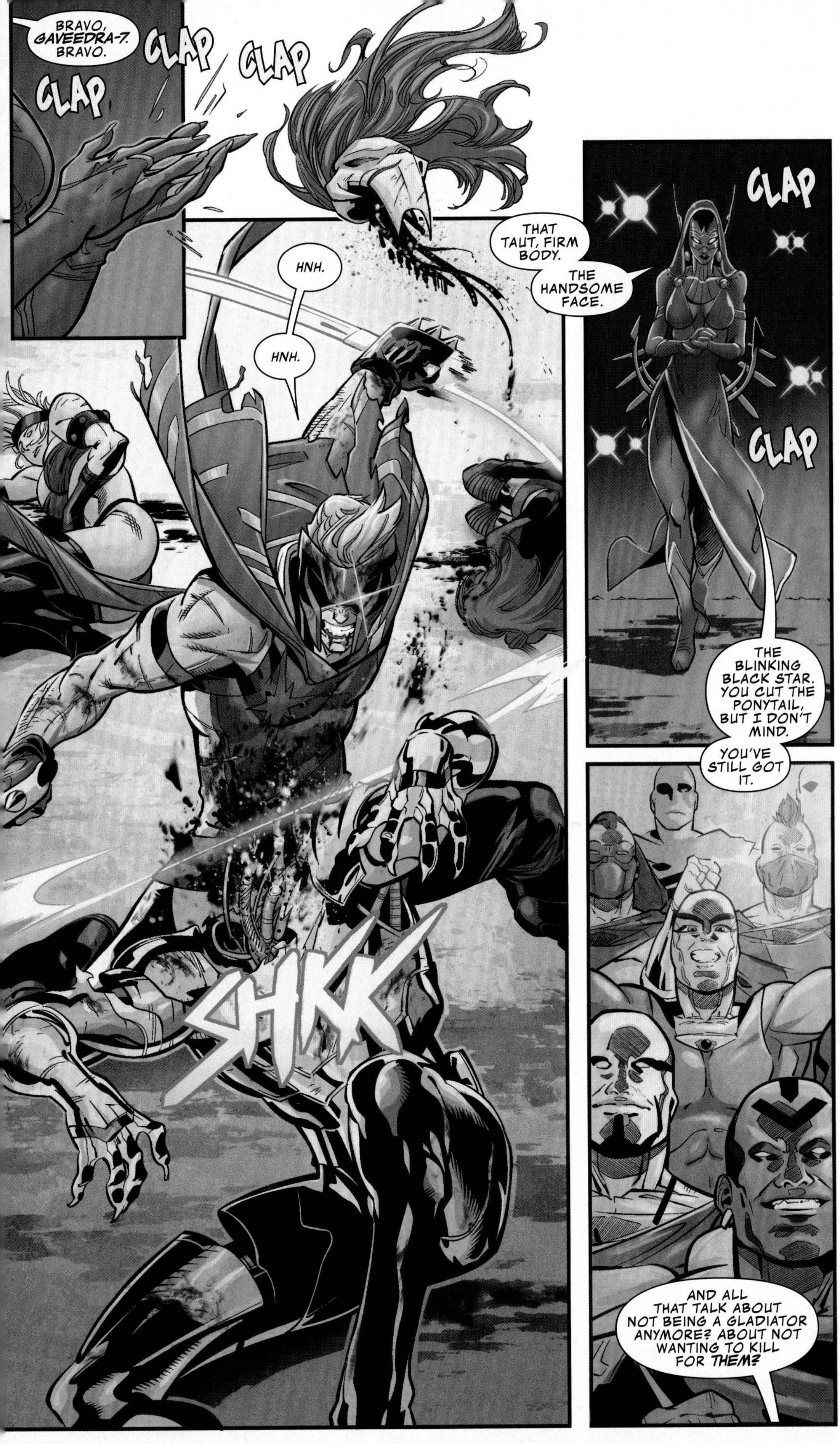
BRAVO, GAVEEDRA-7. BRAVO.
CLAP
CLAP
CLAP
HNH.
HNH.
THAT TAUT, FIRM BODY.
THE HANDSOME FACE.
CLAP
CLAP
THE BLINKING BLACK STAR. YOU CUT THE PONYTAIL, BUT I DON'T MIND.
YOU'VE STILL GOT IT.
SHKK
AND ALL THAT TALK ABOUT NOT BEING A GLADIATOR ANYMORE? ABOUT NOT WANTING TO KILL FOR THEM?

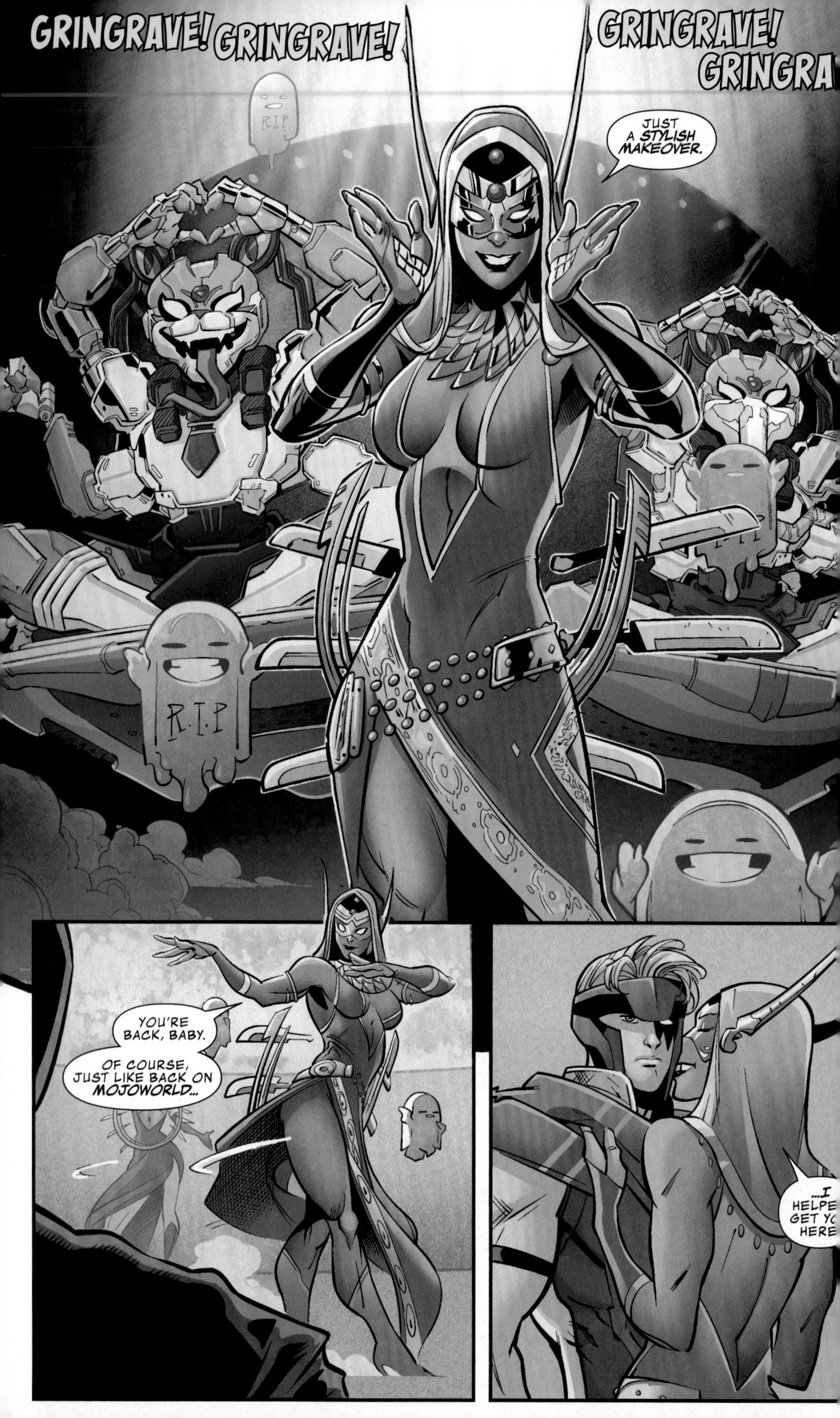
GRINGRAVE! GRINGRAVE!
GRINGRAVE! GRINGRA
JUST A STYLISH MAKEOVER.
R.I.P.
R.I.P.
YOU'RE BACK, BABY.
OF COURSE, JUST LIKE BACK ON MOJOWORLD...
...I HELPE GET YO HERE

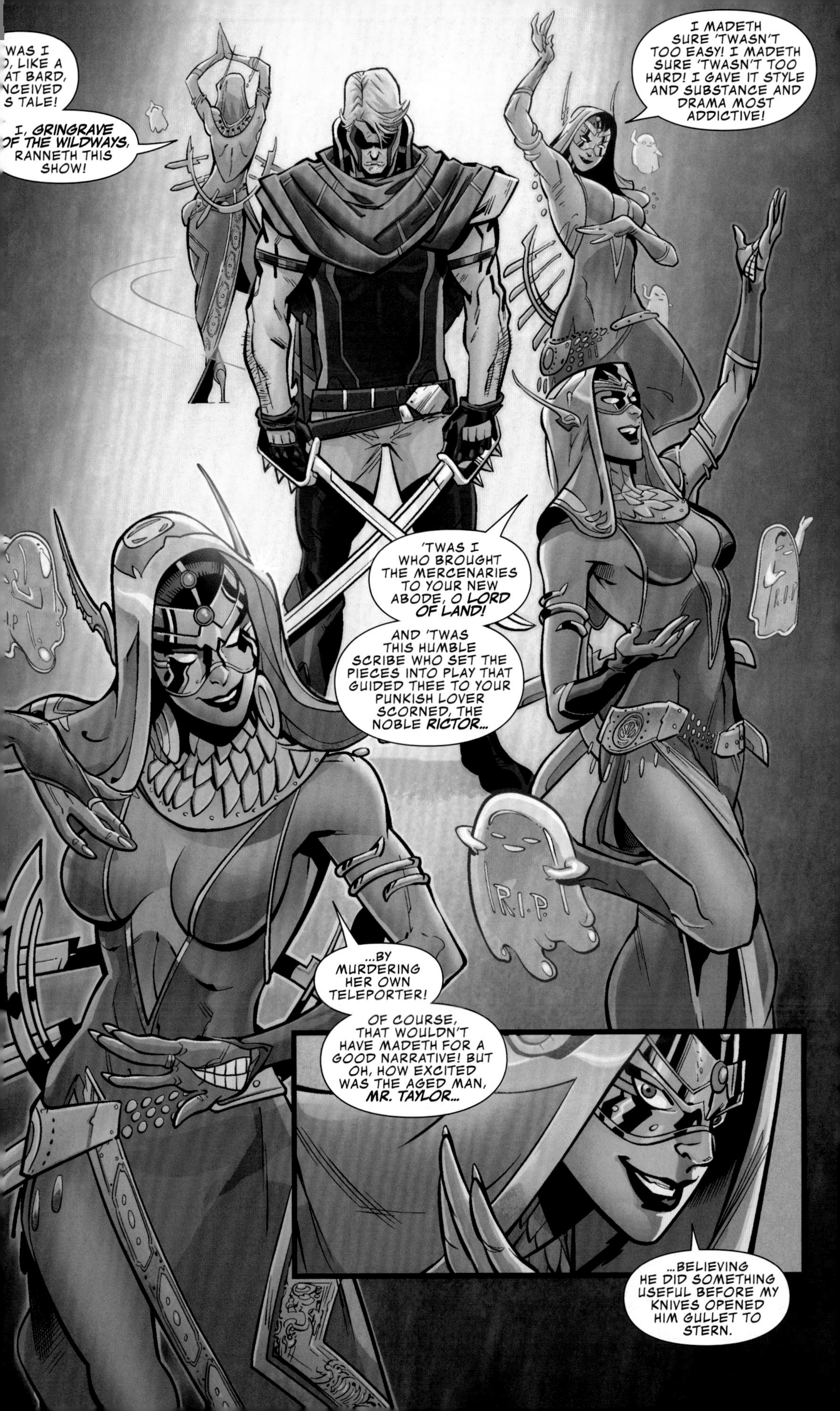
WAS I
D, LIKE A
AT BARD,
NCEIVED
S TALE!
I, GRINGRAVE OF THE WILDWAYS, RANNETH THIS SHOW!
I MADETH SURE 'TWASN'T TOO EASY! I MADETH SURE 'TWASN'T TOO HARD! I GAVE IT STYLE AND SUBSTANCE AND DRAMA MOST ADDICTIVE!
'TWAS I WHO BROUGHT THE MERCENARIES TO YOUR NEW ABODE, O LORD OF LAND!
AND 'TWAS THIS HUMBLE SCRIBE WHO SET THE PIECES INTO PLAY THAT GUIDED THEE TO YOUR PUNKISH LOVER SCORNED, THE NOBLE RICTOR...
R.I.P.
...BY MURDERING HER OWN TELEPORTER!
OF COURSE, THAT WOULDN'T HAVE MADETH FOR A GOOD NARRATIVE! BUT OH, HOW EXCITED WAS THE AGED MAN, MR. TAYLOR...
...BELIEVING HE DID SOMETHING USEFUL BEFORE MY KNIVES OPENED HIM GULLET TO STERN.

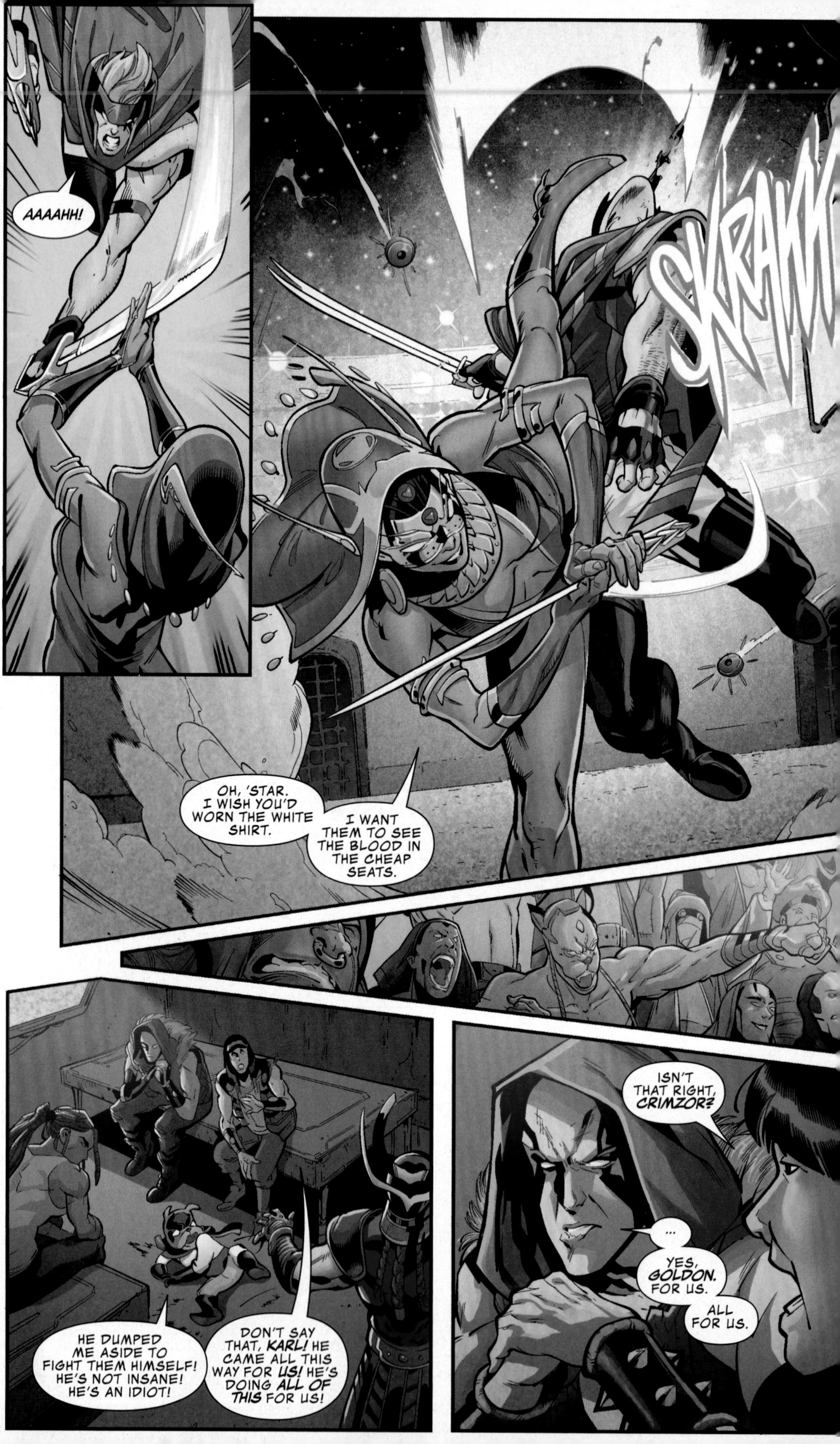
AAAAHH!
SKRAKK
OH, 'STAR. I WISH YOU'D WORN THE WHITE SHIRT.
I WANT THEM TO SEE THE BLOOD IN THE CHEAP SEATS.
HE DUMPED ME ASIDE TO FIGHT THEM HIMSELF! HE'S NOT INSANE! HE'S AN IDIOT!
DON'T SAY THAT, KARL! HE CAME ALL THIS WAY FOR US! HE'S DOING ALL OF THIS FOR US!
ISN'T THAT RIGHT, CRIMZOR?
...
YES, GOLDON. FOR US.
ALL FOR US.

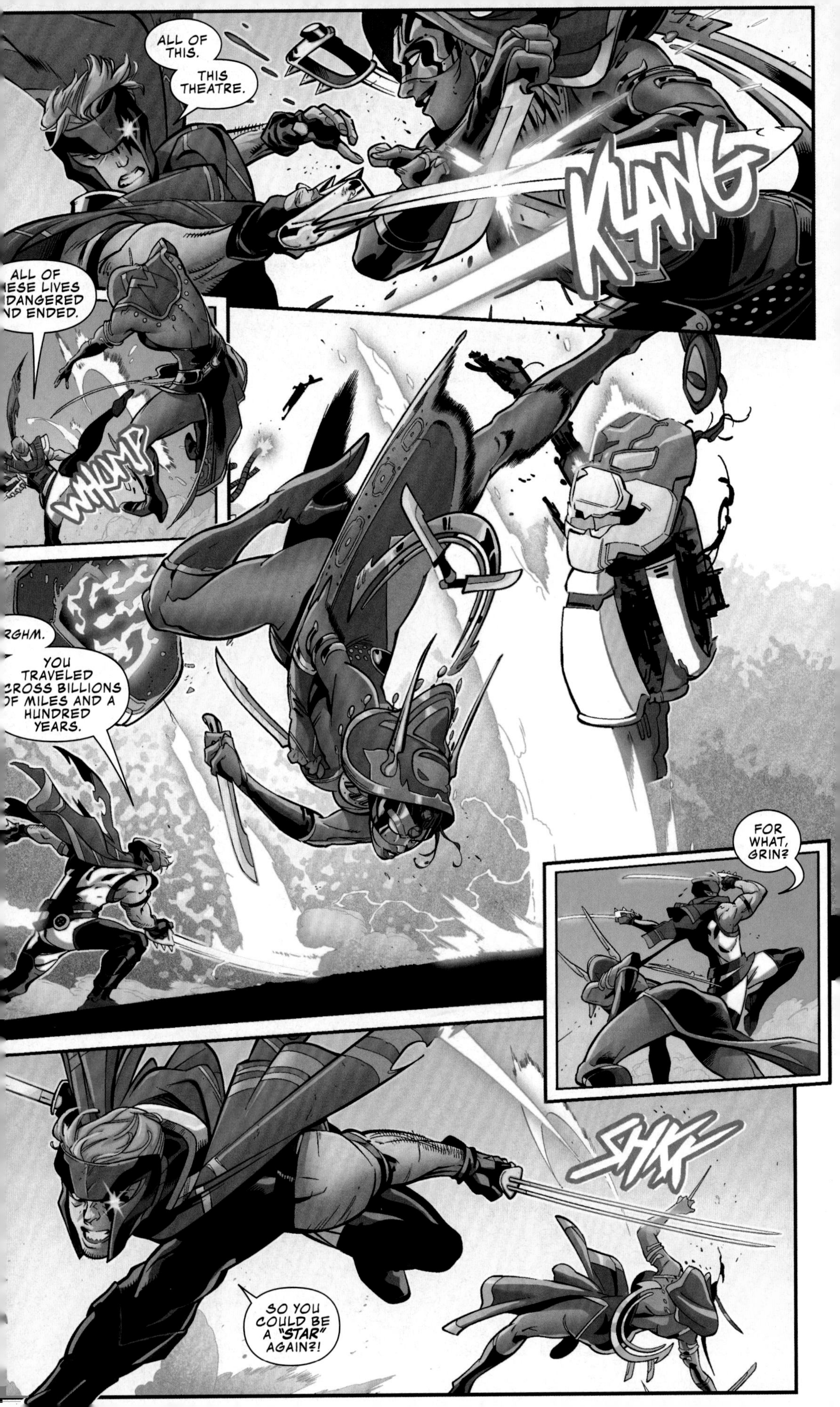

ALL OF THIS.
THIS THEATRE.
KLANG
ALL OF HESE LIVES NDANGERED ND ENDED.
WHOMP
RGHM.
YOU TRAVELED CROSS BILLIONS OF MILES AND A HUNDRED YEARS.
FOR WHAT, GRIN?
SNK
SO YOU COULD BE A "STAR" AGAIN?!

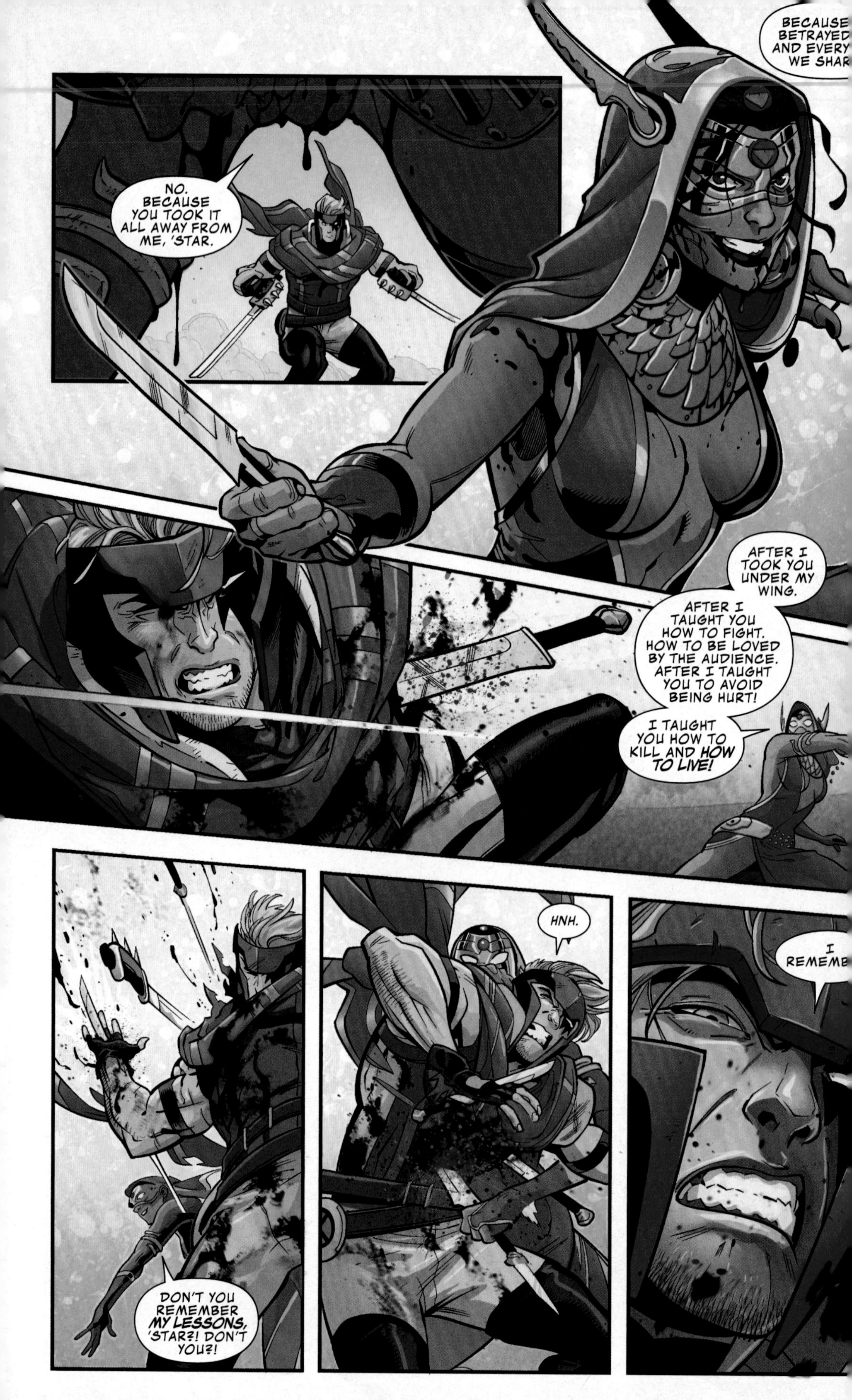

BECAUSE BETRAYED AND EVERY WE SHAR
NO. BECAUSE YOU TOOK IT ALL AWAY FROM ME, 'STAR.
AFTER I TOOK YOU UNDER MY WING.
AFTER I TAUGHT YOU HOW TO FIGHT. HOW TO BE LOVED BY THE AUDIENCE. AFTER I TAUGHT YOU TO AVOID BEING HURT!
I TAUGHT YOU HOW TO KILL AND HOW TO LIVE!
DON'T YOU REMEMBER MY LESSONS, 'STAR?! DON'T YOU?!
HNH.
I REMEMB

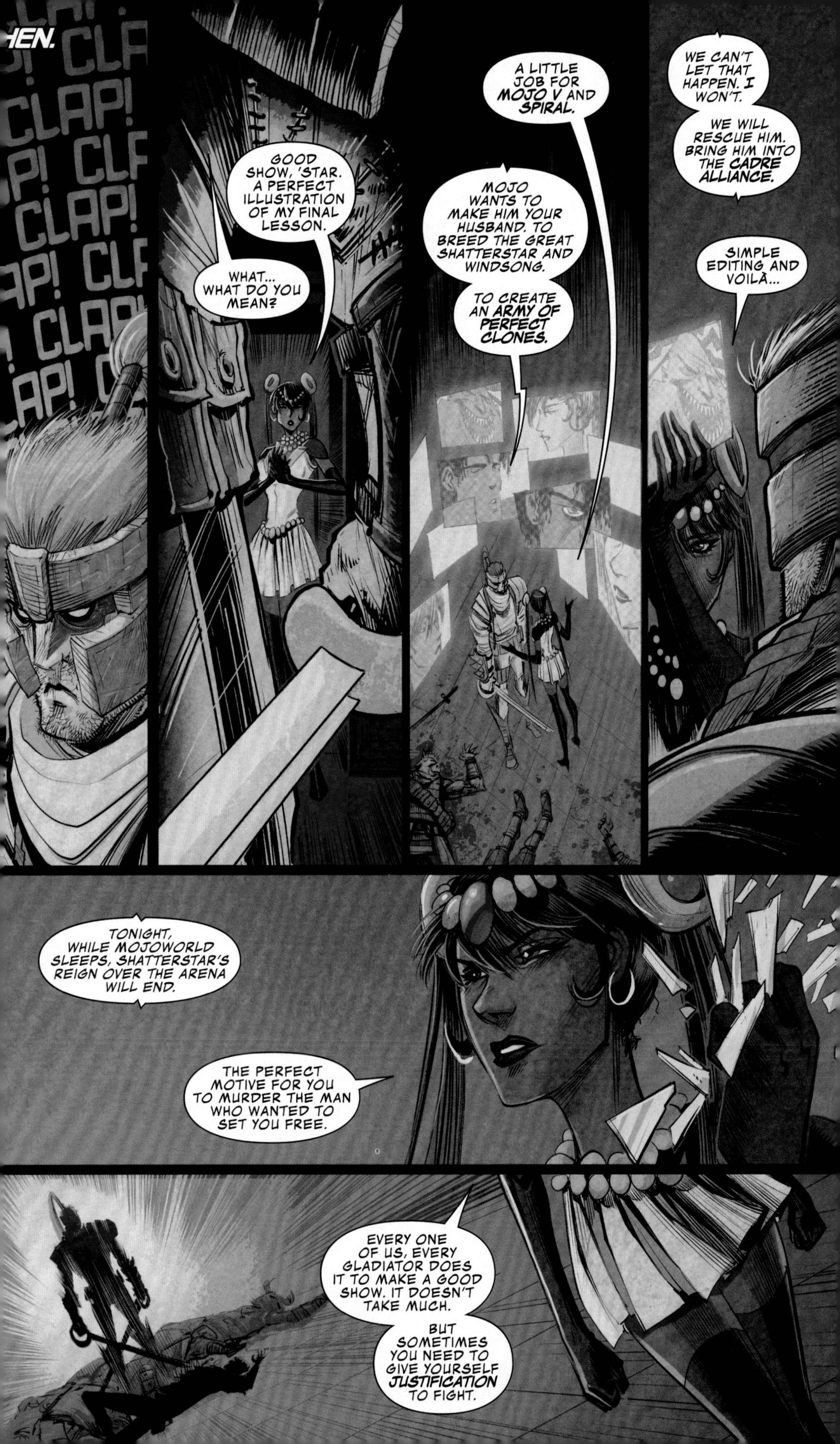

HEN.
CLAP! CLAP! CLAP! CLAP! CLAP! CLAP! CLAP!
GOOD SHOW, 'STAR. A PERFECT ILLUSTRATION OF MY FINAL LESSON.
WHAT... WHAT DO YOU MEAN?
A LITTLE JOB FOR MOJO V AND SPIRAL.
MOJO WANTS TO MAKE HIM YOUR HUSBAND. TO BREED THE GREAT SHATTERSTAR AND WINDSONG.
TO CREATE AN ARMY OF PERFECT CLONES.
WE CAN'T LET THAT HAPPEN. I WON'T.
WE WILL RESCUE HIM. BRING HIM INTO THE CADRE ALLIANCE.
SIMPLE EDITING AND VOILÀ...
TONIGHT, WHILE MOJOWORLD SLEEPS, SHATTERSTAR'S REIGN OVER THE ARENA WILL END.
THE PERFECT MOTIVE FOR YOU TO MURDER THE MAN WHO WANTED TO SET YOU FREE.
EVERY ONE OF US, EVERY GLADIATOR DOES IT TO MAKE A GOOD SHOW. IT DOESN'T TAKE MUCH.
BUT SOMETIMES YOU NEED TO GIVE YOURSELF JUSTIFICATION TO FIGHT.

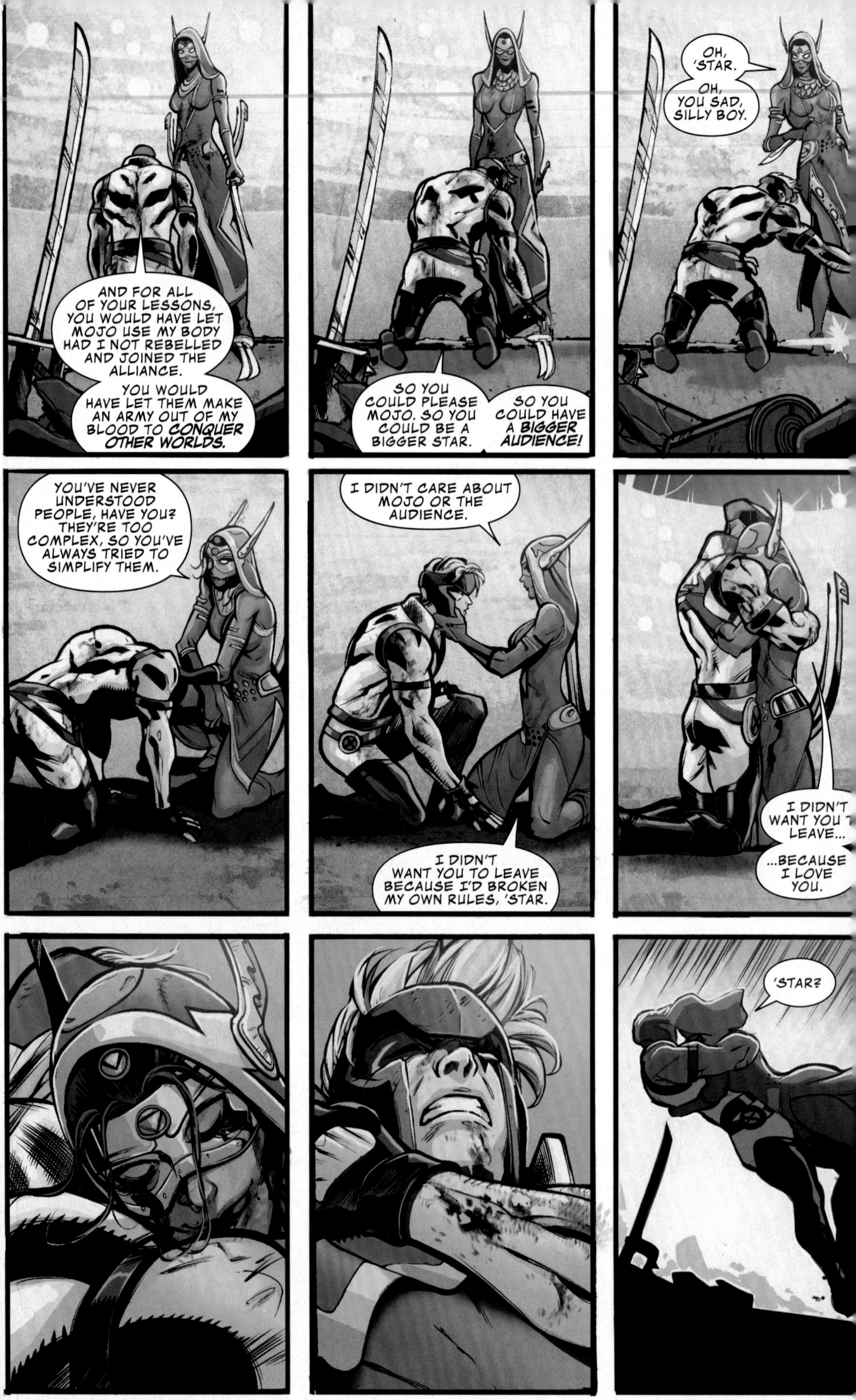
AND FOR ALL OF YOUR LESSONS, YOU WOULD HAVE LET MOJO USE MY BODY HAD I NOT REBELLED AND JOINED THE ALLIANCE.
YOU WOULD HAVE LET THEM MAKE AN ARMY OUT OF MY BLOOD TO **CONQUER OTHER WORLDS.**
SO YOU COULD PLEASE MOJO. SO YOU COULD BE A BIGGER STAR.
SO YOU COULD HAVE A **BIGGER AUDIENCE!**
OH, 'STAR.
OH, YOU SAD, SILLY BOY.
YOU'VE NEVER UNDERSTOOD PEOPLE, HAVE YOU? THEY'RE TOO COMPLEX, SO YOU'VE ALWAYS TRIED TO SIMPLIFY THEM.
I DIDN'T CARE ABOUT MOJO OR THE AUDIENCE.
I DIDN'T WANT YOU TO LEAVE BECAUSE I'D BROKEN MY OWN RULES, 'STAR.
I DIDN'T WANT YOU T LEAVE...
...BECAUSE I LOVE YOU.
'STAR?

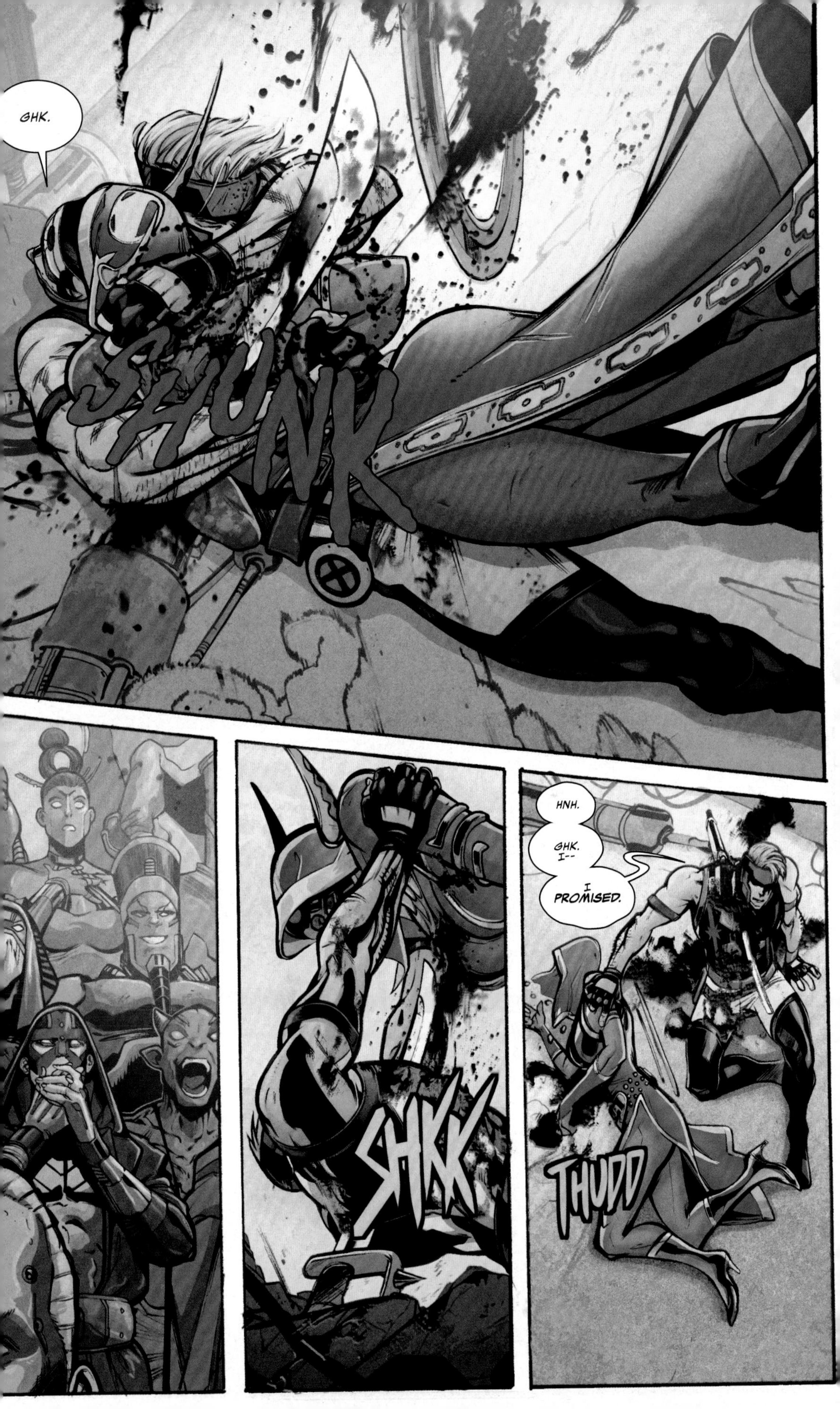
GHK.
SHUNK
HNH.
GHK. I--
I PROMISED.
SHKK
THUDD

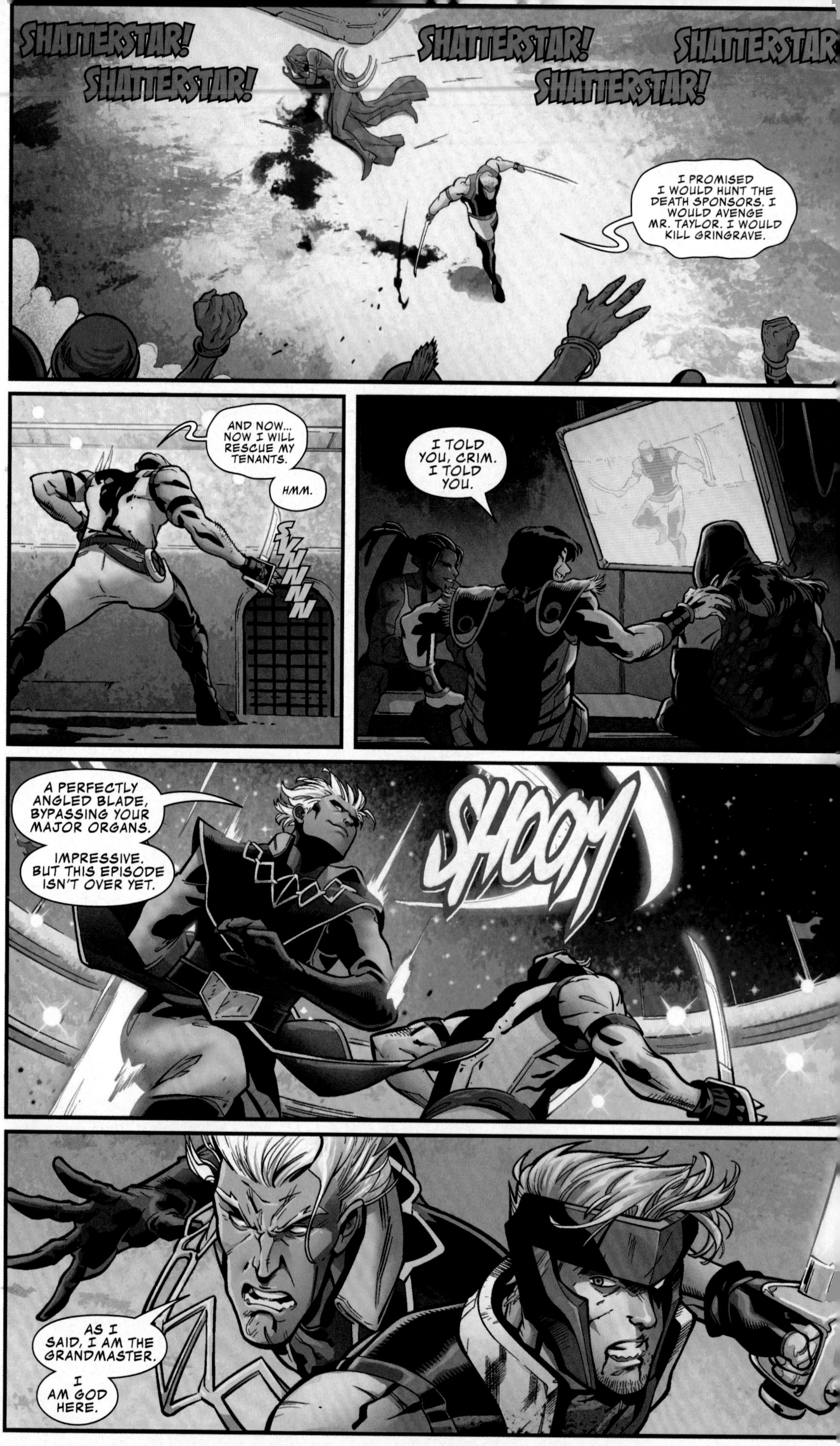
SHATTERSTAR!
SHATTERSTAR!
SHATTERSTAR!
SHATTERSTAR!
SHATTERSTAR
I PROMISED I WOULD HUNT THE DEATH SPONSORS. I WOULD AVENGE MR. TAYLOR. I WOULD KILL GRINGRAVE.
AND NOW... NOW I WILL RESCUE MY TENANTS.
HMM.
SKNNNN
I TOLD YOU, CRIM. I TOLD YOU.
A PERFECTLY ANGLED BLADE, BYPASSING YOUR MAJOR ORGANS.
IMPRESSIVE. BUT THIS EPISODE ISN'T OVER YET.
SHOOM
AS I SAID, I AM THE GRANDMASTER.
I AM GOD HERE.

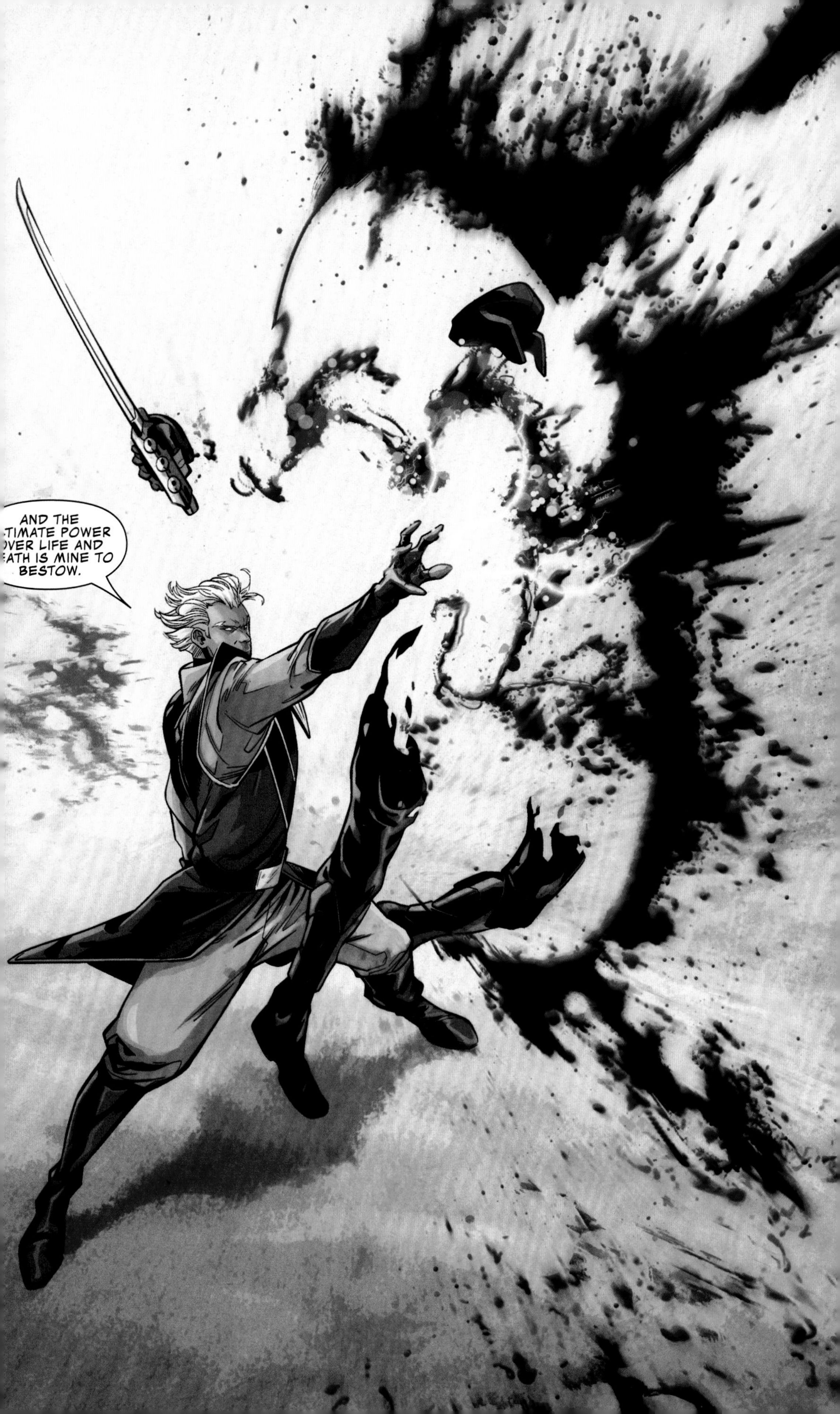
AND THE
TIMATE POWER
OVER LIFE AND
EATH IS MINE TO
BESTOW.

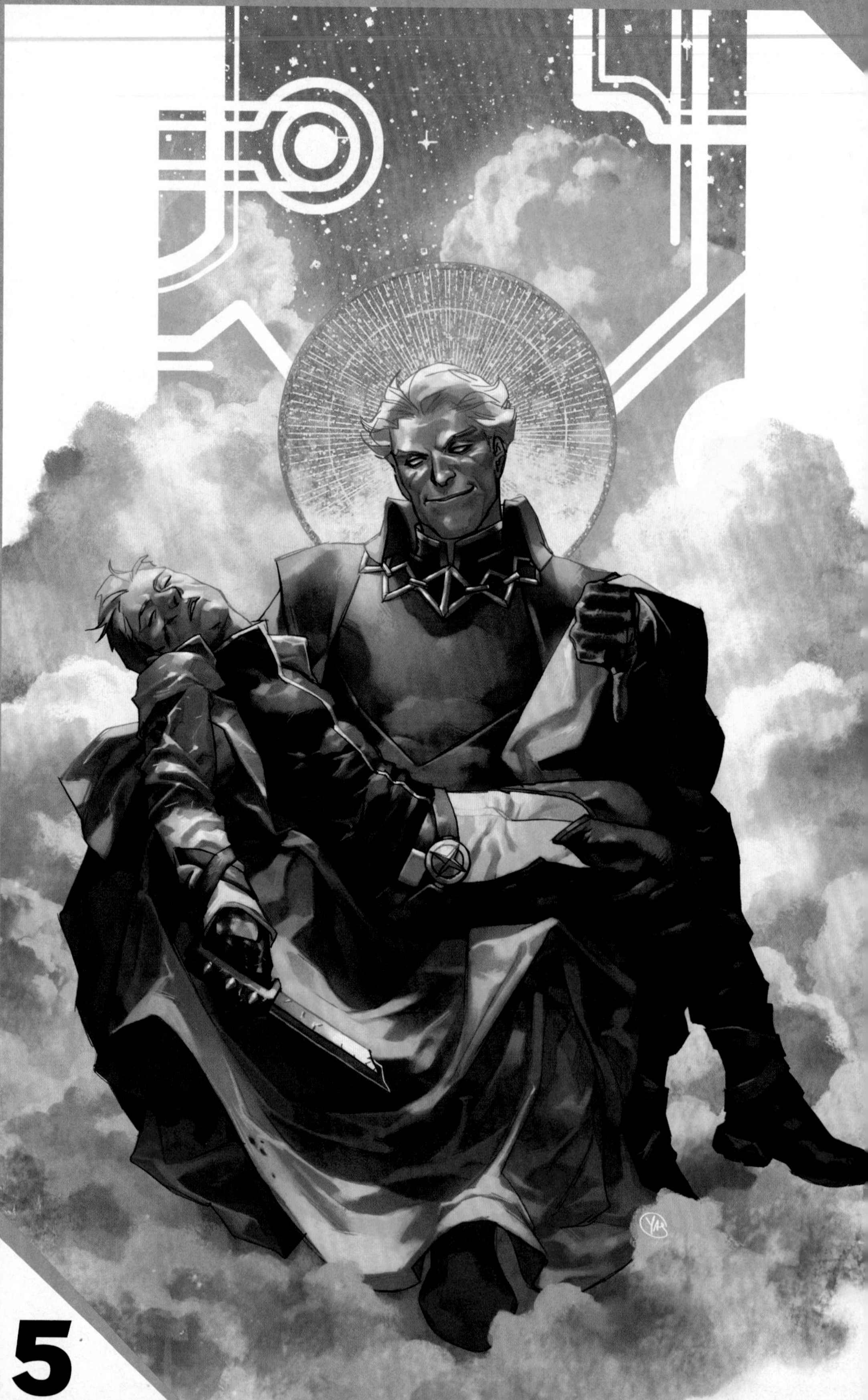
5

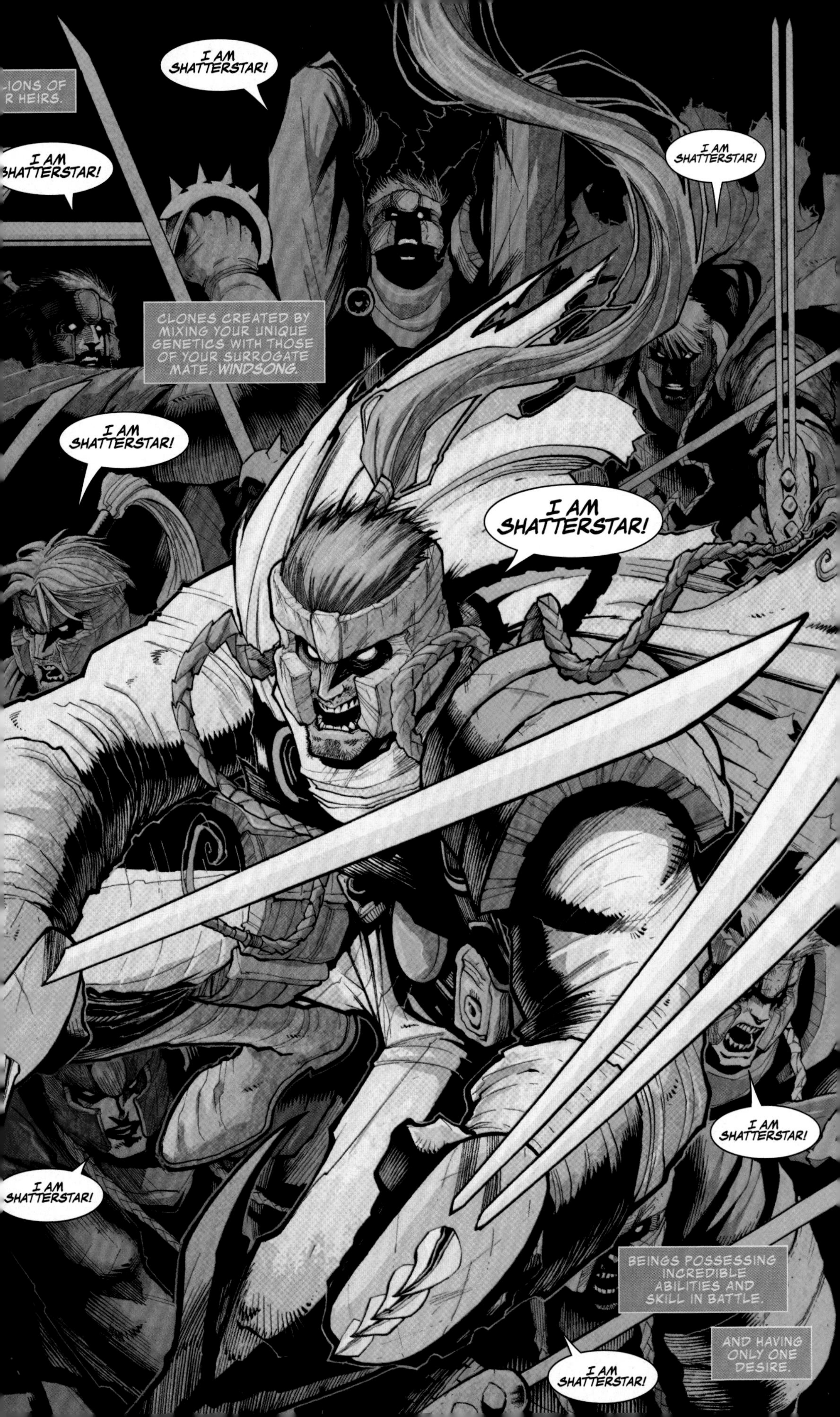

IONS OF R HEIRS.
I AM SHATTERSTAR!
I AM SHATTERSTAR!
I AM SHATTERSTAR!
CLONES CREATED BY MIXING YOUR UNIQUE GENETICS WITH THOSE OF YOUR SURROGATE MATE, WINDSONG.
I AM SHATTERSTAR!
I AM SHATTERSTAR!
I AM SHATTERSTAR!
I AM SHATTERSTAR!
BEINGS POSSESSING INCREDIBLE ABILITIES AND SKILL IN BATTLE.
I AM SHATTERSTAR!
AND HAVING ONLY ONE DESIRE.

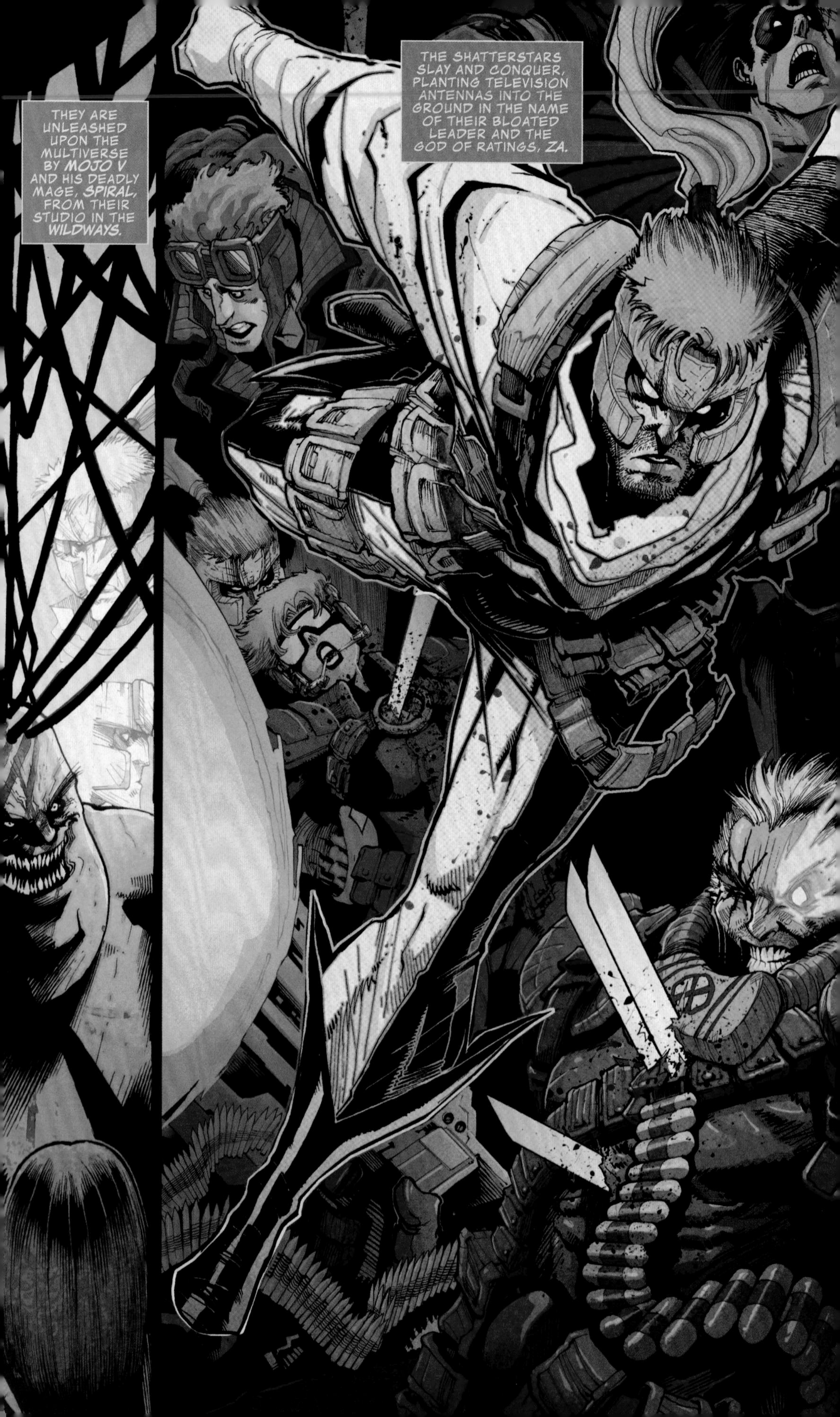
THEY ARE UNLEASHED UPON THE MULTIVERSE BY MOJO V AND HIS DEADLY MAGE, SPIRAL, FROM THEIR STUDIO IN THE WILDWAYS.
THE SHATTERSTARS SLAY AND CONQUER, PLANTING TELEVISION ANTENNAS INTO THE GROUND IN THE NAME OF THEIR BLOATED LEADER AND THE GOD OF RATINGS, ZA.

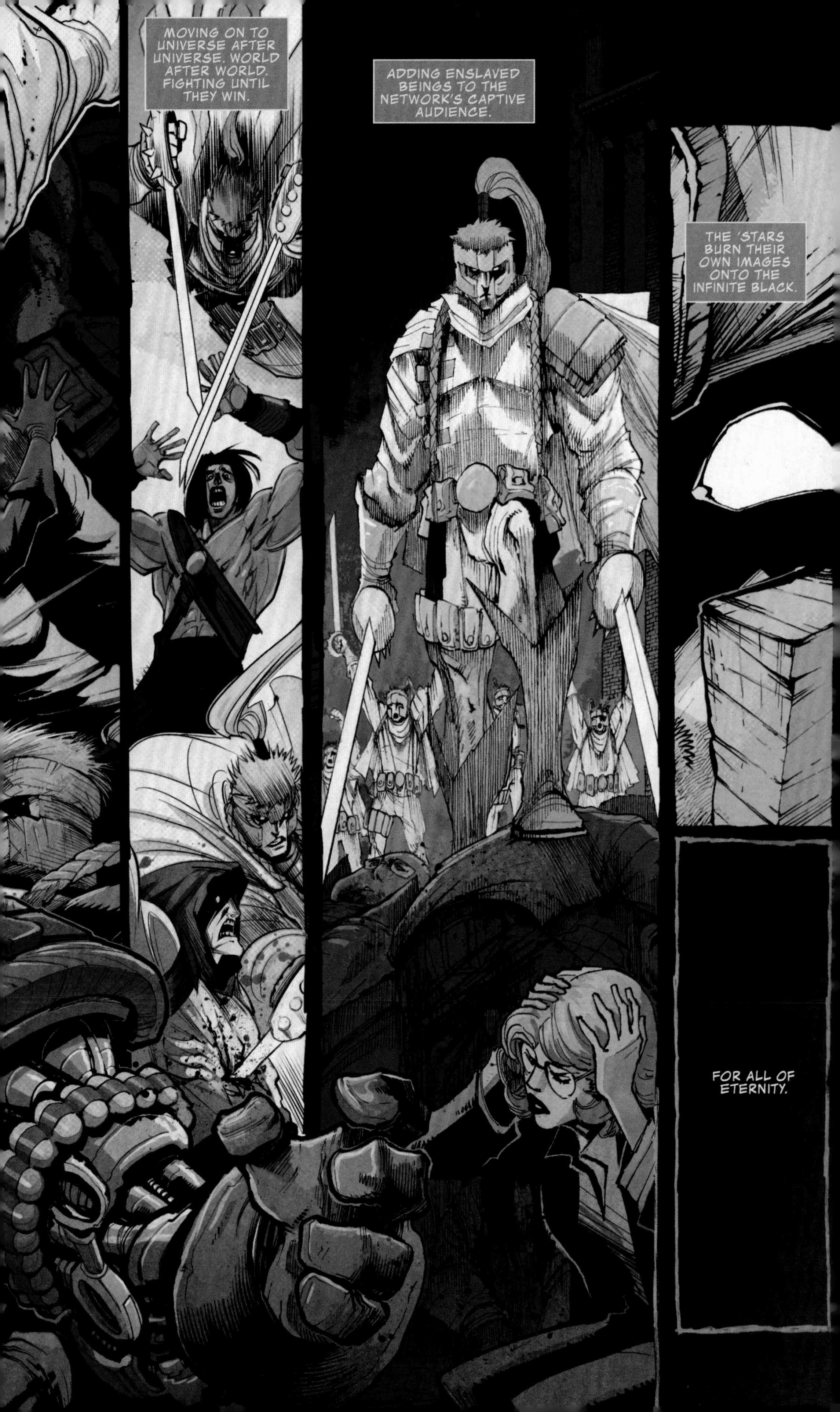
MOVING ON TO UNIVERSE AFTER UNIVERSE. WORLD AFTER WORLD. FIGHTING UNTIL THEY WIN.
ADDING ENSLAVED BEINGS TO THE NETWORK'S CAPTIVE AUDIENCE.
THE 'STARS BURN THEIR OWN IMAGES ONTO THE INFINITE BLACK.
FOR ALL OF ETERNITY.

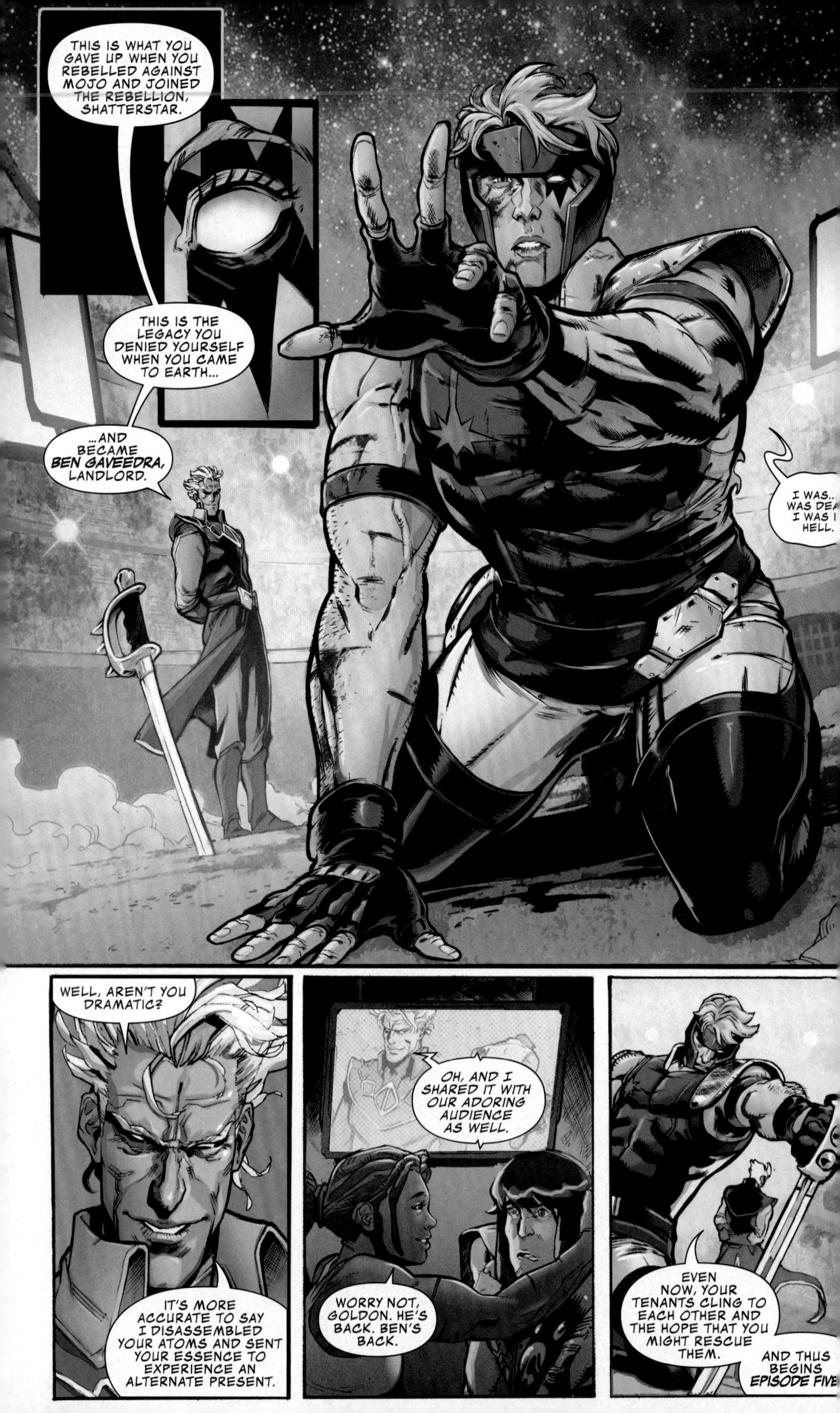
THIS IS WHAT YOU GAVE UP WHEN YOU REBELLED AGAINST MOJO AND JOINED THE REBELLION, SHATTERSTAR.
THIS IS THE LEGACY YOU DENIED YOURSELF WHEN YOU CAME TO EARTH...
...AND BECAME BEN GAVEEDRA, LANDLORD.
WELL, AREN'T YOU DRAMATIC?
IT'S MORE ACCURATE TO SAY I DISASSEMBLED YOUR ATOMS AND SENT YOUR ESSENCE TO EXPERIENCE AN ALTERNATE PRESENT.
OH, AND I SHARED IT WITH OUR ADORING AUDIENCE AS WELL.
WORRY NOT, GOLDON. HE'S BACK. BEN'S BACK.
EVEN NOW, YOUR TENANTS CLING TO EACH OTHER AND THE HOPE THAT YOU MIGHT RESCUE THEM.
AND THUS BEGINS EPISODE FIVE

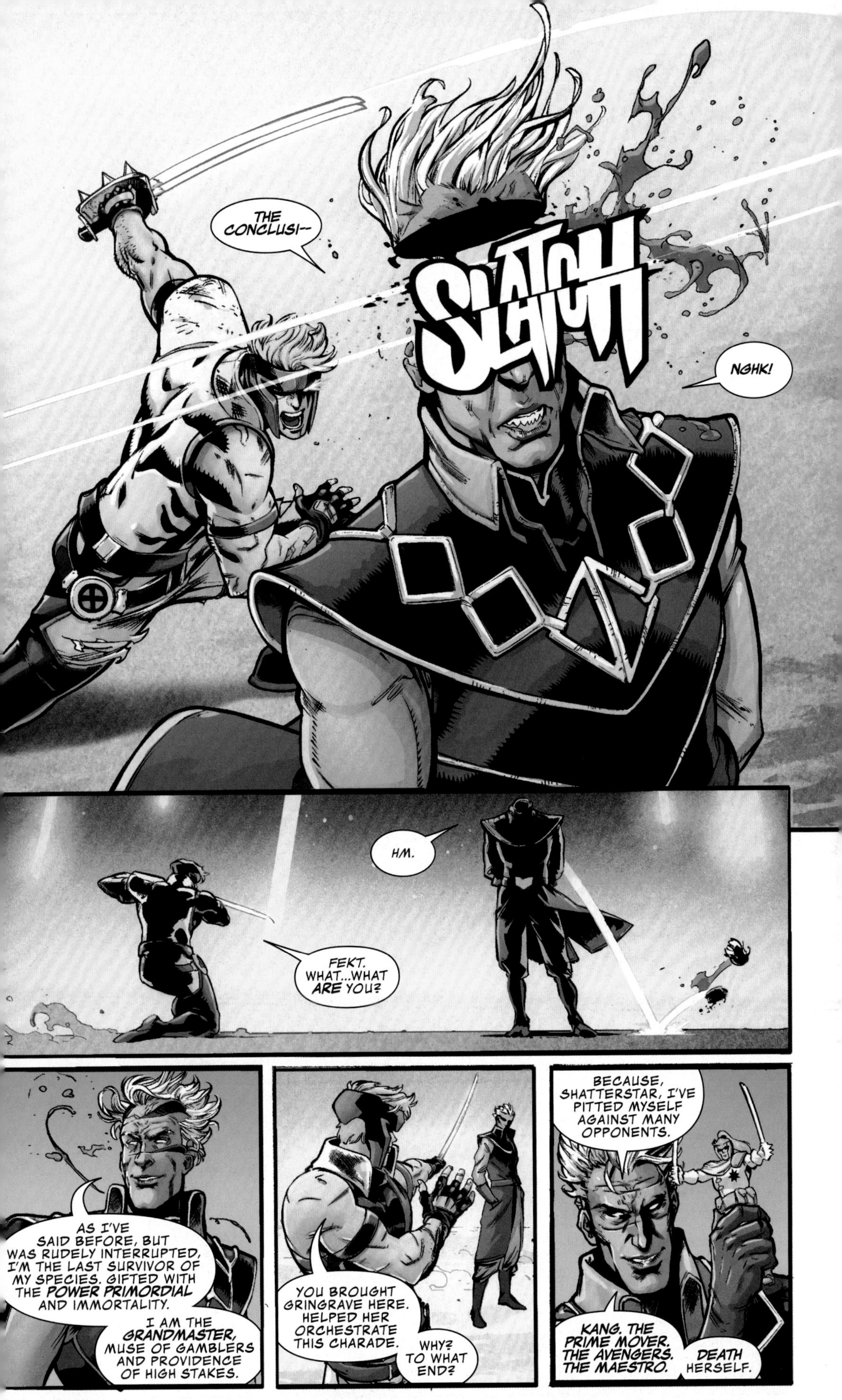
THE CONCLUSI--
SLATCH
NGHK!
HM.
FEKT. WHAT...WHAT ARE YOU?
AS I'VE SAID BEFORE, BUT WAS RUDELY INTERRUPTED, I'M THE LAST SURVIVOR OF MY SPECIES. GIFTED WITH THE POWER PRIMORDIAL AND IMMORTALITY.
I AM THE GRANDMASTER, MUSE OF GAMBLERS AND PROVIDENCE OF HIGH STAKES.
YOU BROUGHT GRINGRAVE HERE. HELPED HER ORCHESTRATE THIS CHARADE.
WHY? TO WHAT END?
BECAUSE, SHATTERSTAR, I'VE PITTED MYSELF AGAINST MANY OPPONENTS.
KANG. THE PRIME MOVER. THE AVENGERS. THE MAESTRO.
DEATH HERSELF.

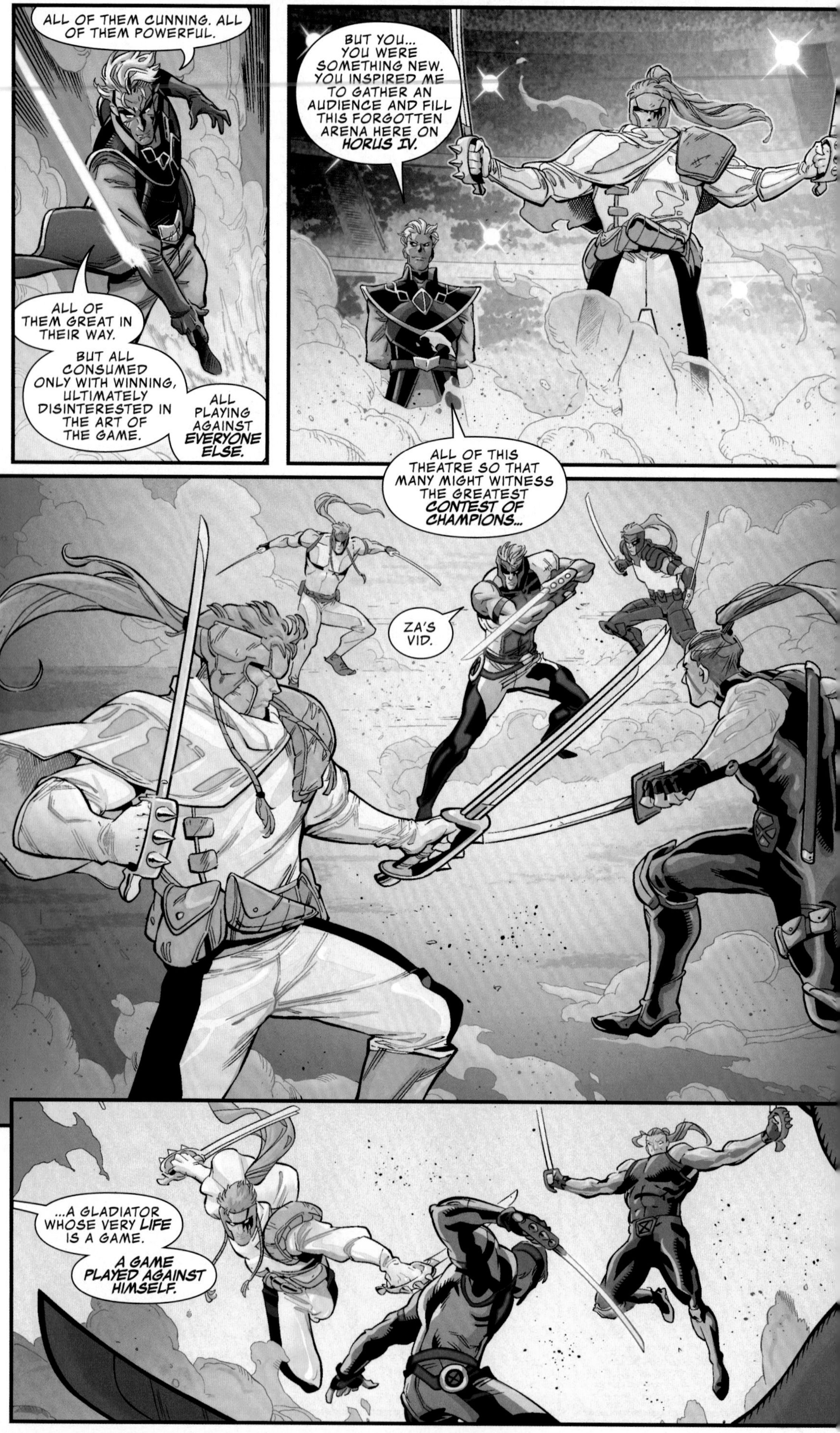
ALL OF THEM CUNNING. ALL OF THEM POWERFUL.
ALL OF THEM GREAT IN THEIR WAY.
BUT ALL CONSUMED ONLY WITH WINNING, ULTIMATELY DISINTERESTED IN THE ART OF THE GAME.
ALL PLAYING AGAINST EVERYONE ELSE.
BUT YOU... YOU WERE SOMETHING NEW. YOU INSPIRED ME TO GATHER AN AUDIENCE AND FILL THIS FORGOTTEN ARENA HERE ON HORUS IV.
ALL OF THIS THEATRE SO THAT MANY MIGHT WITNESS THE GREATEST CONTEST OF CHAMPIONS...
ZA'S VID.
...A GLADIATOR WHOSE VERY LIFE IS A GAME.
A GAME PLAYED AGAINST HIMSELF.

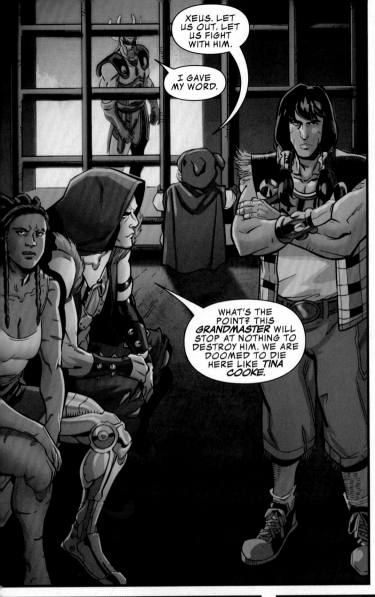

XEUS. LET US OUT. LET US FIGHT WITH HIM.

I GAVE MY WORD.

WHAT'S THE POINT? THIS *GRANDMASTER* WILL STOP AT NOTHING TO DESTROY HIM. WE ARE DOOMED TO DIE HERE LIKE *TINA COOKE*.

NO. BEN GAVE US A HOME TO SHARE.

GABBI. IF I'M NOT THERE WHEN SHE COMES AFTER SCHOOL...

...SHE'LLL THINK *I* ABANDONED HER *TOO*.

IT'S BEN WHO ABANDONED US, *THE END WOMAN.* WHERE WAS SHATTERSTAR WHEN *THE DEATH SPONSORS* AND HIS KINKY EX ATTACKED ANYWAY?

STOP IT, *CRIMZ.* JUST STOP. I'M SICK OF YOUR NEGATIVITY.

OH? IS THAT RIGHT, *GOLDON*? WELL, REMEMBER WHO GOT US CAST OFF TO THAT BACKWATER WORLD WITH ITS GLADIATOR LANDLORD IN THE FIRST PLACE.

WHAT KIND OF KING WOULD YOU HAVE MADE ANYWAY, BROTHER?

IF YOU HAD JUST LET ME RULE *THE SCORPUS CITADEL*, OUR WORLD WOULDN'T HAVE TUMBLED INTO *THE MAW OF NOTHING.*

AHH! SHUT UP, CRIMZOR! *SHUT UP!*

FOOLS!

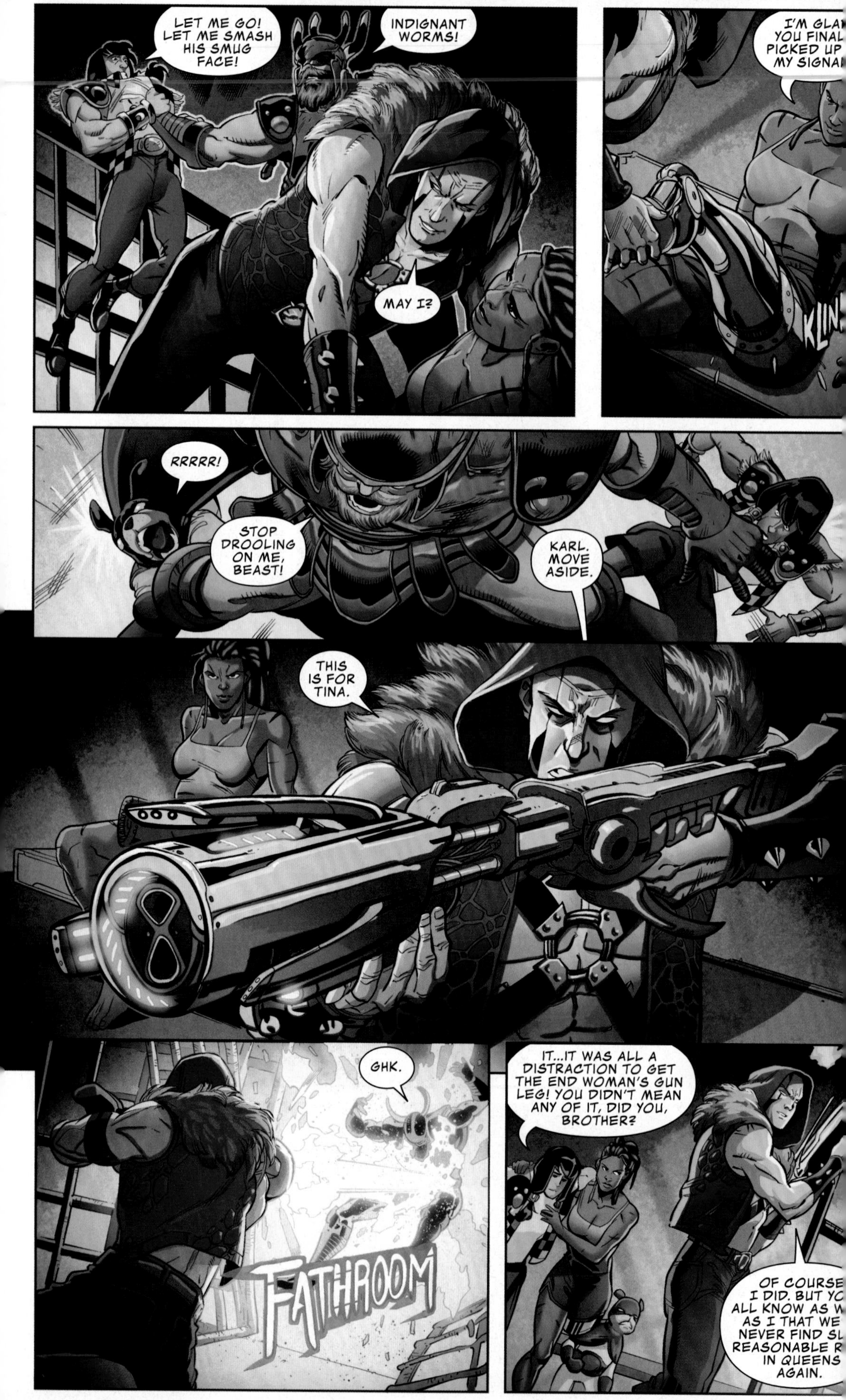
LET ME GO! LET ME SMASH HIS SMUG FACE!
INDIGNANT WORMS!
MAY I?
RRRRR!
STOP DROOLING ON ME, BEAST!
KARL. MOVE ASIDE.
THIS IS FOR TINA.
GHK.
FATHROOM
IT...IT WAS ALL A DISTRACTION TO GET THE END WOMAN'S GUN LEG! YOU DIDN'T MEAN ANY OF IT, DID YOU, BROTHER?

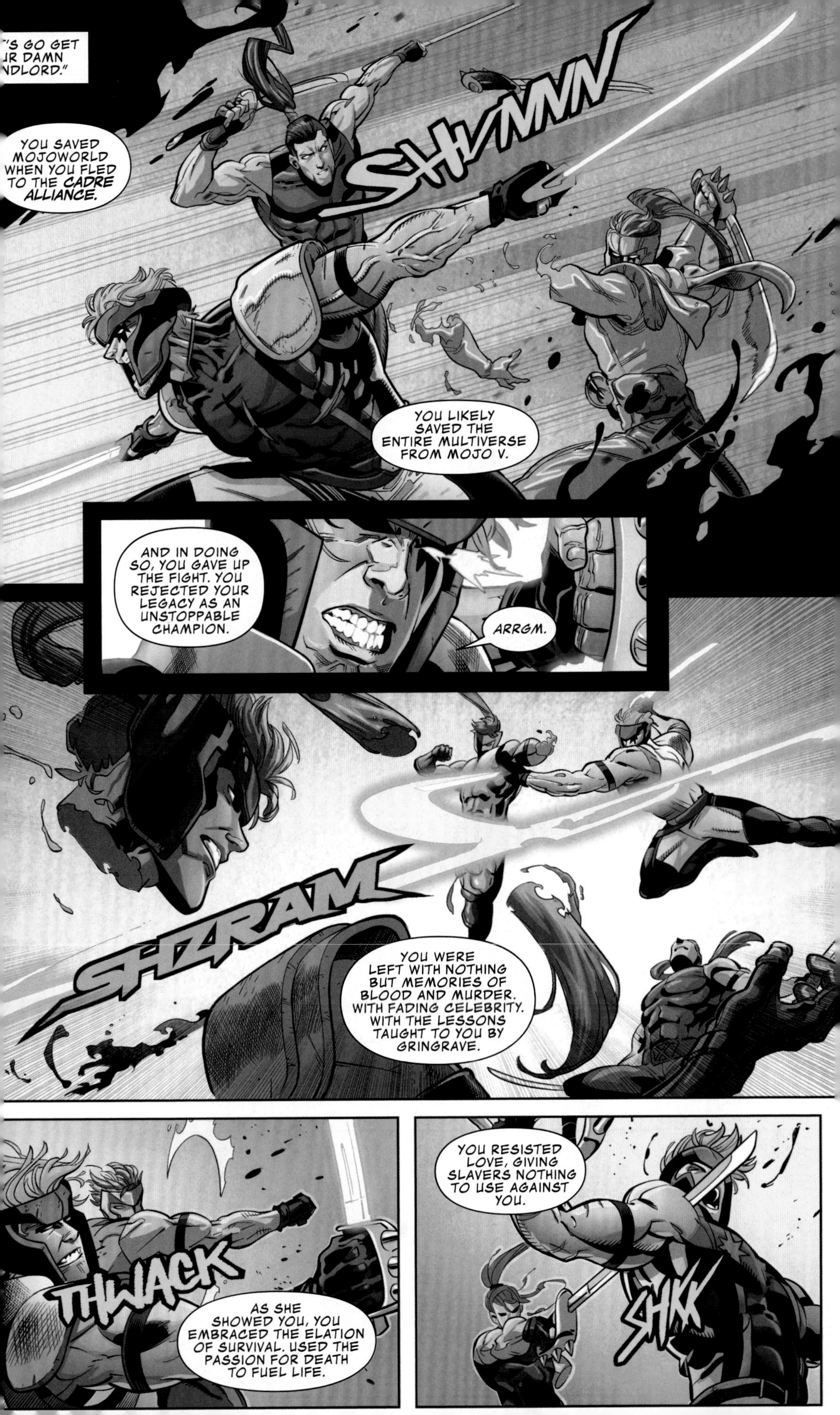
"'S GO GET
R DAMN
NDLORD."
SHWNNN
YOU SAVED MOJOWORLD WHEN YOU FLED TO THE **CADRE ALLIANCE.**
YOU LIKELY SAVED THE ENTIRE MULTIVERSE FROM MOJO V.
AND IN DOING SO, YOU GAVE UP THE FIGHT. YOU REJECTED YOUR LEGACY AS AN UNSTOPPABLE CHAMPION.
ARRGM.
SHZRAM
YOU WERE LEFT WITH NOTHING BUT MEMORIES OF BLOOD AND MURDER. WITH FADING CELEBRITY. WITH THE LESSONS TAUGHT TO YOU BY GRINGRAVE.
THWACK
AS SHE SHOWED YOU, YOU EMBRACED THE ELATION OF SURVIVAL. USED THE PASSION FOR DEATH TO FUEL LIFE.
YOU RESISTED LOVE, GIVING SLAVERS NOTHING TO USE AGAINST YOU.
SHKK

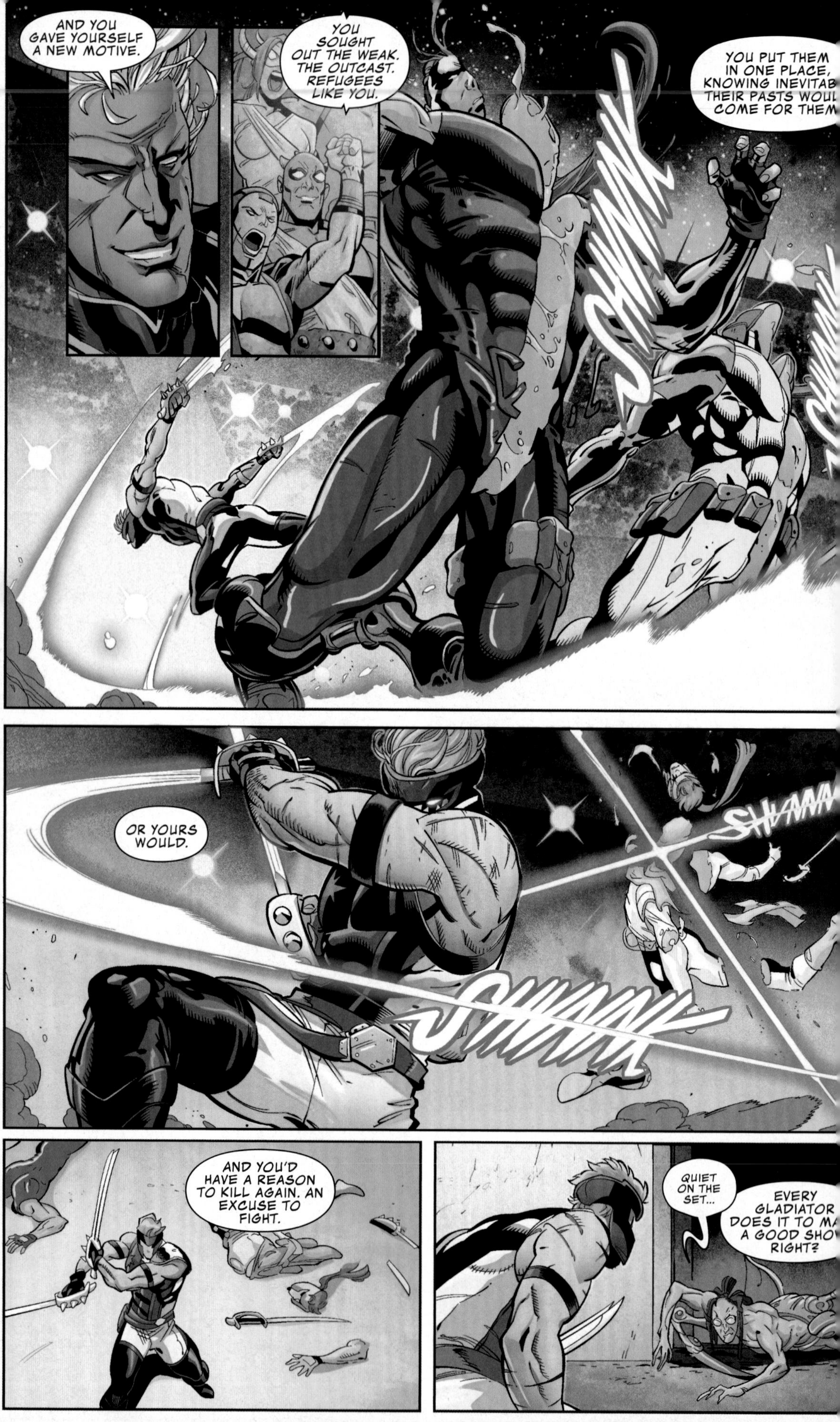
AND YOU GAVE YOURSELF A NEW MOTIVE.
YOU SOUGHT OUT THE WEAK. THE OUTCAST. REFUGEES LIKE YOU.
YOU PUT THEM IN ONE PLACE, KNOWING INEVITAB THEIR PASTS WOUL COME FOR THEM
SHUNK
OR YOURS WOULD.
SHUNK
AND YOU'D HAVE A REASON TO KILL AGAIN. AN EXCUSE TO FIGHT.
QUIET ON THE SET...
EVERY GLADIATOR DOES IT TO MA A GOOD SHO RIGHT?

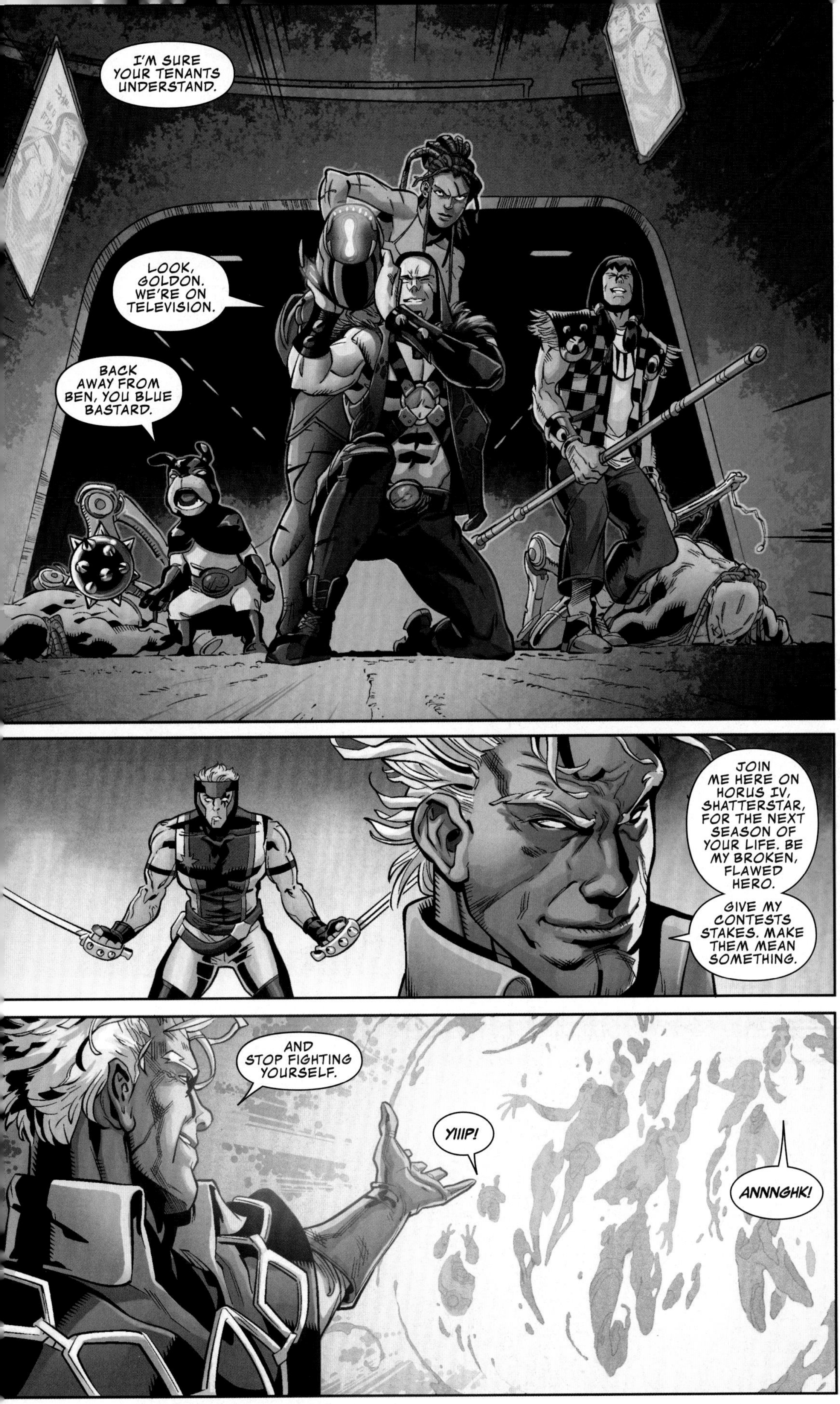
I'M SURE YOUR TENANTS UNDERSTAND.
LOOK, GOLDON. WE'RE ON TELEVISION.
BACK AWAY FROM BEN, YOU BLUE BASTARD.
JOIN ME HERE ON HORUS IV, SHATTERSTAR, FOR THE NEXT SEASON OF YOUR LIFE. BE MY BROKEN, FLAWED HERO.
GIVE MY CONTESTS STAKES. MAKE THEM MEAN SOMETHING.
AND STOP FIGHTING YOURSELF.
YIIIP!
ANNNGHK!

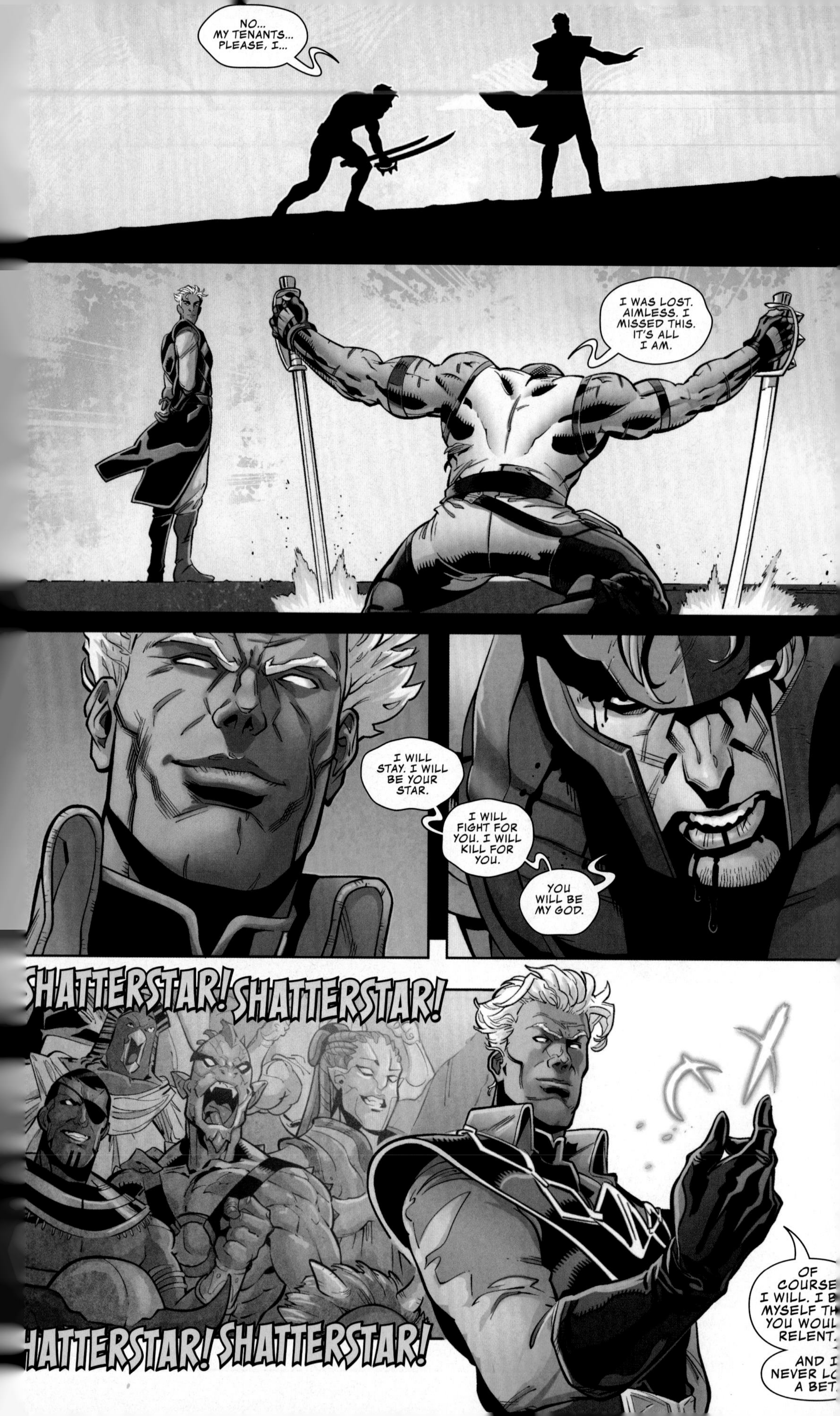
NO... MY TENANTS... PLEASE, I...
I WAS LOST. AIMLESS. I MISSED THIS. IT'S ALL I AM.
I WILL STAY. I WILL BE YOUR STAR.
I WILL FIGHT FOR YOU. I WILL KILL FOR YOU.
YOU WILL BE MY GOD.
SHATTERSTAR! SHATTERSTAR!
HATTERSTAR! SHATTERSTAR!
OF COURSE I WILL. I B MYSELF TH YOU WOUL RELENT.
AND I NEVER LO A BET.

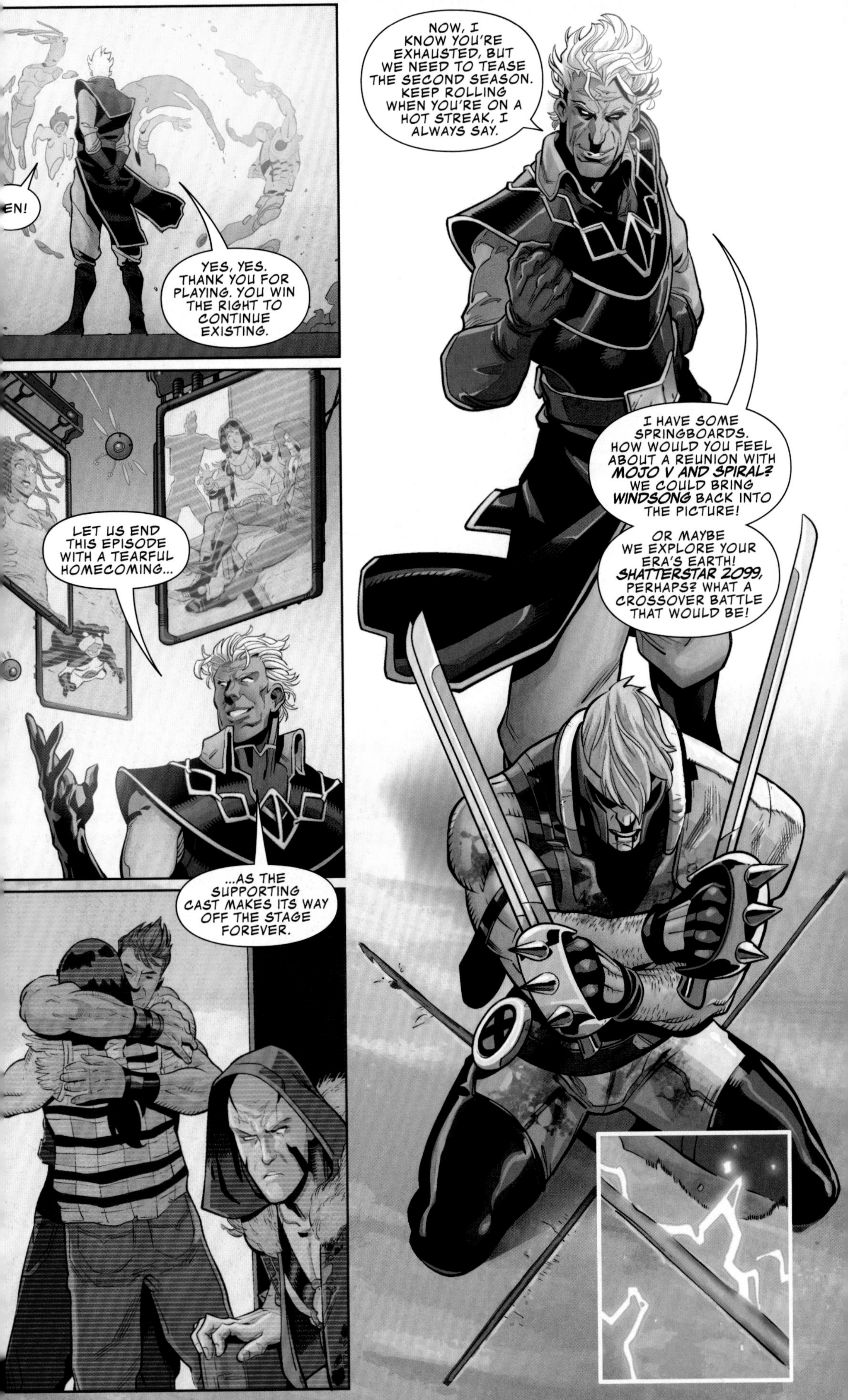
EN!
YES, YES. THANK YOU FOR PLAYING. YOU WIN THE RIGHT TO CONTINUE EXISTING.
LET US END THIS EPISODE WITH A TEARFUL HOMECOMING...
...AS THE SUPPORTING CAST MAKES ITS WAY OFF THE STAGE FOREVER.
NOW, I KNOW YOU'RE EXHAUSTED, BUT WE NEED TO TEASE THE SECOND SEASON. KEEP ROLLING WHEN YOU'RE ON A HOT STREAK, I ALWAYS SAY.
I HAVE SOME SPRINGBOARDS. HOW WOULD YOU FEEL ABOUT A REUNION WITH ***MOJO V AND SPIRAL?*** WE COULD BRING ***WINDSONG*** BACK INTO THE PICTURE!
OR MAYBE WE EXPLORE YOUR ERA'S EARTH! ***SHATTERSTAR 2099,*** PERHAPS? WHAT A CROSSOVER BATTLE THAT WOULD BE!

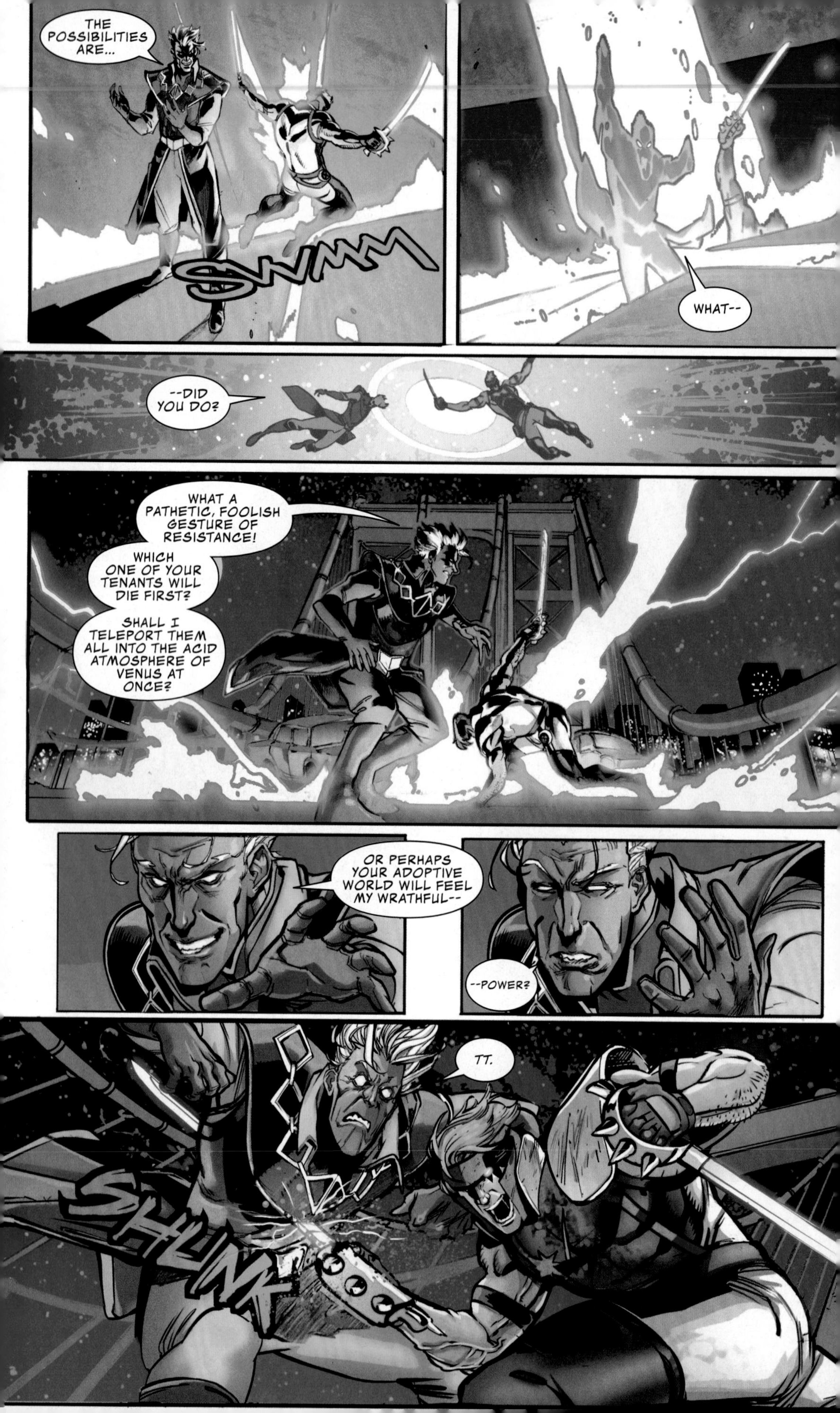
THE POSSIBILITIES ARE...
SWMM
WHAT--
--DID YOU DO?
WHAT A PATHETIC, FOOLISH GESTURE OF RESISTANCE!
WHICH ONE OF YOUR TENANTS WILL DIE FIRST?
SHALL I TELEPORT THEM ALL INTO THE ACID ATMOSPHERE OF VENUS AT ONCE?
OR PERHAPS YOUR ADOPTIVE WORLD WILL FEEL MY WRATHFUL--
--POWER?
TT.
SHUNK

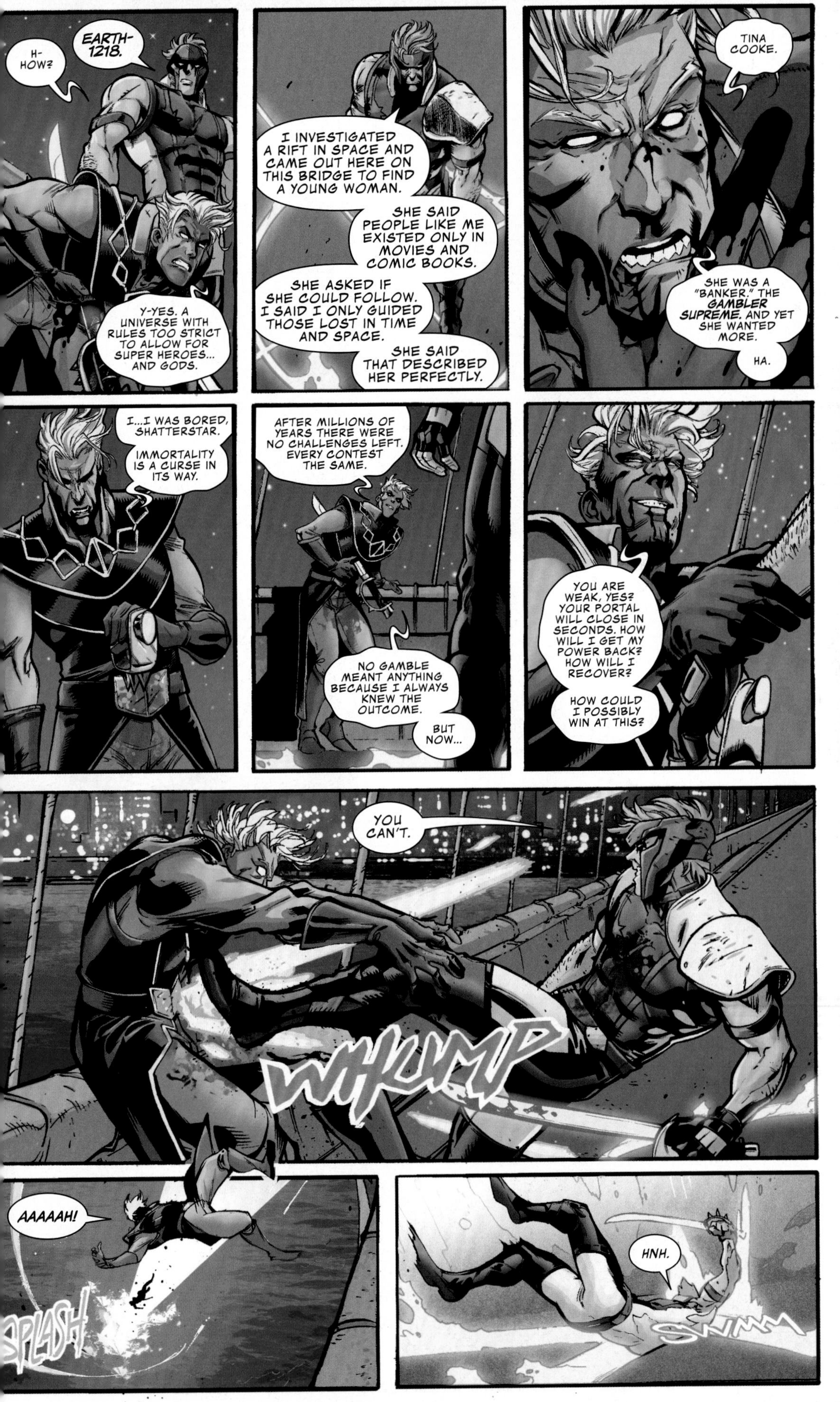
EARTH-1218.
H-HOW?
Y-YES. A UNIVERSE WITH RULES TOO STRICT TO ALLOW FOR SUPER HEROES... AND GODS.
I INVESTIGATED A RIFT IN SPACE AND CAME OUT HERE ON THIS BRIDGE TO FIND A YOUNG WOMAN.
SHE SAID PEOPLE LIKE ME EXISTED ONLY IN MOVIES AND COMIC BOOKS.
SHE ASKED IF SHE COULD FOLLOW. I SAID I ONLY GUIDED THOSE LOST IN TIME AND SPACE.
SHE SAID THAT DESCRIBED HER PERFECTLY.
TINA COOKE.
SHE WAS A "BANKER." THE GAMBLER SUPREME. AND YET SHE WANTED MORE.
HA.
I...I WAS BORED, SHATTERSTAR.
IMMORTALITY IS A CURSE IN ITS WAY.
AFTER MILLIONS OF YEARS THERE WERE NO CHALLENGES LEFT. EVERY CONTEST THE SAME.
NO GAMBLE MEANT ANYTHING BECAUSE I ALWAYS KNEW THE OUTCOME.
BUT NOW...
YOU ARE WEAK, YES? YOUR PORTAL WILL CLOSE IN SECONDS. HOW WILL I GET MY POWER BACK? HOW WILL I RECOVER?
HOW COULD I POSSIBLY WIN AT THIS?
YOU CAN'T.
WHUMP
AAAAAH!
SPLASH
HNH.
SWMM

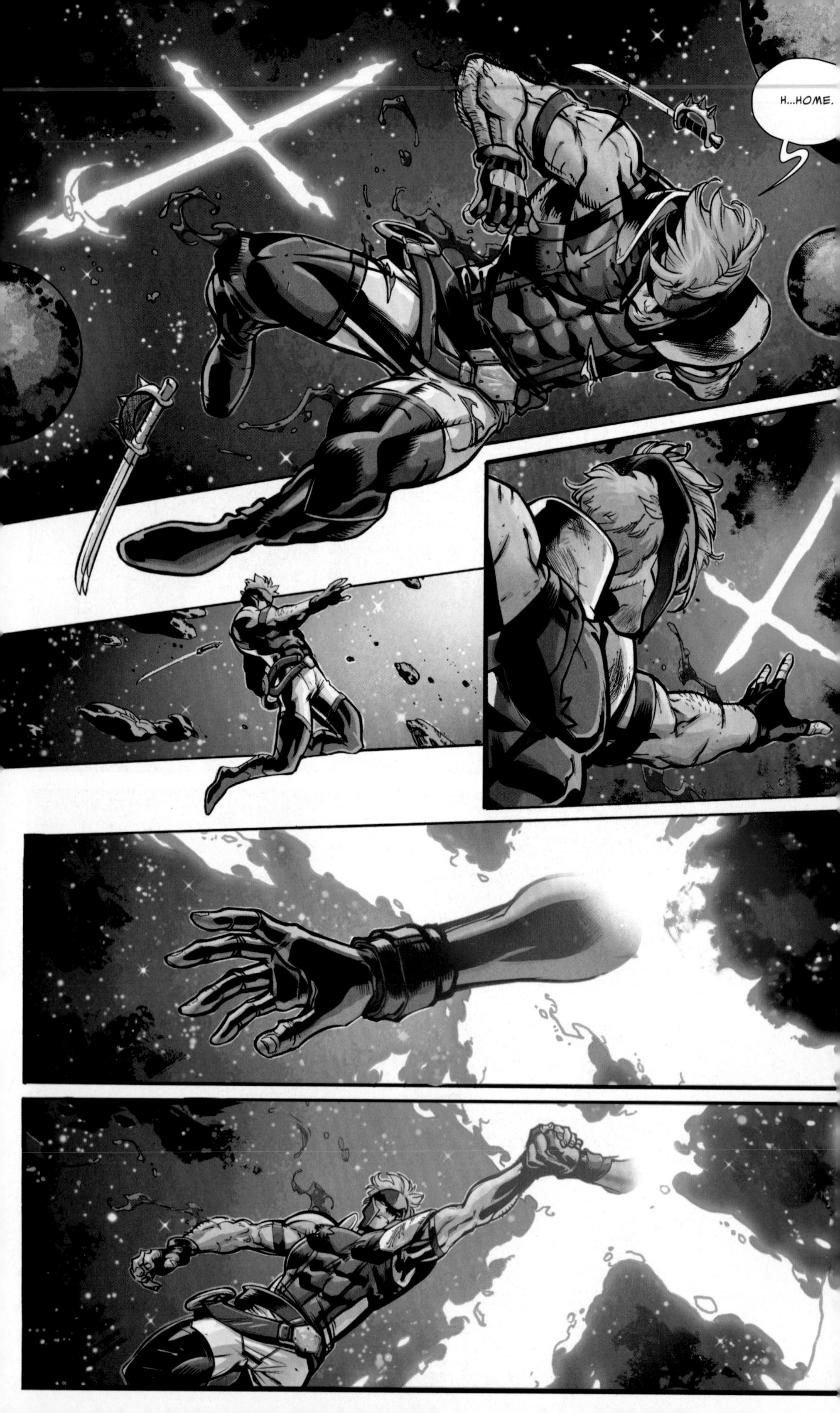
H...HOME.

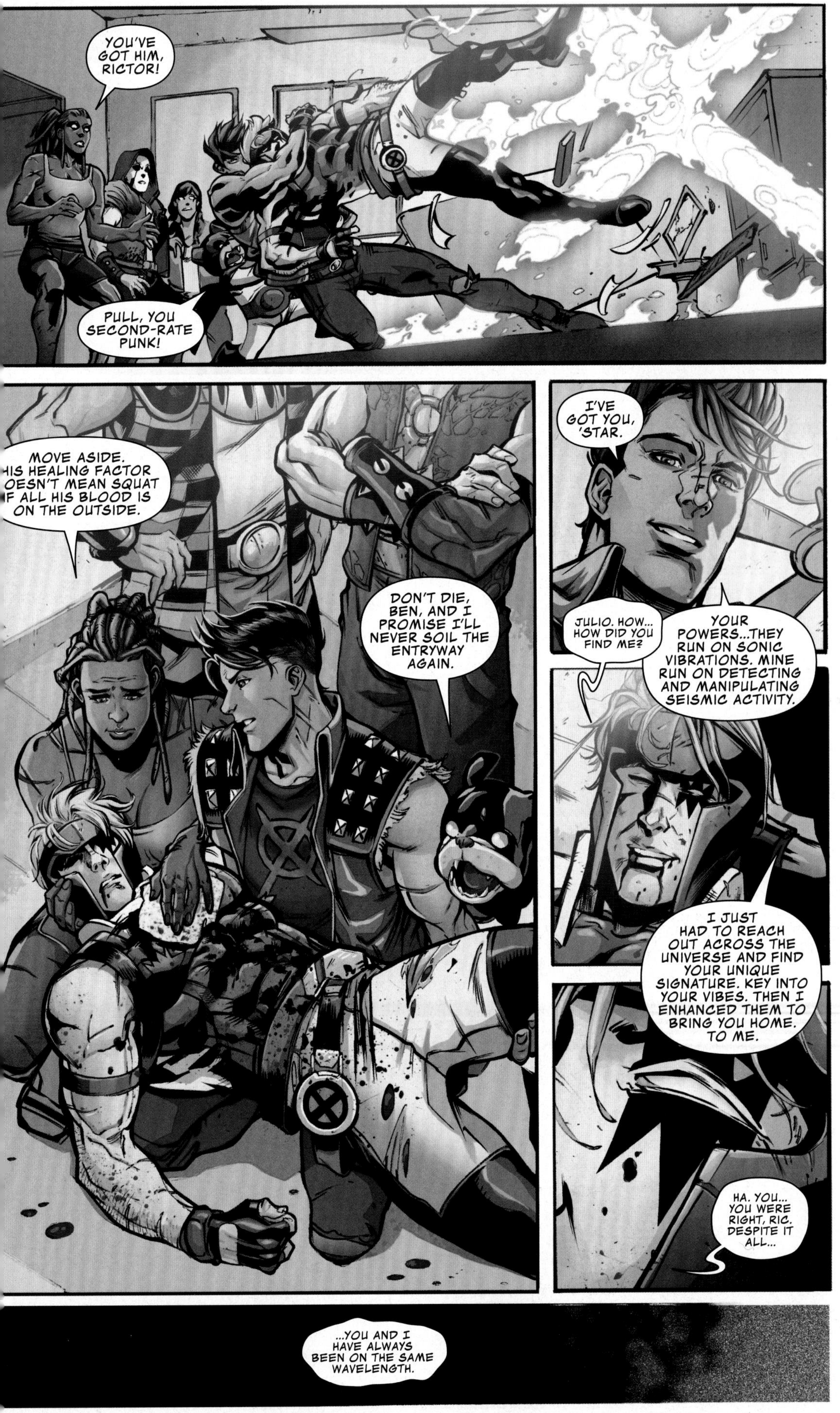
YOU'VE GOT HIM, RICTOR!
PULL, YOU SECOND-RATE PUNK!
MOVE ASIDE. HIS HEALING FACTOR DOESN'T MEAN SQUAT IF ALL HIS BLOOD IS ON THE OUTSIDE.
DON'T DIE, BEN, AND I PROMISE I'LL NEVER SOIL THE ENTRYWAY AGAIN.
I'VE GOT YOU, 'STAR.
JULIO. HOW... HOW DID YOU FIND ME?
YOUR POWERS...THEY RUN ON SONIC VIBRATIONS. MINE RUN ON DETECTING AND MANIPULATING SEISMIC ACTIVITY.
I JUST HAD TO REACH OUT ACROSS THE UNIVERSE AND FIND YOUR UNIQUE SIGNATURE. KEY INTO YOUR VIBES. THEN I ENHANCED THEM TO BRING YOU HOME. TO ME.
HA. YOU... YOU WERE RIGHT, RIC. DESPITE IT ALL...
...YOU AND I HAVE ALWAYS BEEN ON THE SAME WAVELENGTH.

THE MATCH OF THE YEAR...

...NO, MAYBE THE DECADE...

IT'S THE REIGNING CHAMPION...

...FROM BILO MISSISSIPPI, WEIGHING IN 226 POUND

THERE. NOW HE WON'T MISS ANYTHING.

DWAYNE TAYLOR

TRASHER OF THE NIGHT

WAIT...

NEITHE WILL SH

...THE FANTASTIC FOUR FACING OFF AGAINST GALACTUS IN THE BLUE AREA OF THE MOON...

THAT'S A NICE TOUCH, GOLDON.

NOW LET'S GET HOME...

DWAYNE TAYLOR

TRASHER OF THE NIGHT

CHRISTINA COOKE

FRIEND, SEEKER OF TRUTH

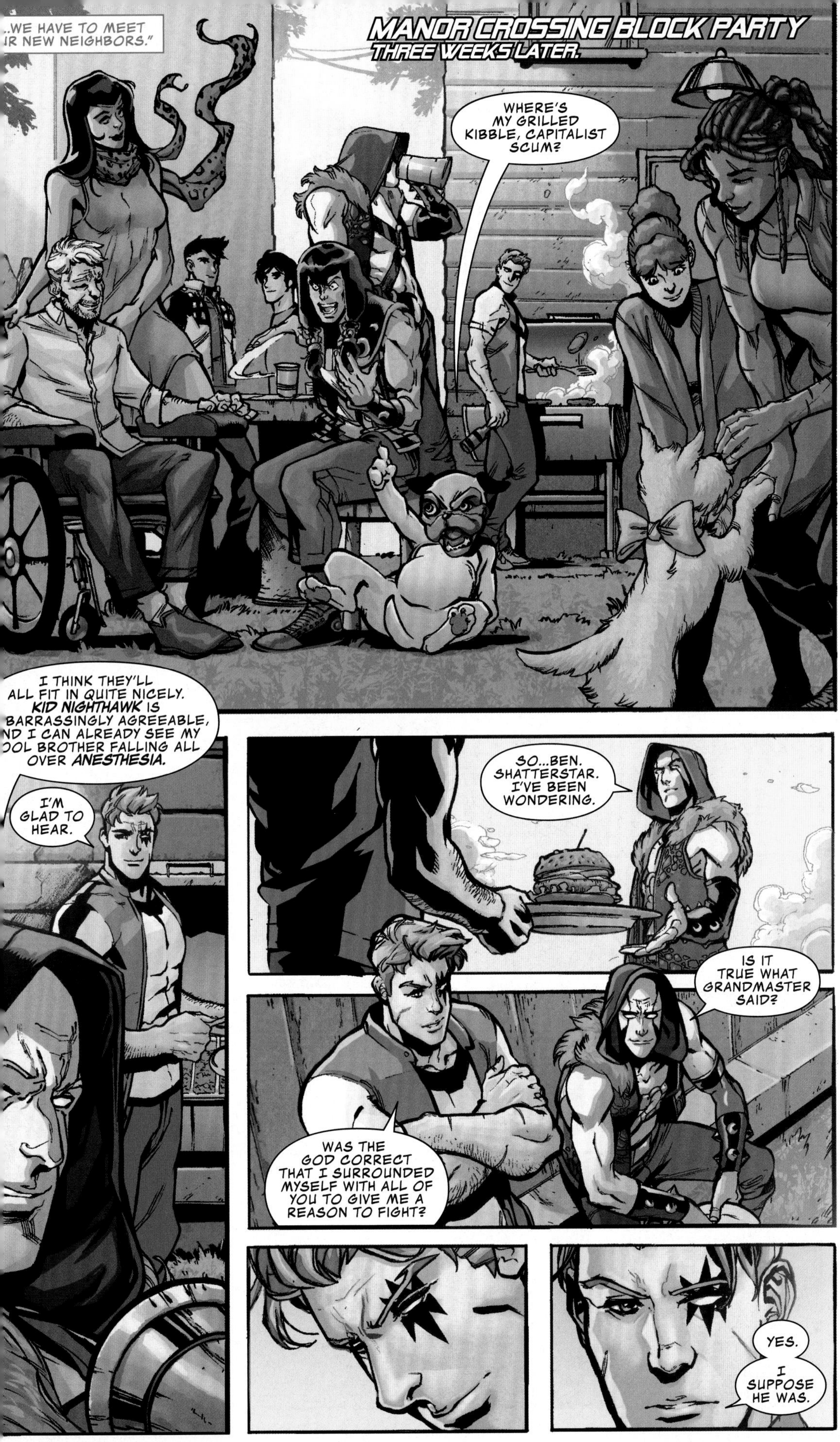

...WE HAVE TO MEET
IR NEW NEIGHBORS."
MANOR CROSSING BLOCK PARTY
THREE WEEKS LATER.
WHERE'S MY GRILLED KIBBLE, CAPITALIST SCUM?
I THINK THEY'LL ALL FIT IN QUITE NICELY. KID NIGHTHAWK IS BARRASSINGLY AGREEABLE, ND I CAN ALREADY SEE MY OOL BROTHER FALLING ALL OVER ANESTHESIA.
I'M GLAD TO HEAR.
SO...BEN. SHATTERSTAR. I'VE BEEN WONDERING.
IS IT TRUE WHAT GRANDMASTER SAID?
WAS THE GOD CORRECT THAT I SURROUNDED MYSELF WITH ALL OF YOU TO GIVE ME A REASON TO FIGHT?
YES.
I SUPPOSE HE WAS.

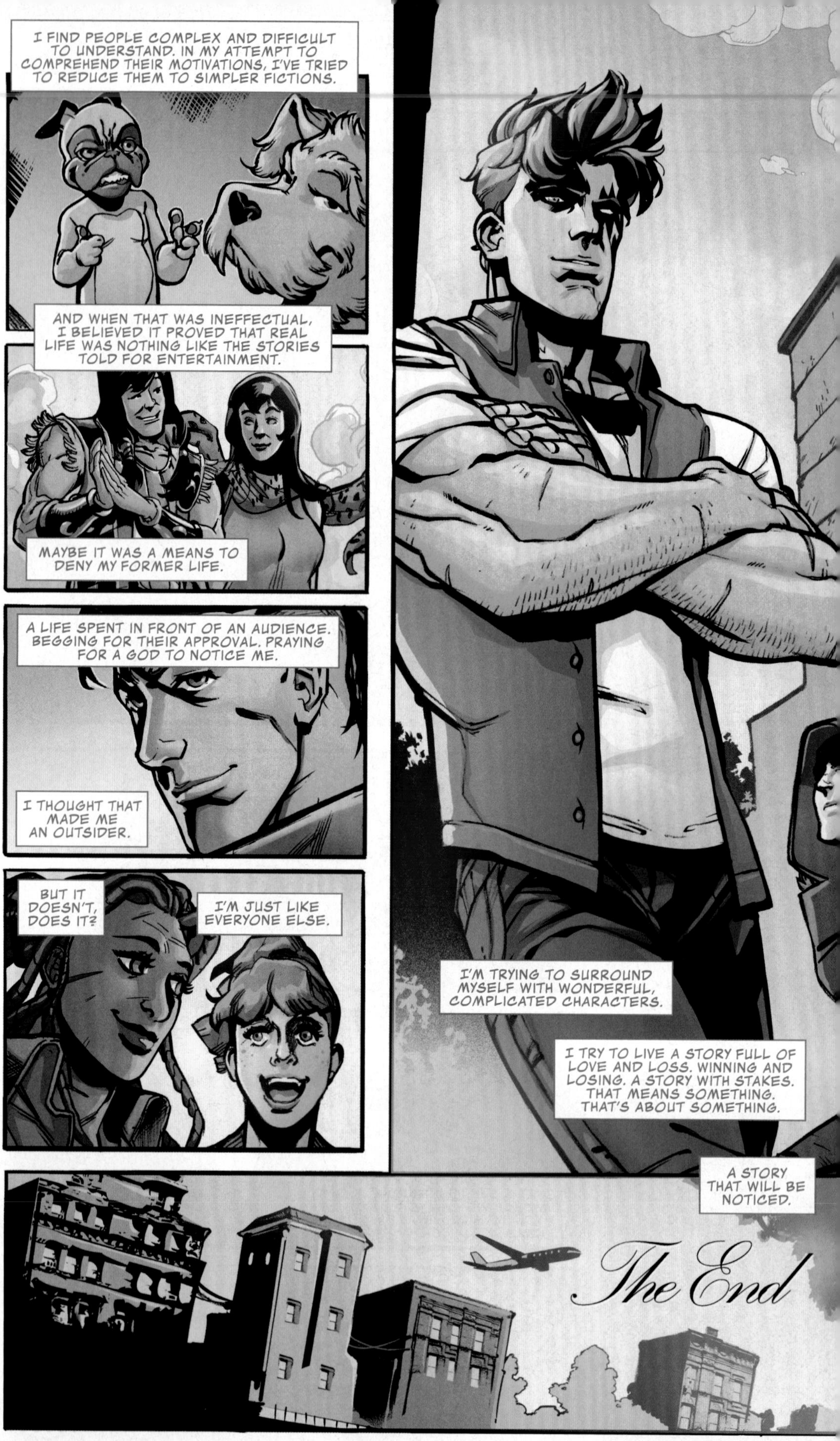

I FIND PEOPLE COMPLEX AND DIFFICULT TO UNDERSTAND. IN MY ATTEMPT TO COMPREHEND THEIR MOTIVATIONS, I'VE TRIED TO REDUCE THEM TO SIMPLER FICTIONS.
AND WHEN THAT WAS INEFFECTUAL, I BELIEVED IT PROVED THAT REAL LIFE WAS NOTHING LIKE THE STORIES TOLD FOR ENTERTAINMENT.
MAYBE IT WAS A MEANS TO DENY MY FORMER LIFE.
A LIFE SPENT IN FRONT OF AN AUDIENCE. BEGGING FOR THEIR APPROVAL. PRAYING FOR A GOD TO NOTICE ME.
I THOUGHT THAT MADE ME AN OUTSIDER.
BUT IT DOESN'T, DOES IT?
I'M JUST LIKE EVERYONE ELSE.
I'M TRYING TO SURROUND MYSELF WITH WONDERFUL, COMPLICATED CHARACTERS.
I TRY TO LIVE A STORY FULL OF LOVE AND LOSS. WINNING AND LOSING. A STORY WITH STAKES. THAT MEANS SOMETHING. THAT'S ABOUT SOMETHING.
A STORY THAT WILL BE NOTICED.
The End

#1 VARIANT BY
**ROB LIEFELD &
ROMULO FAJARDO JR.**

#1 VARIANT BY
IVAN SHAVRIN

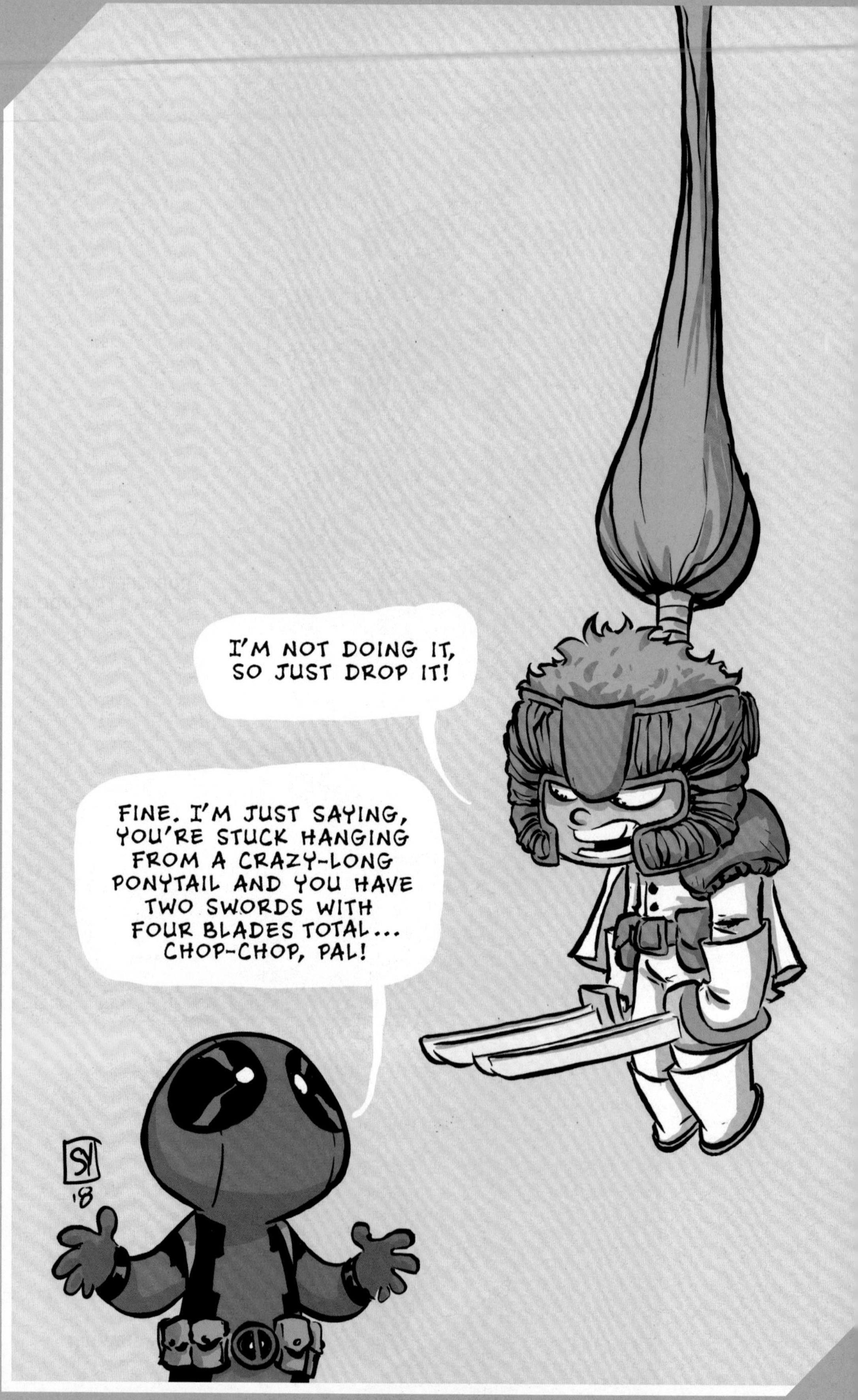
I'M NOT DOING IT, SO JUST DROP IT!
FINE. I'M JUST SAYING, YOU'RE STUCK HANGING FROM A CRAZY-LONG PONYTAIL AND YOU HAVE TWO SWORDS WITH FOUR BLADES TOTAL... CHOP-CHOP, PAL!
SY '18

#1 VARIANT BY **SKOTTIE YOUNG**

CHARACTER DESIGNS

BY **CARLOS VILLA**

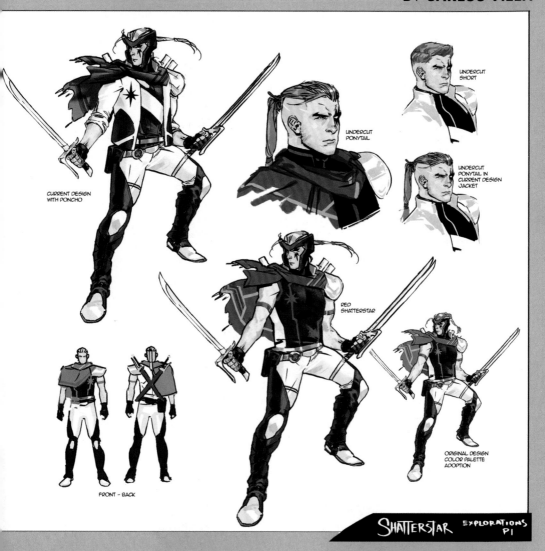

CURRENT DESIGN
WITH PONCHO

UNDERCUT
PONYTAIL

UNDERCUT
SHORT

UNDERCUT
PONYTAIL IN
CURRENT DESIGN
JACKET

RED
SHATTERSTAR

ORIGINAL DESIGN
COLOR PALETTE
ADOPTION

FRONT - BACK

SHATTERSTAR EXPLORATIONS P1

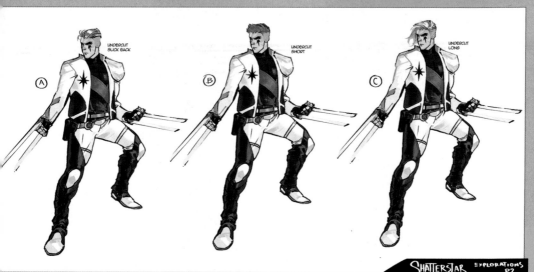

Ⓐ UNDERCUT
SLICK BACK

Ⓑ UNDERCUT
SHORT

Ⓒ UNDERCUT
LONG

SHATTERSTAR EXPLORATIONS P2

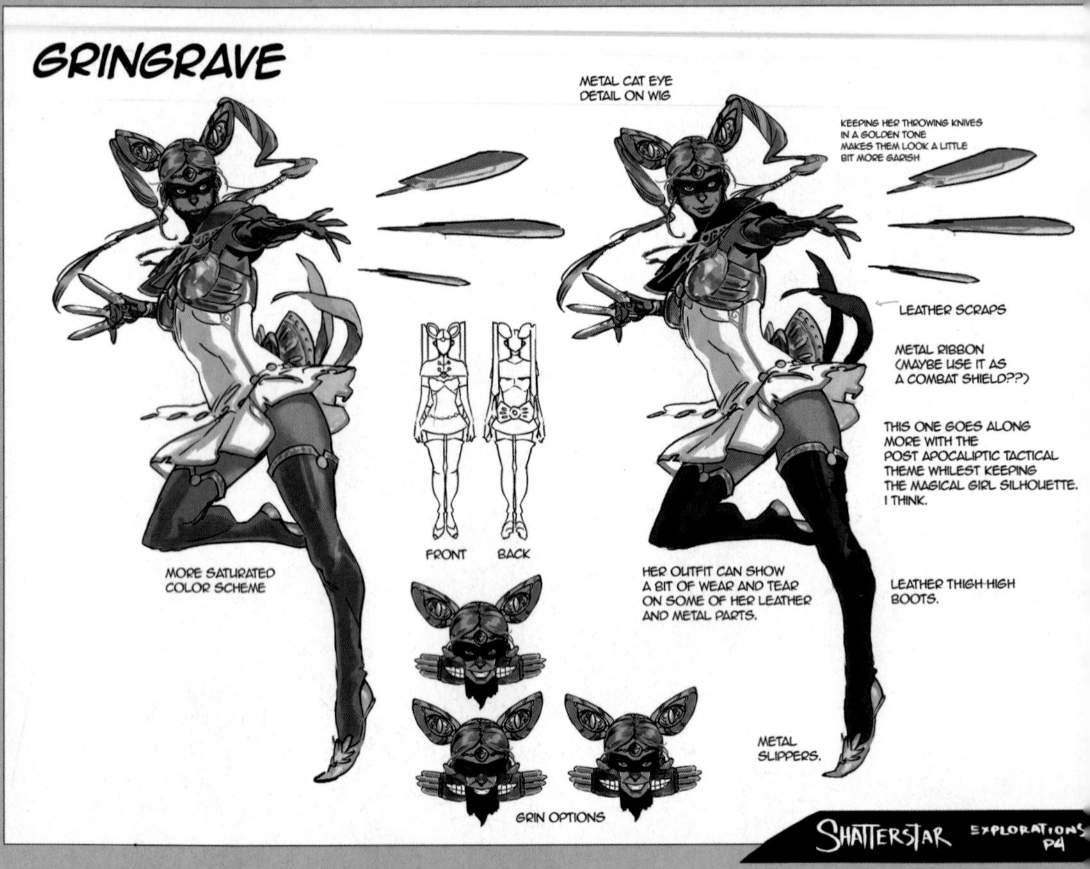
GRINGRAVE
METAL CAT EYE DETAIL ON WIG
KEEPING HER THROWING KNIVES IN A GOLDEN TONE MAKES THEM LOOK A LITTLE BIT MORE GARISH
LEATHER SCRAPS
METAL RIBBON (MAYBE USE IT AS A COMBAT SHIELD??)
THIS ONE GOES ALONG MORE WITH THE POST APOCALIPTIC TACTICAL THEME WHILEST KEEPING THE MAGICAL GIRL SILHOUETTE. I THINK.
FRONT
BACK
MORE SATURATED COLOR SCHEME
HER OUTFIT CAN SHOW A BIT OF WEAR AND TEAR ON SOME OF HER LEATHER AND METAL PARTS.
LEATHER THIGH-HIGH BOOTS.
METAL SLIPPERS.
GRIN OPTIONS
SHATTERSTAR
EXPLORATIONS P4

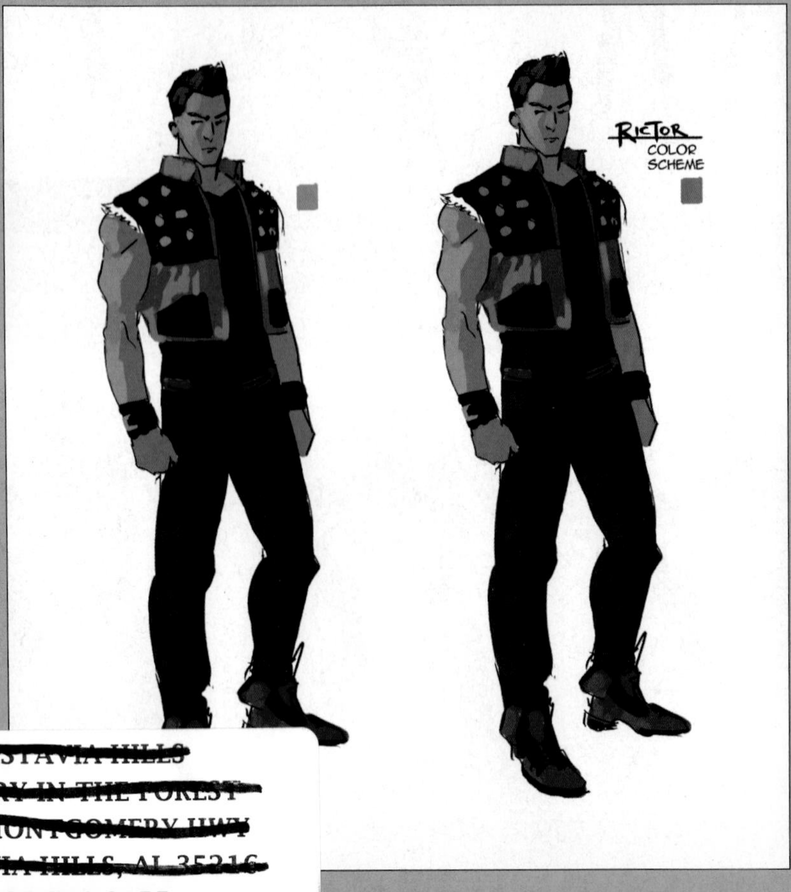
RICTOR
COLOR SCHEME